Transforming the Elite

Transforming the Elite

Black Students and the
Desegregation of Private Schools

Michelle A. Purdy

The University of North Carolina Press CHAPEL HILL

© 2018 The University of North Carolina Press
Set in Merope Basic by Westchester Publishing Services
Manufactured in the United States of America
The University of North Carolina Press has been a member of the
Green Press Initiative since 2003.

Library of Congress Cataloging-in-Publication Data
Names: Purdy, Michelle A., author.
Title: Transforming the elite : black students and the desegregation of private schools /
    Michelle A. Purdy.
Description: Chapel Hill : University of North Carolina Press, [2018] | Includes bibliographical
    references and index.
Identifiers: LCCN 2018010257 | ISBN 9781469643489 (cloth : alk. paper) | ISBN 9781469643496
    (pbk : alk. paper) | ISBN 9781469643502 (ebook)
Subjects: LCSH: Westminster Schools (Atlanta, Ga.)—History—20th century. | Private
    schools—Georgia—Atlanta—History—20th century. | School integration—Georgia—
    Atlanta—History—20th century. | School integration—United States—History—
    20th century. | African American students—Georgia—Atlanta—History—20th century. |
    Pressly, William L. (William Laurens), 1908-2001.
Classification: LCC LD7501.A82 P87 2018 | DDC 371.0209758/231—dc23 LC record available at
    https://lccn.loc.gov/2018010257

Cover illustration: Photo of students from Malcolm Ryder, "First Black Grads Voice Common
Impressions, Ideas," *The Westminster Bi-Line*, June 1972, 3; aerial photo of The Westminster
Schools, ca. 1968. Both photos courtesy of Lewis H. Beck Archives—The Westminster Schools.

This book includes material previously published in a different form in "Courageous Navigation:
African American Students at an Elite Private School in the South, 1967-1972," *Journal of African
American History* 100, no. 4 (Fall 2015): 610-35, and "Blurring Public and Private: The Pragmatic
Desegregation Politics of an Elite Private School in Atlanta," *History of Education Quarterly* 56,
no. 1 (February 2016): 61-89.

For
"My First Teachers"
My mother, Mitchell Pearl A. Purdy
My father, the late Paul W. Purdy Sr.
and
My brother, Paul W. Purdy Jr.

Contents

Figures, Map, and Tables

Abbreviations in the Text

ABC	A Better Chance
ABHMS	American Baptist Home Mission Society
AMA	American Missionary Association
AME	African Methodist Episcopal Church
APS	Atlanta Public Schools
AUC	Atlanta University Center
DAR	Daughters of the American Revolution
ESEA	Elementary and Secondary Education Act
GACHR	Greater Atlanta Council on Human Relations
GEB	General Education Board
HBCUs	Historically Black Colleges and Universities
HOPE	Help Our Public Education, Inc.
ISB	*Independent School Bulletin*
ISEB	Independent Schools Education Board
IRS	Internal Revenue Service
ISTSP	Independent Schools Talent Search Program
LDF	NAACP Legal Defense and Educational Fund, Inc.
MFPE	Minimum Foundation Program of Education
NAACP	National Association for the Advancement of Colored People
NAIS	National Association of Independent Schools
NCIS	National Council of Independent Schools
NDEA	National Defense Education Act

NSSFNS	National Scholarship Service and Fund for Negro Students
OASIS	Organizations Assisting Schools in September
SACS	Southern Association of Colleges and Schools
SAIS	Southern Association of Independent Schools
SCLC	Southern Christian Leadership Conference
SEB	Secondary Education Board
SEEB	Secondary Entrance Examination Board
SNCC	Student Nonviolent Coordinating Committee

Transforming the Elite

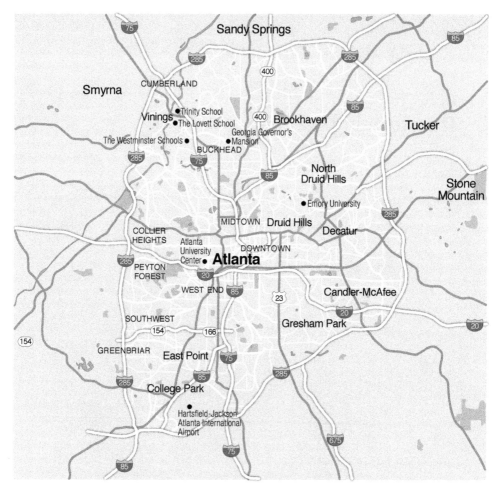

The Westminster Schools, established in 1951, is located on the north side of Atlanta close to Buckhead. The first black students to desegregate Westminster, who lived in Atlanta, primarily resided in neighborhoods close to the West End and Southwest Atlanta. Other first black students were from Norfolk, Virginia, and Houston, Texas. This map shows neighborhoods and landmarks important to *Transforming the Elite*.

Introduction

As far as recommending Westminster to other black students, the consensus was to recommend it to a group of blacks and not to send a black student here by himself.

—MALCOLM RYDER, black alum, Westminster Class of 1972

What they did was incredibly courageous. I don't know how they did it day in and day out.

—HILL MARTIN, white alum, Westminster Class of 1972

In the fall of 1967, the parents of seven black students—Bill Billings, Dawn Clark, Isaac Clark, Janice Kemp, Michael McBay, Jannard Wade, and Wanda Ward—brought them to a new school—a historically white elite private school—nestled on the north side of Atlanta off of the tree-lined two-lane West Paces Ferry Road. Coming from the West End and Southwest Atlanta neighborhoods, they saw the Atlanta landscape change from moderate and well-kept black working- and middle-class family homes to the downtown skyscrapers to larger, more sprawling homes of white middle- and upper-class families in Buckhead, an area of Atlanta now popularly known for its luxurious homes, fine dining, and upscale shopping. Not far from their new school, workers were building the new Georgia governor's mansion styled after Greek Revival design on West Paces Ferry Road. Upon arriving to their new campus, they found school facilities unlike what they had experienced at their segregated black schools; their new school was also not like Atlanta's segregated white public schools. When their parents dropped them off, in front of them was a 180-acre space to learn, to play, to change, to face challenges, and to achieve. They found an administration building (later to be named Pressly Hall) at the center of campus, distinguished by its white columns, grand double staircase, and vaulted ceiling. The older students would spend a good part of their day in college-like academic buildings, such as Askew and Campbell Halls, which housed the then separate boys' and girls' schools for the upper grades. The younger students attended classes in Scott Hall, which was across from the administration building, Askew, and Campbell and connected to the administration building by a covered walkway so that younger students could avoid the traffic lane that once ran through campus.[1] To their delight, they also found playing fields, tennis courts, a football stadium, and a well-outfitted gym. They probably also spotted the dormitories in the distance that were in use at that time; a year later, Malcolm Ryder, the first black male boarding student from Norfolk, Virginia, would arrive. As they looked around, they also saw wealth up close and personal. Wade keenly noticed his classmates' cars, their black maids, and the sizes of their homes: "It was like starting college, in my mind."[2]

These black students had arrived at The Westminster Schools, then and now a leading historically white elite private school or independent school in Atlanta, the Southeast, and the nation.[3] Westminster is a "young" elite school having been founded in 1951. As one of the first schools in the South to offer advanced placement courses, it was known in the mid-twentieth century for its academic rigor. Today, Westminster remains academically rigorous, reflects a commitment to diversity and inclusion, and offers facilities and resources parallel to institutions of higher learning. In 2008, Westminster, then with an endowment of $239 million, was listed as the fourteenth most wealthy independent school in the United States and the second most wealthy in the South. Tuition is presently approximately $25,000 for grades pre-first through fifth grade and $30,000 for sixth through twelfth grades.[4] Westminster now offers twenty-three advanced placement classes, deeming it popularly as "Atlanta's premiere academic power-house."[5] For the middle 50 percent of the 2015 senior class, SAT scores ranged between 1990 and 2200 on the 2400 point scale.[6] In comparison, college-bound seniors nationally averaged a score of 1490 on the SAT in 2015.[7] Graduates attend top universities and colleges throughout the United States and have pursued any number of career paths. There are newer academic buildings, a football stadium used in the recent and very popular movie *The Blindside*, and a state-of-the-art gym. Over 1,800 students attend Westminster, now only a day school and one of the largest private schools in Atlanta and the Southeast. Out of this total population, 31 percent identify as students of color, and the board of trustees, administration, faculty, and staff are comprised of individuals from various racial backgrounds.[8] Westminster's commitment to academic rigor and diversity and inclusion is rooted in what occurred in the mid-twentieth century.

Central to this book is examining how and why leaders of Westminster and other historically white elite private schools chose to desegregate their schools when they were not legally obligated to do so. In the late 1960s and early 1970s, independent schools desegregated and increased their number of black students because of a constellation of factors or a myriad of political, social, and cultural changes, largely driven by African Americans advocating for national change and the enforcement of civil and voting rights. For example, the number of black students attending independent schools nationally more than doubled from 3,720 in 1967 to 7,617 in 1970. Further, by 1969 the percentage of independent schools that enrolled black students also more than doubled: 84 percent versus 33 percent in 1960.[9] Equally important is an analysis of how the first black students navigated Westminster during the early years of school desegregation amid institutional and interpersonal racism. Such institutional racism was codified through "laws, policies, practices, and norms" which are "intentionally and unintentionally maintained and enforced." Combined with interpersonal racism, which is "oppression maintained at the individual level by attitudes or behaviors of individual persons," institutional and interpersonal racism informed a complex and contradictory school culture.[10]

I contend that the lines between public and private blurred as private schools became both focal points of policy and spaces to avoid public school desegregation during the mid-twentieth century. Leaders of independent schools also blurred notions of public and private as they responded to multiple historical, political, social, and economic factors. The first black students to desegregate schools like Westminster were born and raised in the decade after the landmark *Brown v. Board of Education* decision. I posit that they courageously navigated such schools, drawing on their experiences in southern black segregated communities and in southern black segregated schools. Consequently, by virtue of their presence and actions, the first black students and all that they brought with them informed and influenced the Westminster school culture as it underwent institutional change.

This book more forthrightly positions historically white elite schools or independent schools in the racial school desegregation narrative, and this narrative contributes to an expanding understanding of black educational experiences in the third quarter of the twentieth century. This history primarily chronicles Westminster's establishment in 1951 under the leadership of Dr. William Pressly, the school's development in the 1950s and 1960s, and the reasons that led to the 1965 decision to consider applicants of all races. This history continues by documenting the recruitment of the first black students, the desegregation of Westminster in 1967, and the experiences of the first black students. The account concludes with the graduation of the first black students in 1972 and the retirement of the founding school president in 1973. While an institutional history, this book also chronicles, simultaneously, how the National Association of Independent Schools (NAIS) considered and advanced a focus on the recruitment of black students. Together, the institutional and national are linked because of Dr. William Pressly, a national independent school leader. This historical account is bolstered by a deep attention to the relationship among local, regional, and national contexts including public school desegregation, the civil rights movement, increased federal government intervention in public and private schools, and a growing focus to recruit and retain black students to historically white elite private schools and those students' experiences.

Expanding the Desegregation Narrative

When many Americans think of school desegregation, what may come to mind is the iconic 1954 *Brown v. Board of Education* decision which declared "separate but equal" as unconstitutional, followed by the 1955 *Brown v. Board of Education II* decision that directed southern states to move "with all deliberate speed" in desegregating public schools.[11] Next might be the Little Rock Nine and the massive resistance they met from Governor Orval Faubus and everyday white citizens as they desegregated Central High School in Little Rock, Arkansas, in the fall of 1957. Or many may recognize Norman Rockwell's famous painting, *The Problem We All Live With*, that captures Ruby Bridges, then a young black girl, as she desegregated an elementary school with armed escorts in New Orleans, Louisiana, in 1960. Yet in the midst of public school desegregation battles that would continue through the 1960s and 1970s, black students also desegregated a host of other K-12 institutions, including historically white elite private schools.

Such schools, known as college prep schools, academies, or independent schools, include well-known boarding schools Phillips Exeter Academy, Phillips Academy Andover, and Choate Rosemary Hall. Elite day schools include The Dalton School in New York City and Sidwell Friends School in Washington, D.C.; the former is the site of the recent documentary *American Promise*, and the latter is where Chelsea Clinton and Malia and Sasha Obama, children of former presidents and first ladies Bill and Hillary Clinton and Barack and Michelle Obama, have attended school. Independent boarding and day schools are considered to be "the most privileged and prestigious of private schools."[12] During the mid-twentieth century, whites opposed to public school desegregation established segregationist academies so that white students would not have to attend newly desegregated public schools. Some independent school leaders chose to desegregate their schools though they were not legally required to do this.[13]

For many American children and their parents, historically white elite private schools like Exeter, Andover, Choate, Dalton, and Sidwell are elusive, unknown, and mysterious spaces and often only known through books, movies, and television shows including *The Catcher in the Rye*, *School Ties*, and *The Facts of Life*. Currently, private schools constitute 10 percent of all U.S. schools, but independent schools, a subset of private schools, enroll only slightly more than 1 percent of the U.S. school-age population.[14] Other types of private schools include parochial or religious, Montessori, for-profit schools, or culturally distinct schools, such as Afrocentric schools.[15] Yet, as bastions of privilege and prestige, historically white elite private schools, or independent schools, are catalysts for the creation and maintenance of social and cultural capital and are the harbingers of middle- and upper-class white ethos. Former presidents Franklin D. Roosevelt, John F. Kennedy, George W. Bush, and Barack H. Obama have attended these schools that are loci of leadership development for the United States and the world.

Some historically white elite private schools date to the "Age of the Academies" in the eighteenth and nineteenth centuries when private schools abounded prior to the massive increase in public schools.[16] Other private schools were established more recently in the twentieth century. Aware of the negative connotations associated with identifying their schools as "private" in the early twentieth century as the public high school became more commonplace, leaders of historically white elite private schools or college preparatory schools adopted the term *independent*.[17] With membership in NAIS, an organization founded in 1962, many independent schools are defined as "distinct from other private schools in that they are individually governed by a board of trustees and they do not depend on church funds as parochial schools do, or on tax dollars as public schools do."[18] However, "Certain denominational schools think of themselves primarily as independent and secondarily as denominational. This is true generally of the Episcopal, Presbyterian, Quaker, and the few Catholic schools that belong to the NAIS."[19] Further, one of the most salient features of independent schools, though largely nondenominational, is the freedom to provide religious life and training.[20]

Today, many independent schools also promote diversity and inclusion, but how did these contemporary commitments to diversity and inclusion come to be? How did these institutions come to assume these positions on issues of diversity and inclusion given that their schools were largely not built with students of color in mind? How do private school leaders respond to larger political and social changes in U.S. society? Examining the desegregation of a historically white elite private school in Atlanta begins to answer these questions.

Though not the only site of independent school desegregation in the South, Westminster provides a striking case study to answer these questions. Westminster, a "younger" independent school, rose quickly to local and national recognition in the 1950s and 1960s because of Pressly's leadership. In their account of independent schools, Zebulon Vance Wilson, headmaster of St. Albans School in Washington, D.C., and Russell Frank, noted that Pressly was "often mentioned in important discussions about all aspects of private education."[21] Pressly, one of few southern independent school presidents who held positions with the National Council of Independent Schools (NCIS) and NAIS, led Westminster at the same time that other independent school leaders and he grappled with a constellation of factors including the realities of the civil rights movement, public school desegregation, the proliferation of segregationist academies, inquiries into private school admissions policies, and increased federal intervention in public and private schools.

Elite private school leaders could not escape the realities of American apartheid and their complicity in it as black Americans and their white allies were killed, fought, arrested, harassed, insulted, and curtailed at every attempt to force America to contend with racism and inequality. Independent schools leaned toward more inclusivity in contrast to the segregationist academies that sprang up to thwart school desegregation, but whites' fears and resistance helped to increase independent schools' enrollments. On the other hand, the civil rights campaigns and legislation of the 1960s as well as the rise of segregationist academies awakened the moral consciousness of many independent school leaders. Consequently, independent school leaders developed efforts to increase the number of African American students attending independent schools outside of the South and to desegregate independent schools in the South.[22] Policies, publications, and initiatives from NAIS and the further development of recruitment and scholarship programs characterized the efforts of independent school leaders. Concurrently, the question loomed of whether or not schools with discriminatory admissions policies would continue to receive federal tax-exemption status.

Studies commissioned or supported by independent school organizations show that these schools' leaders were heavily concerned with their schools' public image and position within the larger U.S. educational landscape.[23] This concern also contributed to the increased diversity of independent schools in the 1960s; however, research has mostly focused on independent schools outside of the South, especially on the students who participated in programs such as A Better Chance (ABC), which recruited, prepared, and supported African American students enrolling in elite independent schools.[24]

A focus on a southern independent school demonstrates that in the early years of independent school desegregation, no full template for southern schools or African American students in southern independent schools existed. Moreover, William Dandridge, first director of minority affairs for NAIS, suggested that diversity for national leaders in the 1960s and 1970s often meant enrolling "African American children from poor and disadvantaged neighborhoods," reflecting national racial beliefs of the era.[25] How the process of desegregation unfolded at Westminster is indicative of how southern independent school desegregation perhaps was different from schools outside of the South because the first black students at Westminster were in large part from working- and middle-class families. The students' experiences, however, would echo in part those of their counterparts outside of the South.

Although schools like Westminster welcomed their first black students to enroll, these students, like their contemporaries in public K-12 schools and in public and private higher education institutions, endured racial harassment that included physical, verbal, and written attacks. School culture conditions that can be succinctly and best described as complex and contradictory were such that the first desegregation students questioned whether they even belonged in the Westminster school community. The first black students, however, succeeded in large part because of who they were and what they brought with them. Because of their families, the first black students to desegregate Westminster were the beneficiaries of a priceless inheritance rooted in the history of black educational commitments in the South. These students relied on their own educational experiences in mostly segregated black schools, their talents inside and outside of the classrooms, their work ethic, their families and communities, and the efforts of particular white and black individuals at Westminster. The first black students graduated from Westminster having courageously navigated the school's racist and paradoxical school climate by excelling inside and outside the classroom. Isaac Clark, who graduated a year early, enrolled at Morehouse College and then Georgia Tech. Michael McBay, Jannard Wade,

Malcolm Ryder, and Wanda Ward enrolled at Stanford University, More-house College, and Princeton University, respectively. Prior to graduating, McBay, Ryder, Wade, and Ward met to discuss their experiences, which Ryder shared with the school newspaper. The students touched on a number of subjects including friendships, the school culture, their relationships to their home communities, and more. They each experienced Westminster differently, but as Ryder noted, they agreed on the need for black students to be at Westminster with other black students because of the school climate and culture. Their white classmate Hill Martin echoed this by acknowledging the courage needed to attend such a school every day.

No Exemption for Private Schools

This book posits that private schools are not exempt from larger societal changes, and therefore demonstrates the speciousness of the public/private distinction. The public/private distinction emerged as public schools became the leading form of schooling in the United States. In colonial America, there was no universal or standard system of schooling, and there were a number of private schools, supported both publicly and privately. As the United States developed in the late eighteenth century and early nineteenth century, white reformers such as Horace Mann increasingly saw a need to develop a universal school system that would bring standardization, better conditions and resources, help develop an American ethos, and be supported by tax dollars. As the Common School Movement increased the number of public school systems in localities and states in the Northeast and Midwest, schools became categorized as public, private, and parochial because of their origins, funding streams, curricular foci, and administrative organization.[26] Historians and educational researchers, however, have not considered fully how these different types of schools are bound together in relationship to the larger U.S. society.

The history of school desegregation tends to depend on a kind of uncomplicated public/private binary, and the desegregation of historically white elite private schools complicates this relationship. Scholars have not deeply examined how twentieth-century policy issues clouded the distinction between public and private schools. Examining historically white elite private schools shows how leaders of these schools responded to matters affecting the larger public. Concerns about their schools' position in a changing U.S. society incentivized private school leaders, and their actions led to more blurring of public and private lines. There are also limited texts that examine how historically white schools, including those designed to prepare the most elite and the next cadre of leaders, undergo institutional change.

How black students succeeded in historically white elite private schools, in particular those in the South, and how these schools dealt with race relations has also not been readily examined. Such work yields insight into how and why the black freedom struggle intersected with and caused policy and institutional changes, even in private K-12 institutions. The Westminster story centers on how external and internal politics at institutional, local, state, and national levels; the culture of one historically white elite private school; and the matriculation of the first black students influenced and defined institutional change. These interconnected arguments, story lines, and factors illuminate the variables that affect how schools change in relationship to their communities outside and inside their school walls.

The desegregation of historically white elite private schools such as Westminster cannot be understood without the history of public school desegregation because of its direct effect on everyday life in the South and schooling options sought by whites and blacks. Historians have provided accounts of the politics of public school desegregation including "massive resistance" and other forms of opposition to *Brown* from school and city officials, parents, and students. These accounts note the importance of how the 1964 Civil Rights Act, the availability of Title I funding through the 1965 Elementary and Secondary Education Act, and additional court decisions forced southern school districts to desegregate. However, white flight, state-supported privatization, and the establishment of segregationist academies (or schools established by and for whites to avoid public school desegregation) often stymied significant public school desegregation.[27]

More recent accounts have centered the relationship among school desegregation, the political economy, and the development of cities; detailed the segregation that occurs within desegregated schools; pushed the boundaries of regional exceptionalism and possibilities for remedies to school segregation; and considered the long history of school desegregation from the middle to latter twentieth century as legal cases such as *Parents Involved in Community Schools v. Seattle School District No. 1* (2007) and *Meredith v. Jefferson County Board of Education* (2007) continue to determine school desegregation policies.[28] Outside of the South, work has focused on the politics of school desegregation and opposition to busing.[29] Further, scholars are pushing a reconsideration of the often used de facto and de jure demarcation. Historian Matthew Delmont wrote, "Our understanding of school desegregation in the North is skewed as a result, emphasizing innocent 'de facto' segregation over the housing covenants, federal mortgage redlining, public housing segregation, white home owners' associations, and discriminatory real estate practices that produced and maintained segregated neighborhoods as well as the policies regarding school siting, districting, and student transfers that produced and maintained segregated schools."[30] Delmont's account echoes a growing body of work emphasizing the need to historicize racism throughout the United States and to reorient our national narrative around racism; the South is not necessarily the exception.[31]

Yet, the first black students to attend Westminster, who were born between the *Brown* decision and the Civil Rights Act, inherited and experienced the history and realities of southern segregated black schooling as they grew up in segregated black communities. By countering prevailing notions about the inferiority of black schooling and ideological positions that render African Americans as uncaring about education, scholars have richly analyzed and detailed the African American educational experience in the South. Scholars have argued how African Americans—following the Civil War and despite the state-sanctioned terror, violence, and inequality because of Jim Crow laws—advanced universal schooling in the South, sought schooling in both public and private spaces, and participated in the creation of their own educational institutions.[32] Others have interrogated the rich intellectual debates between such leading figures as W. E. B. Du Bois and Booker T. Washington and the intricacies and influence of white philanthropists, white teachers, and white reformers.[33] The individual and collective influence of black teachers and administrators, the strength of segregated black schools, black fights for equalization, and cultural capital and black education have also been documented.[34] Historians and educational researchers have also examined the role of Catholic education, led both by whites and blacks.[35] The first black students inherited this black educational world and a legacy of African American conviction in the power of education for liberation that was adhered to despite great and dangerous consequences. These young people were equipped with tools and traditions that prepared them for a serious and thoughtful approach to schooling even in the face of interpersonal and institutional racism.

The history of black education clearly intersects with that of school desegregation history, but there are histories beyond and outside the particulars of school desegregation politics during the same time period. Memoirs and rich sociological studies add to our understanding of those who desegregated all-white public schools.[36] As desegregation occurred, there were costs to the African American community including the closing of black public and private schools and the dismissal and demotion of black principals and teachers.[37] The centrality of educational programs such as the Freedom Schools and Head Start in Mississippi shows the import of students receiving citizenship training outside of formal schools and the necessity of early childhood education and its possibilities for students and leaders of Head Start, in particular black women, to achieve more economic freedom in the face of continued white resistance.[38] Outside of the South, African Americans also employed strategies to seek educational equity in the decades following *Brown* that did not necessarily center around school desegregation but rather community control.[39] The protests that black youth inspired and led at schools, at institutions of higher education, and on streets during the civil rights movement and Black Power movement position youth and young adults as central to the era.[40] How African American students experienced schools like Westminster extends how we analyze and understand everyday school life and culture during the third quarter of the twentieth century and this particular African American student experience in relationship to the broader landscape of African American education.

Earlier work on historically white elite private schools in Atlanta connects those schools and local politics.[41] While building on this previous scholarship, this book deeply engages the desegregation politics of Westminster through a broader focus that considers the relationship among Atlanta's political and social changes, civil rights, federal policy, the decisions made by independent school leaders, and the national focus on the recruitment of black students to independent schools. The local context, however, holds a special place in this relationship.

Atlanta is the epicenter of the New South and a major Sunbelt city.[42] As home to Martin Luther King Jr. and key civil rights organizations, including the Southern Christian Leadership Conference (SCLC) and the Student Nonviolent Coordinating Committee (SNCC), it is a rich site for studying the intersection of race, class, and school desegregation. In the mid-twentieth century, Atlanta crafted its image as the "City Too Busy to Hate," due in large part both to William B. Hartsfield, the city's long-standing mayor, who sought to position Atlanta as different from other Southern cities, and to the biracial coalition between white moderate businessmen and black leaders. Informed by previous African American struggles for equity and civil rights, local African American citizens, educators, lawyers, activists, and politicians took action in different ways and employed multiple agendas for bringing down Jim Crow during the civil rights movement and Black Power era.[43] Like other southern cities, Atlanta Public Schools (APS) remained segregated until some African Americans pushed for desegregation. Despite Atlanta's position in the New South, the Georgia legislature, largely governed by those from rural Georgia, sought to resist public school desegregation by attempting to "equalize" black schools in the 1950s, by passing laws that called for the closure of any white school that accepted black students, and by allotting public funds for private education.

In 1958, black Atlantans sued the Atlanta school board in *Calhoun v. Latimer*, and Judge Frank A. Hooper ordered the desegregation of Atlanta Public Schools despite state laws. Only after the desegregation of the University of Georgia in January 1961 did the Georgia legislature repeal its laws.[44] As public institutions were desegregated in Atlanta and Georgia, elite higher education institutions, including Emory University in Atlanta, also opened their admissions policies because of multiple factors, including that of "northern foundations, professional academic associations, accrediting bodies," faculty, staff, and alumni who supported desegregation, and "new federal contracting rules."[45] Black students also desegregated Atlanta's leading independent schools as middle- and upper-class whites left the city of Atlanta and populated the expanding northern suburbs. Increasingly, some of these same white Atlantans, who would advocate for desegregation in public spaces, enrolled their children at historically white elite private schools such as Westminster.[46] As with other locations across the South, public school desegregation was gradual in Atlanta. By 1973, many whites had left the city, and local black leadership decided not to adopt busing as a remedy. Rather, they opted for more control of APS.[47]

Recent work by Kevin Kruse, Matthew Lassiter, Melissa Kean, and Tomiko Brown-Nagin builds on previous work on Atlanta, and together, the more recent histories on Atlanta illuminate a city characterized by image concerns; by economic prosperity and extreme poverty; by white and black leaders, who for their own reasons—converging and sometimes diverging—ascribed to pragmatism, gradualism, and moderation; and by white and black activists working separately and together. Atlanta's history dovetails with larger historical debates about conservatism, metropolitan and urban politics, the politics and strategies of the civil rights movement, and black educational opportunity.[48] By analyzing the interplay of this rich, complex local history, institutional politics and culture, regional changes, and national shifts among independent schools, the history of Westminster's desegregation offers a broader examination of the politics of desegregation and black students' experiences in a premier historically white private school in Atlanta.

Turning to the Private and Racial Diversity

As an elite school that garnered both local and national attention, informed by a developing and changing national private school agenda, Westminster provides an important lens for analyzing the relationship among race, class, and school desegregation. Federal regulations also intersected with demographic changes in independent schools as the Internal Revenue Service (IRS) declared as unconstitutional the practice of granting tax exemptions to educational institutions with racially discriminatory practices following the 1970 decision in *Green v. Kennedy*.[49] This case, initiated by black Mississippians, contended that all-white private schools (or segregationist academies) should not receive a tax exemption because of their discriminatory practices. Wanda A. Speede-Franklin, former director of minority affairs and director of information services for NAIS, noted the importance of stricter tax-exemption policies on independent schools by the IRS as the number of black students matriculating to independent schools increased.[50] Keith Evans, current president of Westminster, has discussed how the possibility of losing tax-exempt status would have been detrimental for schools. It would have been difficult to sustain the fiscal operations of independent schools, and school budgets would have needed to account for paying taxes on all expenditures and income. Plus, private institutions would not have been able to offer tax deductions to donors.[51]

How private school leaders such as Pressly positioned their schools in the late 1960s and early 1970s reflects the federal government's increasing role in public and private education and the growing role of the private in American life. By the early 1970s, segments of the American public became even more distrustful of the U.S. government. Many whites increasingly left city centers or turned to private schools as they opposed school desegregation orders and the Supreme Court's decisions in *Engel v. Vitale* (1962) and *Abington v. Schempp* (1963). In the former case, the court declared nondenominational prayer to be unconstitutional, and in the latter the court ruled against daily readings from the Bible.[52] Following Vietnam and Watergate, the American people, who actually valued the increased federal intervention over decades that created Social Security, home finance measures, infrastructure that included highway development, and Medicare, began to distrust the federal government.[53] Historian Thomas Borstelmann argued that as more egalitarian principles seemed to determine social shifts in terms of race and gender, more Americans turned inward and to the private—focusing on themselves, spending more time in their air-conditioned homes, and supporting unfettered deregulation of the economy and reliance on the free market.[54] With this turn to the private, debates about school choice and the privatization of traditional public schools emerged as new topics in schooling reform, and scholars in the coming decades would increasingly argue for institutional reform rooted in the free market.[55]

However, as this turn to the private occurred, race also increasingly became a positive good or marker of status for historically white elite private schools, both at the K-12 level and in higher education. As a constellation of factors pushed independent school leaders like Pressly to engage more directly in recruiting black students to schools like Westminster, the same had held true for historically white elite colleges and universities. Following King's assassination in 1968, black students' protests increased on college campuses of all types. Black students wrote black manifestos calling for the recruitment of more black students, more financial aid to support black students, and the establishment of black studies programs. Because of the weight of King's death and the interconnected protests and calls for attention to matters involving black students, more colleges and universities, including historically white elite institutions, began to recruit and admit more and more black students. According to sociologist Mitchell Stevens, "The historical record leaves little doubt that most institutional leaders required the push of protest and political crisis to move the academy toward racial pluralism."[56] In the same time and space that these pushes for racial diversity occurred, "official diversity very quickly came to be measured by the proportion of a student body that fell into the official minority categories of African American/black, Hispanic, Native American, or Asian. 'Diversity' became a number."[57]

The test for higher education leaders came with the *Bakke* case, initiated in 1974 in the lower courts by Allan Bakke, a white applicant who had been denied admission to the University of California at Davis medical school as they sought to implement affirmative action policies and increase the number of underrepresented minorities enrolled in medical school. With lower courts having found in Bakke's favor, the University of California appealed to the Supreme Court. Elite universities such as Columbia University, Harvard University, Stanford University, and the University of Pennsylvania filed amicus curiae briefs indicating that diversity was necessary since they were charged with producing the next crop of national leaders.[58] To ensure racial diversity meant supporting racial affirmative action in admissions. In 1978, the Supreme Court struck down the lower court decisions and upheld the medical school admissions plan at the University of California–Davis. With this decision and the efforts of the previous thirty years, race became an even more important factor in student admissions, especially at historically white, highly selective, elite institutions. Similar to the institutions in which they sought to enroll their graduates, leaders of historically white elite K-12 institutions simultaneously sought more black students through a host of different means. Alongside their counterparts in higher education, these leaders were redefining what it meant to have a quality education at historically white elite institutions.

Today in independent schools, even in those that began as segregationist academies, there is increased focus on the recruitment of more diverse students, racially and otherwise, and an increased number of diversity coordinators.[59] As Shamus Khan wrote in his study of St. Paul's in New Hampshire, "Today the school seeks to be a microcosm of our world. Rich and poor, black and white, boys and girls live in a community together . . . they make up a diverse and idealized community."[60] In these diverse settings, according to Khan, a new elite is emerging in which hierarchies are no longer fixed, experiences are important, and being privileged means adaptability in different settings. Schools such as St. Paul's seem to be "increasingly open" in a "relentlessly unequal" society in which those with the highest incomes experienced the greatest increases over the last half century.[61] Although these schools seemingly lead on these matters and the notions of elite may be changing or masking true hierarchy, "access is not the same as integration."[62]

Historically white elite private schools such as Westminster, that now actively promote diversity and inclusion, occupy an interesting position in the U.S. schooling landscape. The current national climate includes resegregated public schools. Many black and brown students attend school primarily with other students of color and many white students go to school primarily with other white students.[63] In the 2007 ruling in *Parents Involved*, a case in which white parents argued that student assignments for public schools based on race was unconstitutional, Chief Justice John Roberts in the majority opinion declared, "The way to stop discrimination on the basis of race is to stop discriminating on the basis of race."[64] This decision found unconstitutional school districts' explicit use of race in deciding where students should attend public schools. In an increasingly unequal society in which debates swirl around school choice, most notably about charter schools and vouchers and the privatization of public schools, parents of students (and students themselves) from the most vulnerable populations—whether marginalized by any combination of identities including race, class, gender, language, religion, sexual orientation, or ability—still seek equitable, inclusive schooling environments where they will succeed and be prepared to enter and thrive as full citizens in the current political economy. On one hand, independent schools represent a desirable schooling option for many regardless of race or other marginalized identity, but on the other hand, they still contribute to the development of power and leadership for those already privileged in society.

In the mid-twentieth century, historically white elite private schools that help to make and remake power embarked on a campaign to recruit black students. For some institutions this meant increasing their small enrollment of black students; for other institutions like Westminster this meant desegregating. One may ask how did having black students become an asset to these institutions as they did to elite colleges and universities? How did independent schools, created within an inequitable society undergirded by racism, change their policies and why? Further, what happened on such campuses like Westminster's before and after the first black students enrolled and graduated? What did such experiences mean for individual black students and the larger black community?

Looking Within

Transforming the Elite draws on both bottom-up social history and top-down institutional and organizational history. To capture these histories, I analyzed multiple collections at Westminster, including Board of Trustee minutes, Annual President's Reports, and promotional materials, as well as every school newspaper and yearbook published between 1951 and 1973. I also researched materials in additional archival collections as well as the *Independent School Bulletin*, the NCIS *Report*, the NAIS *Report*, and Reports from NAIS's annual conferences. To capture the lived experience, I employed oral history, and I interviewed black and white alumni of Westminster, black and white parents of Westminster alumni, and black and white leaders in the independent school world. This combination of sources yields an examination that blends microhistory and case study design.[65] If microhistory is defined as how the "individual [life] serves as an allegory for broader issues affecting the culture as a whole," then the individual is Westminster, and it is analyzed for deep institutional understanding over time.[66] Further, the oral histories are undergirded by particular sensibilities, including the importance of trust between interviewer and interviewee, and they are informed by historical ethnography and qualitative inquiry as well as the research on oral history and memory.[67] Together the archival documents and interviews underlie a multifaceted history of one school's desegregation story. The convergence of story lines, including Atlanta's pragmatic desegregation politics, public school desegregation, civil rights, federal policy for public and private schools, and national changes among independent schools, provides context for analyzing Westminster's desegregation politics, its school culture, its local, regional, and national position, and the black student experience. Although the African American alumni interviewed have reconciled with aspects of their experiences, being black in an elite independent school in the 1960s and 1970s was not easy.

While *Transforming the Elite* addresses many themes of the era, it is primarily organized chronologically with a focus on the rhythm and experience of everyday school life over time, and students' first and last names are used interchangeably. Westminster's desegregation politics, its school culture, and the experiences of the first black students interact with institutional history and local, regional, and national contexts. Interwoven throughout the narrative are considerations of the multiplicity of historical actors involved in black educational opportunities in the South, individual and collective black educational advocacy, and the characteristics that defined positive southern black educational experiences. Additionally, this examination is informed by black and white responses to civil rights and school desegregation, and it considers the import of independent schools to civic and business leaders, to the politics of race and desegregation occurring in cities such as Atlanta, and to the range of educational opportunities available in that metropolitan area. Altogether, the push and pull of different contexts illuminate the desegregation of Westminster.

Chapter 1, "The Inheritances of a New Elite Private School," chronicles how early decisions by Pressly and other private school leaders began to blur the boundaries between public and private. During its first few years of existence, Westminster became the school that middle- and upper-class Atlanta needed in the midst of the postwar population boom. By 1957, Pressly became the first southerner to lead NCIS, thereby making him privy to the longer history of independent schools in the United States, including their early attention to race and recruitment of black students during the mid-twentieth century. As Pressly assumed national leadership, a school culture developed that reflected "Old South" sentiments and racist traditions. Not long after Westminster was born, so were the first black students, including Michael McBay, Malcolm Ryder, Jannard Wade, and Wanda Ward, who desegregated the school in the late 1960s. The first desegregation generation were recipients of a priceless black educational inheritance that equipped them to desegregate Westminster.

Chapter 2, "Contending with Change and Challenges," captures the development of Westminster in the late 1950s and early 1960s. By the late 1950s, Westminster's student body had quadrupled, and the school was now housed on the current West Paces Ferry Road campus. School leaders prepared for the possible closing of Atlanta Public Schools (APS) as black Atlantans called for desegregation in the face of oppositional state policies. State leaders ultimately repealed their laws, and nine black students desegregated APS in the fall of 1961. As the civil rights movement increased in momentum, Westminster and other local Atlanta schools received inquiries into their admissions policies from interracial organizations such as the Greater Atlanta Council on Human Relations (GACHR), leading civil rights activists including the Kings, Abernathys, and Youngs, and black families such as the Rosses. Private school leaders such as Pressly worked to find a balance among multiple contexts and influences, including the enlarged federal presence in education and increased questions about federal tax-exempt status for private schools. Concurrently, a school culture developed in ways that continued to reflect the "Old South" and included racist traditions while some white students earnestly debated and discussed the issues of the day.

Chapter 3, "The Blurring of Public and Private," analyzes Westminster's development and its adoption of an open admissions policy in 1965 alongside an increasing national effort to recruit black students to independent schools. The civil rights movement and possible changes in federal tax-exemption policies for their institutions captured the attention of independent school leaders, and these leaders then increasingly sought to diversify their student bodies through shifts in policies, practices, recruitment programs, and scholarship funds. Westminster became a southern exemplar of this national agenda with its striking and political announcement of its open admissions policy, but the school was also emblematic of the pragmatic desegregation politics of Atlanta. As Westminster prepared to desegregate, the first black students learned of Westminster through several avenues including the Stouffer Foundation.

Chapter 4, "The Fearless Firsts," documents the first years of school desegregation at Westminster. By 1967, Westminster was a nationally known school whose alumni attended colleges and universities across the nation, but black students like Michael McBay and Dawn Clark endured overt racial harassment. Following the assassination of Dr. King in April 1968, the pivotal and tumultuous decade concluded with increased protest in the nation at the same time that NAIS further advanced its recruitment efforts of black students. At Westminster, Malcolm Ryder, Ron McBay (Michael's younger brother), Joia Johnson, and others enrolled also experienced racial harassment. The first black students, however, began to find their niches inside and outside the classroom. The school culture included increased volunteer efforts in black neighborhoods, celebrations of black workers in the yearbooks and newspapers, and visits by notable black individuals. Nevertheless, some school traditions reflecting racial subordination continued. The fearless firsts found their way by largely relying on their skills and talents, the support of their families, and the dedication of black workers and select white administrators and teachers.

Chapter 5, "Courageous Navigation," examines the early 1970s, including the last years of Pressly's tenure at Westminster, a legal turning point in the enforcement of open admissions policies at private institutions, and the graduation of the first black students from Westminster. During the summer of 1970, Pressly spoke out against segregationist academies. Following a legal case filed by black Mississippians challenging the tax-exemption status of segregated white private schools, the IRS required private institutions with tax-exempt status to establish nondiscriminatory admissions policies. Under the leadership of William Dandridge, NAIS gave more attention to the quality of the black student experience in independent schools. Yet these changes could not fully interrupt the institutional and interpersonal racism that black students experienced in independent schools. As shifting politics occurred in Atlanta, the black students at Westminster immersed themselves in academics and extracurricular activities, and the students became even more important to the institution. Michael McBay, who had been harassed, became the activist, in the more traditional sense, among the black students. As the first group graduated, new black students like Corliss Blount and Donata Russell joined Westminster. Altogether, thirty-five black students matriculated at Westminster during the first years of desegregation, and over half graduated in time as they individually succeeded, broke barriers, and courageously navigated an institution not originally created to accommodate them.

Transforming the Elite concludes by addressing how formal schooling for many African Americans is still an avenue for upward mobility in a society very much grappling with race and racism. The decisions African Americans make about schooling are not simple, and black families struggle with the many variables that affect black students' academic, social, psychological, and emotional outcomes. As African Americans continue to face dilemmas about schooling options and endure gaps in access to equitable public schools, they sometimes believe that historically white private schools are the better choice for their children. Yet racism and racial matters transcend school type, and many are challenging school cultures, no matter the type of institution, to be more inclusive and diverse.[68]

WHEN I FIRST BEGAN this project, I considered what I knew of African American educational history and school desegregation history. Similar to my previous research on higher education and equity in Mississippi, I looked within. As an African American woman born and raised in Jackson, Mississippi, who attended St. Andrew's Episcopal School, an independent day school, and graduated "alpha and omega" (meaning that I attended from kindergarten through twelfth grades), I began this project wanting to know who had come before me in such schools as St. Andrew's. This study clearly has evolved into much more than a personal quest to understand.

Knowing that most of our nation's children, especially those who racially identify as I do, attend public schools has pushed me to think about the relationship of this history to the racial inequities in public schooling. Because black students have been educated in different types of school settings, their schooling experiences call on both historians and contemporary researchers of African American education to examine this multitude of educational spaces. By doing so, we more fully understand black student achievement and black students' experiences. Access to quality public schooling has informed and shaped the African American educational experience, but African Americans have been educated in any number of institutions because of the promise and belief that schooling, public or private, can lead to better preparation and full participation in the political economy and polity.

Understanding the experiences of African American students in a historically white elite private school in the South adds to and modifies what we know about African American educational experiences and leadership development in a changing American society. Because of forces at institutional, local, regional, and national levels, black students desegregated and attended independent schools and other historically white K-12 and higher education institutions in greater numbers in the 1960s and 1970s. With family, community, and previous experiences as anchors, the first African American students at schools like Westminster navigated institutions that had not been established for them. That Westminster and other elite schools became accessible to more blacks as the nation underwent significant changes signaled a shift in student demographics, but the work continues to make every student's experience one of high quality.

CHAPTER ONE

The Inheritances of a New Elite Private School

By the mid-twentieth century, independent school leaders had increasingly become more cognizant of their schools' image and homogeneity. One independent school leader penned a piece in 1949 entitled "Colored Students Are an Asset." Mira B. Wilson, a white woman and principal of the Northfield School for Girls in East Northfield, Massachusetts, noted that twenty-two independent schools had "committed themselves to a nondiscriminatory policy."[1] Though three schools had declared their intentions to enroll "colored" pupils, they had not done so. In calling into question the low enrollment numbers of black Americans in historically white elite private schools, Wilson concluded by arguing "the policy of inclusion is in line with the best interests of both religious and national life."[2]

The attention that Wilson brought to the low enrollment number of black students in independent schools did not prevent the further establishment of schools, such as Westminster, with all-white student populations. Founded in 1951 under the leadership of Dr. William "Bill" Pressly, Westminster joined the cadre of old-line private schools in the South like Episcopal High School in Alexandria, Virginia, established in 1839, and the McCallie School in Chattanooga, Tennessee, established in 1905. Born out of a segregated southern context, Westminster, a "younger" elite private school, emerged as a nonsectarian school with a close affiliation with the Presbyterian Church.

In 1952, those marketing Westminster promoted it as "The School Atlanta Needs." The promotional materials stated: "Atlanta is not able to point with pride to the campus and buildings of a single nationally known independent preparatory school, where both boys and girls in elementary and secondary grades can obtain an education of recognized academic worth and Christ-centered in purpose."[3] Westminster leaders characterized the school as a viable alternative to the private education offered in the Northeast: "Richmond, Chattanooga, Nashville, and Memphis have some excellent independent schools, but by and large, the South provides few educational opportunities on par with those offered by the leading preparatory schools of the Northeast states. Therefore, hundreds of our young people are sent away to school year after year."[4] Such promotions appealed to white southerners who perhaps wanted to keep their children nearby and who increasingly came to support private schools as the population grew in Atlanta. More white Atlantans backed private schools as threats of public school desegregation and the desegregation of public facilities unsettled their way of life. Middle- and upper-class white Atlanta citizens needed and wanted Westminster and other private schools in the 1950s. Private schools allowed middle- and upper-class whites to enroll their children in schools that perhaps they thought would be untouched by desegregation politics and that offered academic rigor and, in some cases, a religious focus.

Within its earliest years, Westminster's stature increased locally and nationally as a particular school culture developed. To build Westminster, Pressly capitalized on the interests of Atlanta's white leading citizens and the pragmatic politics that city leaders deployed. Such politics contrasted with the state of Georgia that passed legislation to resist the implementation of *Brown v. Board of Education* (1954). Pressly also became a leader of the National Council of Independent Schools (NCIS). Simultaneously, Westminster's administrators, faculty, staff, and students cultivated an early school culture that reflected "Old South" sentiments and included racist traditions.

Westminster did not have an explicit statement that denied admission to black students, but school leaders did not seek them either. The first black students who would desegregate and navigate Westminster were born at the same time the school developed. The first black students to attend Westminster were to be nurtured in segregated black communities that had been created and sustained behind the veil of Jim Crow that "denied [African Americans] the basic rights of citizenship in the land of their birth." African Americans, who whites had deemed inherently inferior, were still "expected to provide the basic labor of the South even as they complied with the perverse etiquette of Jim Crow."[5] Despite this harsh reality and state-sanctioned racism, African Americans fostered vibrant communities that included a multiplicity of educational options and experiences. That terror and vibrancy coexisted and continue to coexist marks the lives of marginalized communities in the United States. Understanding the world into which the first black students were born extends what we know about Jim Crow and black communities that formed during the early and mid-twentieth century and how those communities undergirded those black students who led societal change in the mid- to latter twentieth century. The history of black education in the South is complex, but the first black students to desegregate Westminster, because of their families, communities, and their schooling experiences in segregated black schools prior to attending Westminster, were recipients of a priceless inheritance. These students inherited and benefited from African Americans' enduring belief in and commitment to the possibility of education as a means of freedom and liberation.

By leading Westminster in the early to mid-1950s to become a school needed and wanted by middle- and upper-class whites, Pressly, its founding president, began to negotiate multiple contexts, including that of the city of Atlanta, the state of Georgia, and independent schools nationally. The overlapping and conflicting dynamics among these contexts would define Westminster's internal debates, public relations, and school culture. Pressly, having worked in independent school education, recognized these intersecting contexts and began to blur public and private in his actions as he led the development of Westminster and as private schools became part of states' plans to avoid desegregation and focal points of other societal discussions and concerns. In these initial years, whites established segregationist academies after the *Brown* decision. These schools became havens for white students whose parents did not want them to attend desegregated public schools. Because it was founded just prior to the *Brown* decision, Westminster is not technically a segregationist academy. Private spaces, however, like Westminster, allowed for whites to retreat from the realities of the crumbling Jim Crow South. These new realities informed how public and private school leaders deliberated on the direction of their schools during the post-World War II era and early stages of the civil rights movement. At the same time, the first black students that would desegregate Westminster were being born and would be raised in segregated black communities and schools developed because of and in spite of Jim Crow. What they gained as young boys and girls born in the mid-twentieth century would help equip them for experiences that they did not even know lay ahead—desegregating and attending Westminster.

"The School Atlanta Needs"

During the mid-twentieth century, as the city's population continued to grow, political changes reflected Atlanta's growing pragmatic politics which differed from state resistance to end Jim Crow. In the decade prior to Westminster's founding, Atlanta's population increased from 302,299 to 331,314, and African Americans, who in 1940 made up 35 percent of Atlanta's population, continued to push against segregation laws and practices.[6]

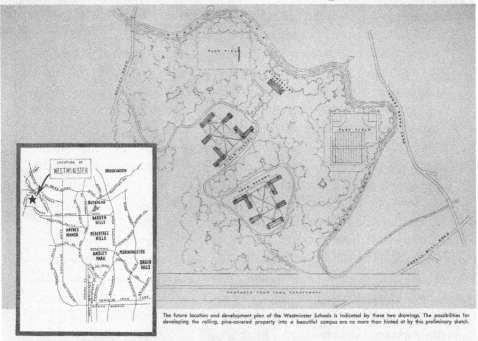

The future location and development plan of the Westminster Schools is indicated by these two drawings. The possibilities for developing the rolling, pine-covered property into a beautiful campus are no more than hinted at by this preliminary sketch.

In the 1952 promotional materials, The Westminster Schools were marketed as "The School Atlanta Needs." School leaders envisioned a Christian school on Atlanta's north side that would parallel other historically white elite private schools, or independent schools, throughout the Southeast and the nation. Over time, the Westminster campus would include more academic buildings, athletic facilities, and additional resources, rivaling other independent school campuses and those campuses of some institutions of higher education. Source: "The School Atlanta Needs," RG 13.07, box 1, folder: 1952 Promotional Materials (3 of 3). Office of Institutional Advancement, Campaigns and Promotional Materials, Beck Archives-Westminster.

For example, "A. T. Walden filed a pay equity suit in 1942—his first foray into civil rights litigation."[7] Following the decision in *Smith v. Allwright* (1944) which declared Texas's all-white primaries to be unconstitutional, black Georgians successfully challenged Georgia's all-white primary in 1945.[8] In the days following this legal victory and reflective of the Double Victory (or Double V) campaigns following World War II, more and more Africans Americans registered to vote. By the summer of 1946, 100,000 African Americans had registered throughout the state, and 21,244 blacks had registered in Atlanta. African American agency and advocacy resulted in significant legal victories. Although racism persisted, increased voter registration enlarged the power of the African American vote, and black leadership influenced the city's white leadership even more.

Atlanta's role in the New South, the south that emerged after the Civil War and that would lead the region economically, politically, culturally, and socially, increased in the early to mid-twentieth century. Led by Mayor William B. Hartsfield beginning in 1937 (and almost without interruption until 1962), Atlanta experienced significant events during his early tenure as mayor. *Gone with the Wind*, a cinematic representation of the "Old South," premiered in December 1939, and Atlantans celebrated the one hundredth anniversary of the Atlanta municipality and the twenty-fifth anniversary of Coca-Cola, an economic driving force in Atlanta led by the Woodruff family. Hartsfield also led the expansion of what is now Hartsfield-Jackson International Airport, the nation's busiest airport. Because of the abolition of the Georgia white primary and the subsequent recognition of the power of the black vote, the white business community in North Atlanta established a loose political alliance with the city's black leaders; this partnership became known as the Northside-Black alliance.[9] White leaders of the alliance included Mayor Hartsfield, Ralph McGill, editor of the *Atlanta Constitution*, and Robert Woodruff, president of Coca-Cola; they represented the essence of "business conservatives." Business conservatives, as educated, wealthy individuals and moderates on race relations, were "less inclined than the lower classes or rural communities to view strict segregation by any means necessary as the only option."[10] These leaders wanted to preserve their economic interests, and therefore would employ more pragmatic racial politics. Black leaders included John Wesley Dobbs and A. T. Walden, founders of the Atlanta Negro Voters League in 1949. Dobbs and Walden were two members of Atlanta's black middle class, which included leaders of Atlanta's black churches, businesses, and educational institutions such as the historically black colleges and universities (HBCUs) which then comprised the Atlanta University Center (AUC) — Atlanta University, Morehouse College, and Spelman College.[11] During the 1949 mayoral election, Hartsfield, a segregationist, knew the importance of appealing to black Atlantans, so he appeared before the Atlanta Negro Voters League. The league only endorsed Mayor Hartsfield after he agreed to support: "hiring more black police; opening a fire station with black firemen in Westside Atlanta's black areas; getting more parks, playgrounds, public housing, and land for private homes; and upgrading black city workers."[12] With the endorsement of the Atlanta Negro Voters League and 50.1 percent of the vote, including 82.5 percent from two predominantly black precincts, Atlantans reelected Hartsfield as mayor, and he hired eight black police officers who desegregated the Atlanta Police Department. However, "whatever Hartsfield's rhetoric, Atlanta's blacks were still treated as second-class citizens. No white leader sought to end segregation. As stated in the early 1950s, 'I'm a true friend of the Negro and will be as long as he keeps his place.'"[13]

Gains on the local level for African Americans were limited in the 1940s, but despite opposition, the advancements illuminated the shifting tide in the post–World War II era. Southern states like Georgia, which was still heavily governed by rural leaders, did their best to thwart any possibility of desegregation. In 1947, under Governor Herman Talmadge, the state legislature devised a statewide system of school finance, the Minimum Foundation Program of Education (MFPE). Supported by the Georgia Educators Association, Superintendent Mauney Douglass Collins, and Roy V. Harris, a leading Georgia politician, MFPE served as Georgia's last-minute attempt to create actual "separate but equal" black and white public schools. Three years later, the National Association for the Advancement of Colored People (NAACP) filed *Aaron v. Cook* against the Atlanta school board. The NAACP Legal Defense and Educational Fund (LDF) also earned victories in *Sweatt v. Painter* (1950) and *McLaurin v. Oklahoma* (1950) that solidly chipped away at *Plessy v. Ferguson* (1896). Both cases helped to set the tenor for the five cases known as *Brown v. Board of Education*, which were already being heard in lower courts. Though *Sweatt* and *McLaurin* concerned black access to higher education, they contributed to establishing legal precedent for *Brown* by pointing to the intangibles of educational opportunity.[14] That same year, the Georgia General Assembly approved a record-breaking $207,505,708 state appropriations bill; half of this appropriation was to fund MFPE so that state leaders could attempt to equalize funding between black and white schools. Similar to other southern states, the Georgia legislature wanted to make separate but equal schools a reality in order to avoid the possibility of desegregation on the grounds that white and black schools were unequal. Another part of the bill included a state law that "required the state to cut off funds to all public schools in Georgia in the event of the admission of one black to one public school."[15]

Private schools, however, were not beholden to the threat of having funds cut, and MFPE was a factor in ongoing accreditation conversations for independent schools. That MFPE affected some aspect of independent schools indicated an early sign of increasing governmental influence in private schools and how private schools were not operating completely on their own accord. In 1950, qualification in the Southern Association of Independent Schools (SAIS) was by accreditation from the Southern Association of Colleges and Schools (SACS).[16] Yet at SACS's November 1950 meeting in Richmond, Virginia, attendees discussed "proposals for the establishment of new standards by the association," including the requirement that a school be accredited by its local state before being approved by the association. Private school leaders objected because they thought that state accreditation requirements, intended for public high schools, would constrain independent schools' curricular offerings and impose new requirements for the length of the school year and teacher certification.[17] By March 1951, independent school leaders tabled discussions because states appeared lenient toward independent schools although state departments still favored state approval prior to SACS offering schools accreditation.[18] The increasing discussion about how schools qualified for SAIS and the potential requirement of state accreditation reflected how private schools were very much a part of debates by individuals who oversaw public matters such as the accreditation of public schools.

State accreditation of Georgia's independent schools depended on compliance with MFPE. Without compliance, schools risked losing accreditation by SACS.[19] Additionally, along with providing money to "equalize" white and black schools, MFPE included funds to increase public school teachers' salaries. This raise in salaries caused concern among independent school leaders because they did not know if they could match the new salaries when hiring teachers for their schools. By September, when Westminster opened its doors, the salary policy had been eased for private schools, allowing private schools to follow the state salary schedule for the 1950-51 school year.[20] Further, in March 1952, a compromise was reached regarding private schools' accreditation. A school could be eligible for accreditation upon applying to SACS's state commission. Additionally, the SACS executive committee made provisions so that independent school leaders, including the president of SAIS, could be represented.[21]

With enrollment increasing in area public schools, "Atlanta's explosive population growth created a market niche for private schools."[22] Atlanta's population swelled in the 1950s jumping from 331,314 to 487,455 in 1960, and in 1951 the city expanded with the annexation of Buckhead, enlarging the city limits from 37 to 118 square miles. In the same year that Westminster began, Trinity School was founded on the north side of Atlanta, and the

Lovett School, another private school, continued to grow, indicating expanding support for private schools among middle- and upper-class whites in Atlanta. The threat of public school closure per Georgia law if local school districts complied with *Brown* fortified private schools' growth. Therefore, "while the Atlanta business community worked behind the scenes to keep open schools, they were not going to be unprepared for the possibility that the schools might be closed."[23] Westminster would exemplify the importance of a historically white elite K-12 school in the city of Atlanta during the 1950s as city leaders employed pragmatic desegregation politics, as the state legislature of Georgia did its best to avoid public school desegregation, as massive resistance occurred throughout the South, as segregationist academies sprouted, and as support increased for all private schools.

Before leading Westminster, Pressly had been coheadmaster of McCallie, where he had begun working as a teacher in 1936. Pressly had spent his childhood in Louisville, Georgia, and Chester, South Carolina, and learned about slavery, including about slave auctions, from Henrietta Cummings (or Aunt Hen), a former slave who worked for his family. He began his college career at Erskine College, an institution that his great-grandfather founded and that his grandfather led. He later transferred to Princeton and graduated. His wife, Alice McCallie, whom he married in 1940, was the daughter of Spencer McCallie, one of the founders of the McCallie School.[24]

Pressly, having been at the McCallie School for a number of years, came to Atlanta when the white establishment sought his advice about the need for a new leader of a struggling school, the Napsonian School, founded in 1909 under the leadership of Dr. Richard Orme Flinn, pastor of North Avenue Presbyterian Church. In 1942, the school's leadership "passed to an incorporated board of trustees, affiliated with both the Presbytery and the Synod" and adopted the school name. Although boys had been accepted in the lower grades since the school's establishment, Napsonian only admitted girls to upper grades.[25] With a well-rounded curriculum which included a focus on Christianity and physical education, SACS accredited the school in 1921, and graduates attended colleges such as Agnes Scott College in Atlanta and Randolph-Macon College in Virginia.[26] But by the mid-twentieth century, Napsonian's enrollment declined. Dr. James Ross McCain, president of Agnes Scott and board member of Napsonian, wrote in 1951 to Pressly, a family friend, asking him to recommend a leader for a new school. Rather than nominate someone else, Pressly nominated himself.[27]

From 1951 to 1973, Dr. William "Bill" Pressly led Westminster as the school's founding president. During his tenure, he also held a number of leadership roles outside of Westminster including chair of the National Council of Independent Schools (NCIS) and founding trustee of the National Association of Independent Schools (NAIS). Such positions helped to link Westminster to national conversations among independent school leaders concerning race and the recruitment of black students in the 1950s and 1960s. Source: *Lynx* (Yearbook) 1965, 5, RG 21.02, Beck Archives-Westminster.

Under Pressly, Westminster soon became a fixture in the political and social climate of Atlanta. Pressly relied on specific criteria to develop Westminster into a leading college preparatory school. He directed the formation of a board of trustees, hired "well-trained faculty," and led the recruitment of "a student body of bright and talented youngsters."[28] Pressly also garnered community support for the school by recognizing the importance of whites in the Northside-Black Alliance, the alliance that had been formed among leading white businessmen and leading black civic leaders. He capitalized on Atlanta's white power structure. Even prior to accepting the offer from McCain, Pressly sought the advice of leading Atlantan white businessmen, such as Woodruff, Harrison Jones (also of Coca-Cola), and John Sibley, chairman of the Trust Company of Georgia. Though Pressly received the support of all three men, Woodruff made it clear that he would not support the school financially because of his financial commitments to Emory University's medical school.

The Westminster board of trustees included well-known members of Atlanta's white community: Dr. Vernon S. Broyles Jr., pastor of Atlanta's North Avenue Presbyterian Church and former chair of the board for the Napsonian School; McCain; and Welborn Cody, the school's attorney and a member of North Avenue Presbyterian Church. Broyles served as chair for more than twenty years, and McCain served until his death in 1965. Pressly stated that the "Board of Trustees must accept its share of responsibility for raising these funds . . . I want the Board of Trustees to realize that no school head coming into town can be expected to raise funds without the wholehearted cooperation of each member of the Board of Trustees."[29] He appealed for the development of boarding school components in addition to day schools for boys and girls, a tuition increase from $300 to $400, a salary of $9,000 with a $1,500 house allowance, and a new name for the school—The Westminster Schools.

In the fall of 1951, Westminster began with three units—a junior school (consisting of kindergarten through seventh grade), a girls' school (eighth through twelfth grades), and a boys' school (eighth through twelfth grades). In the facilities of the Napsonian School, eighteen faculty and staff taught and administered the new school with 240 students. The school operated on a budget of $75,000 and included 2,500 volumes in the library.[30] During the summer of 1953, Washington Seminary, an all-girls' school begun in 1878, merged with Westminster.[31] Additionally, Westminster began receiving significant financial contributions in November. Robert Woodruff changed his mind, and Pressly announced what would be the first of many gifts from the Woodruff Foundation—a donation of $50,000 for the campaign, with a total fundraising goal of $840,000.[32] Such support from Coca-Cola's first family indicated Westminster's growing standing among members of the white establishment. Westminster's receipt of $7,000 as part of a grant from the Fund for the Advancement of Education in December 1953 also indicated the strength of the school's faculty and students. The grant supported an initial "experiment in enrichment and acceleration of the educational program." This program would later become the Advanced Placement (AP) Program.[33] By the late 1950s, Westminster occupied its current campus on West Paces Ferry Road on Atlanta's north side, close to Buckhead. The school enrolled close to one thousand students, quadruple the size of its original student body, and tuition hovered around $200 for lower grades, $450 for junior high and high school, and close to $1,500 for those who boarded.[34]

Westminster increased in stature within the community, and the local press praised Pressly's leadership. An April 1952 article by Celestine Sibley, noted columnist for the *Atlanta Constitution*, reported on a three-day convocation about educational opportunity in the Atlanta area that Pressly hosted. In the summer of 1953, Sibley reflected on Pressly's demeanor and his accomplishments. She conveyed that Pressly quickly acquired a sense of loyalty from those affiliated with the Napsonian School and Washington Seminary. Although individuals had deep ties to the former schools, Pressly had worked tirelessly in his efforts to grow Westminster and had shown "a tremendous amount of tact and patience" as he worked with people who found it difficult to let go of their old schools. As Sibley noted, "People, particularly Southern people, are fond of their old institutions and their old ways. . . . Your mind may tell you that the new thing is good but your heart rebels."[35] Sibley's sentiments not only captured this reluctance but spoke to a larger theme that would resonate in future years as civil rights activists forced the overturning of Jim Crow laws.

City leaders would move tepidly toward desegregation so as not to disrupt its economic prosperity, although the state legislature had already passed laws in an attempt to equalize black schools under the guise of "separate but equal" and to deny funding to any segregated white school that admitted a black student. On the heels of the desegregation of the Atlanta Police Department, Atlanta citizens elected Dr. Rufus Clement, president of Atlanta University, to the Atlanta school board in 1953. Clement, along with Dr. Miles Amos and Austin Walden, who were newly elected as representatives of Atlanta's Third Ward, had become Atlanta's first black officials since Reconstruction.[36] Indicative of its audience, however, the Westminster promotional materials did not include these changes occurring in the city. The promotional materials were intended for white Atlantans and when describing the city, there was no discussion of race relations. While some whites most likely knew of these racial shifts in the city, the lack of attention to such changes showed the school's position on such matters and how they were able to appeal to white Atlantans.

Westminster's 1954 promotional materials, entitled "A Great City, A Great School," described Atlanta as follows: "For her greatness is not something she was born with, nor something 'thrust upon her'; it is something she has achieved. It is the product of opportunity, vision, and creative effort." Likewise, Westminster capitalized on this same combination. Pressly discussed the freedom of independent schools: selecting students "who have the ability and desire to do the hard work it requires, and to meet the high standards it sets," the inclusion of Bible instruction, and the ability "to concentrate on the special task of college preparation."[37] Pressly noted how leaders in both higher education and in the public schools, including Ida Jarrell, superintendent of APS, positively received the addition of Westminster.[38] Leaders from all types of institutions seemingly viewed Westminster as a good addition to the city as public schools became sites of desegregation battles.

As Atlanta's leaders employed pragmatic desegregation politics, Westminster enjoyed the growing support of Atlanta's leading white citizens. Ivan Allen Jr., then president of the Chamber of Commerce and future mayor of Atlanta from 1962 to 1970, and his wife, Louise Richardson Allen, sent their sons to Westminster, and Louise served on the school's board. During Westminster's second major fundraiser in 1954, Ivan Allen and Pressly together met with "60 key prospective donors" and the campaign "surpassed its goal" of $430,000.[39] Pressly had carefully positioned Westminster to be on the minds of leading white Atlantans who would support the school.

Resistance to *Brown*

On May 17, 1954, the Supreme Court ruled in *Brown* the unconstitutionality of "separate but equal" in public schools. Their decision rested on the argument that segregation had stamped a badge of inferiority on black children. The unanimous decision was met with mixed reactions. The NAACP LDF waged the case as a way to overturn *Plessy v. Ferguson*, but African Americans hesitated to celebrate too much because they did not know what the decision meant for the schooling of black children and their jobs as teachers and school administrators. As Richard Kluger wrote, "Too many proclamations of white America's good intentions had reached African Americans' ears in the past to permit premature celebration now."[40]

A year later, the Supreme Court issued *Brown v. Board of Education II* which allowed for states to move "with all deliberate speed" in implementing school desegregation. Because of this decision, most leaders of southern states stymied the implementation of school desegregation. Whites used massive resistance and other intimidation tactics in an effort to stop African Americans from desegregating public schools. For example, in the state of Virginia, officials closed schools in Prince Edward County for five years. At the same time, the Georgia state legislature became more entrenched in its opposition to school desegregation, reflecting the southern political leaders who wrote and signed the Southern Manifesto in 1956. Georgia state legislators continued to pass laws to avoid complying with *Brown* while also allocating more resources to improve black schools in hopes to achieve "separate but equal" educational systems for black and white students. Talmadge and the General Assembly continued to increase expenditures for black schools while simultaneously advancing the private school plan initiated in 1953 through a new amendment—Amendment 4. The proposed amendment gave the General Assembly the ability to "discharge" themselves "of all obligation" of providing "adequate education for the state's citizens." The amendment also provided citizens with "grants from state, county, and municipal funds . . . for educational purposes."[41] Critics of the amendment, which included members of the Georgia Education Association, the Georgia Teachers and Education Association, and the state Parent-Teachers Association, questioned the legality of the plan and the fate of teachers' retirement monies.[42] Talmadge and the state Democratic Party, however, championed the amendment "as the only way to maintain a system of common schools and segregation."[43] With a vote of 210,458 to 181,148, Amendment 4 passed.[44]

Such opposition to school desegregation, the murder of Emmett Till in Mississippi in 1955, and the Montgomery Bus Boycott begun in December 1955 only escalated the civil rights movement. But black students did begin to desegregate schools in cities such as Washington, D.C., Baltimore, Maryland, Louisville, Kentucky, St. Louis, Missouri, and in smaller communities like Clinton, Tennessee. What occurred in Clinton, Tennessee, is emblematic of both early school desegregation processes and massive resistance even before the desegregation of Central High School in Little Rock, Arkansas. Nine black students desegregated Clinton High School on August 27, 1956, but protests followed what had been a relatively peaceful day at Clinton High. (The small number of black students to desegregate schools would be the norm until the mid-1960s.) By the end of the week, only about half of the student body, including the nine black students, attended Clinton High. That Friday night, segregationists violently protested, and by Sunday afternoon, six hundred National Guardsmen arrived in Clinton, helping to end the protests.[45] The fall semester progressed with the nine black students being escorted to school each day by three white escorts. Yet, school leaders temporarily closed Clinton High in December following the beating of one escort.[46] When the school reopened in the spring of 1957, the black students felt ostracized and isolated, reflecting the experiences of the first black students to desegregate formerly all-white schools elsewhere.[47] However, despite the racism encountered, Bobby Cain graduated in the spring of 1957, becoming the first black student to graduate from Clinton High. One year later, without as much publicity, Gail Ann Epps became the first black young woman to graduate.

Ultimately, how southern leaders opposed school desegregation inside and outside of Georgia would intersect with the more pragmatic politics of Atlanta. The Georgia General Assembly continued to pass laws that would thwart the possibility of public school desegregation. Legislators enacted new laws including the Private School Plan of 1956, which authorized the state to lease public school buildings for private educational purposes and to extend retirement benefits to nonpublic school teachers. In January 1957, the General Assembly gave Governor Talmadge the power to abolish compulsory school attendance laws and provided funds for the Georgia Commission on Education to create and promote prosegregationist propaganda.[48] Furthermore, to oversee its resistance, the state equipped the commission with surveillance equipment to spy on those thought to be threats to compliance with state law. Consequently, by 1957, "the total effect [of the actions of the Georgia Assembly] was a climate where any diversity was unacceptable."[49]

Atlanta's political leaders differed from the approach of the state legislators. Through orchestrated plans and court orders, blacks began to desegregate city services, including golf courses in 1955 and city buses in 1959. In a city committed to economic prosperity and a state committed to segregation in the midst of a growing civil rights movement, Westminster had developed into a well-known elite private school in Atlanta. It benefited from Atlanta's expanded population, overcrowded and segregated public schools, and white citizens' increasing support of private schools. As Pressly assumed a prominent national leadership position in 1957, Westminster's stature would only enlarge.

National Leadership, National Changes

In 1957, the nation witnessed firsthand the depth of white massive resistance when nine black students desegregated Central High School in Little Rock, Arkansas. They faced such immense opposition, including that of Governor Orval Faubus, that the federal government intervened. President Eisenhower federalized the Arkansas National Guard and sent the 101st Airborne Division, making Little Rock an example of federal intervention.[50] As Herbert Brownell, then U.S. attorney general, stated, "We felt that this was the test case that had to be made in order to dramatize to everyone that when it came to a showdown, the federal government was supreme in this area."[51] As segregationist academies only grew in number in the mid-1950s, private school leaders continued to debate their place in the United States as they had done during the first half of the twentieth century, and at the helm was Pressly.

That same year, elite private school leaders had elected Pressly chair of the NCIS executive committee, the first southerner to hold the position.

Before becoming chair of NCIS, Pressly was a charter trustee for the College Entrance Examination Board, vice president of SAIS, chairman of the Georgia State Committee of SACS, and a member on the Georgia Accrediting Commission. Through his positions, Pressly was most likely aware of changes among independent schools during the twentieth century as private school leaders became concerned with their schools' public image, their schools' position in the U.S. educational landscape, and their schools' homogeneity.

By virtue of Pressly's national position, Westminster not only developed within a city that employed pragmatic desegregation and a state that attempted to avoid school desegregation at all costs but also within a gradually changing independent school world. These changes in historically white elite private schools began as academies declined in the nineteenth century with the rise of public high schools in the late nineteenth century and early twentieth century. Private schools found themselves addressing similar issues as their public counterparts. As southern leaders institutionalized segregated schooling, educators and policymakers throughout the nation used schools to contend with the social, economic, and political realities of the era, which also included new waves of immigration, domestic migration, continuing industrialization, and mounting economic stratification. From 1900 to 1950 the U.S. population nearly doubled, from approximately 76 million to 151 million. The percentage of those living in urban areas rose from 35 percent to 64 percent.[52] Further, with the passage of school compulsory attendance laws, schooling became more of a focal point in everyday American life, and the public high school became more available.[53] Some of the nation's largest school districts continued to develop, and schools increasingly became sites for how to contend with the "other" whether that "other" was a new immigrant from southern or eastern Europe, Mexico, or Japan. Educators and others used schooling to Americanize these and other populations, such as Native Americans, while these groups also forged their own sense of being American.[54]

Schools, both public and private, became sites for expanding the curriculum and the purposes of schools, and schools reflected the sentiments of the nation following World War I about the need for increased focus on democratic ideals and engagement.[55] In Iowa, for example, the state legislature mandated in 1919 that public and private schools teach about citizenship.[56] In other parts of the country, swelling democratic fervor served as a backdrop for challenges to private schooling. As parents complied with school compulsory laws, policymakers challenged those parents who chose private schools for their children. For instance, in Oregon, policymakers passed legislation championed by protestant activists, the Ku Klux Klan, and other nativist groups that called for children to attend public schools. In *Pierce v. Society of Sisters* (1925), the U.S. Supreme Court ruled the law unconstitutional, thereby giving parents the option to decide between public and private schools.[57] Collectively, these changes framed how historically white elite private schools sought to solidify their position in the changing U.S. educational landscape.

The rise of professionalization in education also influenced changes among independent schools; similar to the public sector, independent schools began to form their own organizations, including NCIS, which Pressly found himself leading in 1957. In the early twentieth century, emphasis on the scientific and demands for specialized labor, expert knowledge, and bureaucratic efficiency affected how school and educational leaders organized and operated schools, school districts, state departments of education, and national policies. Educators became professionalized and "formed national ties through new associations, conferences, publications, networks, and university training programs, and also developed a science of education that provided a common language and models to which states and localities often turned."[58] Educational leaders established professional organizations, including the National Council of Teachers of English in 1911, the American Educational Research Association in 1916, the National Council of Teachers of Mathematics in 1920, and the National Council for the Social Studies in 1921. Independent school leaders moved in a similar fashion and sought to avoid "excess regulation" by creating organizations at all levels including the national, regional, state, and local. As Arthur Powell noted, "By such devices as accreditation procedures, principles of good practice (including financial-management practices), regional and national training workshops, and membership standards (even if minimal ones), membership associations enhanced the reputations of schools and dampened ardor for government intervention."[59]

Concerned about standardizing admission requirements for the lower grades of the secondary schools, "a handful of private school people" began the Secondary Entrance Examination Board (SEEB) in 1923, and they started "a series of information meetings at The Fessenden School in West Newton, Massachusetts."[60] In its initial development, the board "published 'Definition of Requirements' and examinations," adopted by nineteen schools, and became an official organization on the occasion of its first conference on October 31, 1925, at the Harvard Club in Boston. The number of member schools grew to one hundred by 1930 and "an elaborate substructure of committees dealing with every aspect of the curriculum and not a few extracurricular questions was gradually built."[61] The SEEB (later named the Secondary Education Board [SEB] in 1928 and then the Independent Schools Education Board [ISEB] in 1958) developed entrance exams and requirements, researched school practices, and provided varied activities for school personnel. In the 1930s, SEEB also began publishing *The Independent School Bulletin* (*ISB*), which has become a leading publication (currently titled *Independent School*) on independent school education, addressing leadership, teaching and curriculum, student experiences, school events and announcements, and programs and initiatives.

By the 1940s, private schools or "prep" schools increasingly wanted to be "free of the unfortunate connotations often associated with the word 'private.'" As in the mid-nineteenth century, these connotations included "elitist," "undemocratic," and "un-American."[62] School leaders therefore adopted the term *independent school*, which became commonplace in the 1930s and 1940s.[63] Moreover, school leaders wanted to "distinguish fiscally and educationally responsible nonpublic schools from fly-by-night or profit-making con games."[64] Independent school leaders developed a second national organization, NCIS, in the early 1940s.[65] NCIS had less tangible goals than SEEB, and NCIS was more informed by the growing negative reputation of independent schools and the desire to monitor possible federal regulations.[66]

Morton Snyder, head of Rye Country Day School in New York, initially proposed NCIS during a meeting of the SEEB in 1929. The SEEB board hesitated to take on the task of developing "a national federation of Private School Associations." Snyder wanted a group or organization that would defend private schools amidst "'hostile climate,'" prejudice and lack of public understanding. He envisaged a federation that would explore what could be done to promote the interest of private schools in different areas of the country."[67] NCIS came to fruition through the joining of the SEB Committee on Public Service, established in 1941, and a special committee of the Country Day School Headmasters' Association, seeking to explore Snyder's plan. NCIS initially formed in August 1942 as a "loose knit confederation of constituent members; some regional associations (such as the California Association), [and] some 'type' organizations (such as the Headmistresses' Association of the East or the Secondary Education Board)."[68] The organization primarily served "purposes very similar to those of the SEB Committee on Public Service (which subsequently disbanded)—

furthering the concept of public service, speaking on behalf of all independent schools, enhancing unity among them, and providing contact with other branches of education."[69]

In 1943, SEB formed its own Committee on Public Relations. The formation of NCIS and this committee caused confusion about direction of its efforts. To eliminate confusion, a special meeting was held in February 1947 in Cleveland. During this meeting, representatives of NCIS's executive committee and SEB's Committee on Public Relations decided that a national organization was needed to address independent schools' issues, to better connect independent schools with public schools and the larger community, and to promote independent schools nationally.[70] The group chose Francis Parkman, formerly the head of Saint Mark's School in Massachusetts, as executive secretary in January 1948. NCIS leaders, primarily school heads from various types of independent schools throughout the country, took up the challenge of combating negative stereotypes about independent schools by focusing on a variety of matters, including relevant legislation, public relations, topics pertaining to teachers (i.e., training, recruitment, and retention), reports from local and regional associations, accreditation, annual statistics, and the function of NCIS as an organization. The focus on legislation and public relations revealed their importance to national independent school leaders.

As independent school leaders organized and contemplated their external identity, they also became concerned about their schools' homogeneity, especially as they identified their schools as independent schools by the 1940s. Some independent school leaders also sought to increase the availability of financial aid. Schools wanted financially needy yet academically able students because independent schools sought to maintain their high academic standards. With additional economic prosperity, independent schools were able to offer some financial aid. For example, 12 percent of students in 1950 received aid. Providing funds, however, became difficult as there were fluctuations in annual gifts from parents, and these gifts helped to underwrite how much financial aid schools could distribute. School leaders also began to expand the religious, ethnic, and gender diversity among their students. For example, Jewish students sought admission to independent schools. Although Jewish families could sometimes pay tuition fees, independent schools maintained low Jewish student populations. For instance, only 5 percent of Andover students in the 1940s were Jewish. Administrators pushed to reduce the percentage to avoid "frightening" the "Protestant constituency."[71]

Independent Schools, Black Students, and Mid-Twentieth-Century Politics

These concerns about student demographics informed Wilson's 1949 article that considered "colored students" an asset. Although Wilson's call may not have been universal, especially in the South, changes at other independent schools indicated a slightly shifting focus on the recruitment and admission of black students to independent schools. In 1944, black students desegregated Francis W. Parker School in Chicago.[72] Shortly after Wilson's article appeared, an announcement in January 1950 read "two Negro students have been enrolled in the Junior I class at Calhoun School, New York City." The article described the students and their admission as follows: "One of the girls is a graduate of the Modern School, a private elementary school for Negro children in New York City; the other was, for five years, a student at the Lincoln School. The girls have already taken an active part in the extracurricular activities in dramatics, music, and writing for school publications. The school feels that they have a valuable contribution to make to the life and breadth of understanding of the student group."[73] In 1951, the National Scholarship Service and Fund for Negro Students (NSSFNS) in coordination with northern independent schools began a program for recruiting black students to independent schools. As the NAACP earned victories in *Sweatt* and *McLaurin* and began to develop the cases that would become *Brown*, "the NSSFNS, a nonprofit talent identification organization, was quietly integrating and placing Black students in some of the leading White private colleges and New England preparatory schools."[74] Felice Nierenberg Schwartz started NSSFNS in 1947; Schwartz was a wealthy white Smith College graduate who was concerned about the small number of black students matriculating through the elite Seven Sister colleges. With the support of 146 college presidents and a diverse group of board members and officers, NSSFNS launched its higher education and preparatory school programs. Through its prep school program that began in the early 1950s and continued for over a decade, NSSFNS "succeeded in placing 275 Negro students in 46 schools," some of whom came from the South. The prep school program both provided opportunity to African American students and countered their white teachers' and fellow students' notions of their perceived social and intellectual inferiority.[75]

By the mid-1950s, admissions policies continued to change for independent schools. The May 1956 *ISB* included an announcement of the newly adopted open admissions policy of the Sidwell Friends School in Washington, D.C. The announcement, presumably in an effort to appeal to the greater public and the goals of independent schools nationally, indicated that the process would be gradual, which was similar to public school desegregation. The blurb also outlined the advantages of a Sidwell education: "to provide college preparatory training at a high level of academic excellence, with an awareness of an obligation to train for subsequent leadership and good citizenship." Yet, only qualified black children, according to Sidwell's standards, were to receive this education so "that they, too, may be better prepared for ultimate professional and civic leadership."[76] The Sidwell announcement foreshadowed a constant theme about black children (no matter their family's socioeconomic status), independent schools, and the unwavering of academic standards.

While some schools admitted a small number of African American students in the 1940s and 1950s, whites did not always treat them well. Phillips Academy in Andover, Massachusetts, had accepted African American students in the 1940s, but when an alumnus asked about recruiting more black students in 1944, the headmaster responded that there were currently two black students at the school and that accepting more might "cause trouble."[77] Civil rights leader Julian Bond attended the George School in Newtown, Pennsylvania, in the 1950s and viewed the school as a "hotbed of racism" and noted "that his fellow students were not very concerned about hiding their prejudices." Richard Zweigenhaft and G. William Domhoff also reported about the directions an administrator once gave to Bond that upset him. Bond and his white girlfriend would walk in Newtown, a normal dating activity for George School students, and "Bond recalls with some bitterness that the school dean asked him not to wear his much loved George School jacket when he was walking into town with his girlfriend."[78] Although black students may have been admitted to such schools, the quality of their experiences reflected the perpetuation of racism in U.S. society and the structural and interpersonal changes that would need to occur in independent schools.

In addition to desegregation matters, all K-12 educational institutions found themselves in the midst of concerns about the quality of U.S. math and science education in response to Sputnik and the Cold War. As 1957 came to a close, NCIS, under Pressly's leadership, reported that it had received numerous inquiries about the role of academies in the U.S. educational crisis. In addition to releasing a statement to member schools concerning the quality of curriculum and teaching, the NCIS executive committee encouraged schools "to continue and to expand their activities in certain specific areas such as the Advanced Placement Program, summer activities, opportunities for teacher refresher and advanced courses and the like."[79]

During the first half of the twentieth century, lines between public and private had blurred. As public high schools and high school education increasingly became part and parcel of U.S. life, leaders of historically white elite private schools sought to strengthen the position of their schools. They began describing their schools as "independent" because they were concerned about how the larger public reacted to the label *private*. They created new national organizations and questioned their homogenous populations. These changes did not prevent how some black students negatively experienced independent schools, but the students did inform how independent school leaders would continue to respond to advocacy for equal rights and opposition to that advocacy in the mid- to latter twentieth century. Discussions ensued about the requirements for schools' accreditation, and state governments had enacted plans that would use private schools to thwart public school desegregation. Although the *Brown* decision legally only affected public schools, the private world felt the reverberations. In 1957, Arthur Miller wrote a legal analysis, *Racial Discrimination and Private Education*, that made it clear that private schools were not exempt from the conversation concerning the implementation and reach of public school desegregation.[80] Miller's analysis coincided with the increased enrollment in independent schools nationally and the continued development of private schools' relationship with national matters."[81]

Miller, an Emory University law professor, discussed the legal status of nonpublic education with respect to state control of education, cases involving curriculum, instruction, and administration, and religious training being offered in private schools and not in public schools. Miller specifically addressed the lack of definitive measures or limits of state governments regulating private schools. Some states considered "'so-called' Fair Educational Practices designed to require that certain private schools ignore race or religion as a criterion for matriculation. On the other hand, a number of Southern states have statutes that appear to require segregation in nonpublic schools."[82] For example, the Georgia Constitution and statutes operated "in such a fashion that any private school accepting both white and colored students loses its tax exemption."[83] Tax exemption of private school property had been a benefit that many private schools had enjoyed without ever being challenged. Though Miller provided a possible legal argument that black individuals could employ in a case calling for the desegregation of private schools, he did not foresee black individuals being successful.

A Developing Southern School Culture

Pressly, as chair of NCIS and the president of a growing southern independent school, was presumably quite aware of the era in which he lived. As Westminster's leader, he would have to respond to the politics of its city and state as well as changes occurring among independent schools nationally. In the midst of this balancing act, those at Westminster were cultivating a school climate into which African American students would enter; this culture reflected a contradictory and complex racial climate.

The theme for the 1952 May Day Pageant was "Song of the South" featuring "Uncle Remus and his various friends." Characters represented in the pageant included "Br'er Bear, Br'er Fox, and Br'er Rabbit."[84] This production was most likely based on the 1946 Disney release *Song of the South*, its first live action dramatic film. Joel Chandler Harris, a native of Eatonton, Georgia, and former editor of the *Atlanta Constitution* in the late nineteenth century, first told the stories featured in the production. With the 1880 publication of *Uncle Remus: His Songs and His Sayings*, Harris's African American storyteller Uncle Remus came to life. Harris's work contributed to developing nostalgia for the Old South that depicted "perfect race, class, and gender harmony," according to historian Grace Elizabeth Hale.[85] Cultural production related to "the Old South" "culminated with David O. Selznick's 1939 film of Margaret Mitchell's *Gone with the Wind*."[86] In reproducing Uncle Remus stories, the Westminster students echoed images of the Old South and the loyal ex-slave.

Westminster's climate revealed racist and southern traditions. For example, advertisements in the school newspaper for the Pickaninny, a coffee shop, featured three black figures gleefully running. The Pickaninny was operated by Mammy's Shanty, a restaurant on Peachtree Street, Atlanta's central thoroughfare that connects the downtown to the north side.[87] These images illuminated a powerful and dominant caricature of black children in the twentieth century. According to sociologist David Pilgrim, pickaninnies or picaninnies were "child coons." They "had bulging eyes, unkempt hair, red lips, and wide lips. . . . They were routinely shown on postcards, posters, and other ephemera being chased or eaten. Picaninnies were portrayed as nameless, shiftless natural buffoons running from alligators and toward fried chicken."[88] Similar to the inclusion of Uncle Remus stories in the May Day celebrations, advertisements for the Pickaninny marked how Westminster students thought about the appropriateness of including such an advertisement in the school newspaper, thereby showing how their school culture was a product of a particular old white southern heritage. The ad, in conversation with other racist school traditions, show that leaders and students of Westminster in the early 1950s gave little consideration for stopping the racism that was deeply embedded in the developing school culture.

This lack of deliberation about racist implications continued. At the beginning of the 1955-56 school year, the girls' school produced the *Westminster Chimes*, and the boys' school produced the *Mark Sheet*, both school newspapers. The papers continued to focus on school activities and student accomplishments and contained examples of the school's racial climate. For example, the 1956 Mardi Gras celebration was based on the theme "Favorite Old Song." A picture of the freshman float "Dixie" appeared in the newspaper. The picture shows a leading lady on the float with a basket of cotton in front of her and two float pullers, who seem to be in black face. Based on the caption, all students appeared to be Westminster students.[89] In January 1956, "Slave Market Provides Rat's Revenge on Seniors," one can see how students discussed the slave auction, an annual fundraiser for the Atlanta Child's Home. One description of the auction involved the sons of Ivan and Louise Allen Jr. The reporter wrote, "Ivan Allen became the unworthy slave of Inman [Allen] who had as his assistant John Mullin, Jimmy Fluker, and Tommy Rains. Ivan started off Wednesday by crawling around the gymnasium floor and then serving Inman and Tommy a Coke just before Mr. Austin's English Class." Pressly also seems to have participated by purchasing a student who appeared the next day at "the Girls' School with tied hands and feet and a lipstick covered face. After finding a 'Help' note pinned to [him], one of the girls finally rescued him."[90] Students with the highest bids won, and the descriptions that accompanied the documentation of the auctions indicated that auctioned students did jobs. Such adherence to racist traditions shows how students were taught about the institution of slavery and enslaved African Americans. It is not clear whether any students opposed such depictions at the May Day festivities or the slave auction.

These racially charged pictures, depictions, and events at Westminster point to how Westminster embraced racist forms in the years before desegregation as a southern institution that attempted to provide a nationally recognized education. Based on how they conceptualized U.S. slave auctions of those of African descent, young men auctioned one another, and

Westminster publications, including student newspapers and yearbooks, captured facets of school life and Westminster's local context in Atlanta, Georgia. The Pickaninny Coffee Shop advertisement appeared in a 1954 edition of the *Westminster Tattler*. This advertisement is one indication of the school's culture, which included racist traditions such as slave auction fundraisers and certain performances during school events, that continued through the early years of school desegregation. A cadre of white students (and ultimately black students) would use the school newspapers to question and examine the status quo concerning race and racism. Source: "The Pickaninny," advertisement, *Westminster Tattler*, April 1954, 3, RG 21.03, Beck Archives-Westminster.

the event seemed popular among students, faculty, and staff. As this southern school would continue to develop, it would include a school culture that manifested values related to race. The first black students would ultimately navigate this culture during the latter part of the next decade.

A Priceless Inheritance

The first black students to desegregate Westminster were born at the same time that Westminster grew and developed, and they were bequeathed a priceless inheritance that included a deep adherence by African Americans to the power of literacy and education. Their parents and relatives had been educated in public and private segregated black schools, including Booker T. Washington High School, the first black public high school in Atlanta and one of the early black public high schools in the South. Additionally, some family members had graduated from historically black colleges and universities, including Morehouse College, Spelman College, Paine College, Atlanta University, Morris Brown College, and Norfolk State University, and worked as educators in grades K-12 and in higher education. By virtue of being born in the 1950s, the first black students to desegregate

Westminster experienced a fully developed black educational world that helped to advance their parents and family members. When desegregation would begin at Westminster, the first black students carried their books, binders, pens, and pencils in their backpacks, as well as their culture, curiosity, confidence, talents, skills, and knowledge that were nurtured by their families and communities and by their schooling in segregated black schools. As of the mid-twentieth century, the black educational world inherited by the first black students was shaped by public and private schools. This world developed because enslaved African Americans sought opportunities to learn despite harsh consequences. Further, African Americans helped create educational opportunity in the Jim Crow South while debating the philosophy and direction of black education and negotiating relationships with white reformers and benefactors.

Enslaved Africans already possessed great skills and knowledge. As they became African Americans and as slavery grew and dominated the South in the nineteenth century, whites legally denied African Americans the opportunity to become literate during enslavement. For example, Georgia state leaders passed their first antiliteracy law in 1770. For enslaved African Americans during the antebellum period, acquiring literacy, which was a dangerous activity, became that much more important as it challenged the very institutional structure of slavery. The number of slaves grew to four million by the Civil War, but African Americans resisted their conditions in small and large ways. Such actions as Gabriel Prosser's slave rebellion in Virginia in 1800, Denmark Vesey's insurrection in Charleston, South Carolina, in 1822, and the publication of David Walker's *Appeal* in 1829 scared whites and led them to pass laws to quell African American literacy acquirement.[91] White legislators passed antiliteracy laws throughout the South, including a second law in Georgia in 1829, and those enslaved literally had "to steal" an education.[92] Enslaved and free African Americans learned from one another and some whites, had schools both public and secret, and found ways to pass knowledge on to one another whether by camouflaging textbooks or by eavesdropping. Heather Andrea Williams wrote, "Literacy provided the means to write a pass to freedom, to learn of abolitionist activities, or to read the Bible. Because it most often happened in secret, the very act of learning to read and write subverted the master-slave relationship and created a private life for those who were owned by others."[93] On the other hand, gaining the right to literacy was not always easy to absorb and the very tasks of reading, and especially writing, could be difficult because coming into new freedom was not a simple process for African Americans.[94] Literary scholar Christopher Hager opined, "As emancipation progressed more and more freed people were learning to write, but they were also finding that the written medium involved many of the same challenges, restrictions, biases, and perils as the social and political world to which it granted them access."[95]

As in other parts of the South, the Freedmen's Bureau and missionary organizations, including the American Missionary Association (AMA) and the American Baptist Home Mission Society (ABHMS), supported and influenced early black schooling after the Civil War. Although few African Americans could attend school with any regularity, white women taught children and adults who wanted to learn to read and write, in spite of the new realities such skills brought. These teachers combated sexism and patriarchy as they imparted a curriculum that included both perceptions of African American racial inferiority and the desire to cultivate freedmen and women in the image of Victorian and Protestant values that had and continued to undergird the common schools of the Northeast and Midwest. For example, in Georgia, the teachers' motivations and their values of "evangelical piety, self-control, and hard, steady work formed the trinity of northern-sponsored freedmen's education."[96]

From enslavement through Reconstruction, African Americans found ways to acquire literacy and schooling even when whites legally denied these opportunities. Their advancements in education could not be avoided by southern whites, and ex-slaves led in making schooling in the South a reality. With ex-slaves having already established schools, black politicians and leaders pushed for public schooling to be included in state constitutions during Reconstruction constitutional conventions, and by 1870, each constitution included such requirements.[97] Although constitutions allowed for schooling, it would be a decade before many white southerners realized that any attempt to reverse the thrust of the ex-slaves' school campaigns could invite greater black resistance and northern intervention, and they began to make an uneasy peace with Reconstruction-era educational reforms. Further, lower-class whites in concert with populists began advocating for schooling in the late 1880s and 1890s.[98] The rise of a literate black working class and middle-class whites' inability to wipe out black educational gains led to demands for educational reforms in the early twentieth century. However, white enforcement of Jim Crow laws advanced by the 1896 decision of "separate but equal" in *Plessy v. Ferguson* precluded any hope for equal funding or that public schooling systems could be equal and separate in the South. With the institutionalization of separate and unequal, white leaders did not provide equal funding for instructional services, the number of teachers, and the number of schools, and this inequality only increased in the first half of the twentieth century.[99]

In the late nineteenth and early twentieth centuries, African American efforts to advance educational opportunity continued through a system of segregated public and private schools and institutions of higher education. The intertwinement of philosophical differences among black educators, and the negotiation of relationships with white reformers and white benefactors shaped the efforts of everyday African Americans as they championed educational opportunity through their monetary support, commitment, and activism at all levels. Central to the philosophical differences were the positions of Booker T. Washington and W. E. B. Du Bois, two of the foremost leading thinkers about black education during the era.

Washington, often characterized as a pragmatist and accommodationist, focused on preparing ex-slaves to be effective laborers and foregrounded industrial education. At this time, industrial education called for black Americans to learn applicable skills and knowledge for their everyday work that could be deemed blue-collar, working-class, menial, or physical labor jobs. Washington, born a slave in 1856 and later educated at Hampton Institute in Virginia, founded the Tuskegee Institute in 1881 following the lead of Samuel Armstrong, a white missionary and educator, who had taken Washington under his tutelage at Hampton. On the other hand, Du Bois was born and raised in Great Barrington, Massachusetts, and was twelve years younger than Washington. Du Bois initially advocated for classical liberal education and the role of the talented tenth in elevating the majority of African Americans. Classical liberal education included courses in English, math, science, and history, and other subjects thought to develop the mind intellectually rather than practically. Having attended Fisk University in Nashville, Tennessee, Du Bois was the first African American to earn a doctorate from Harvard University. He publicly challenged Washington in his well-known chapter, "Of Mr. Booker T. Washington and Others," in *The Souls of Black Folk*, published in 1903. Du Bois contended that Washington asked black people to give up, "First, political power, second, insistence on civil rights, and third, higher education of Negro youth—and concentrate all of their energies on industrial education, the accumulation of wealth, and the conciliation of the South."[100]

Influenced by their respective childhoods in the South and North, Washington and Du Bois held different beliefs about the purposes of black education, but those beliefs, and even their public opposition, did not preclude them from engaging one another, though with some level of skepticism. Following Washington's death in 1915, Du Bois, a prolific scholar and editor of the NAACP's *The Crisis*, continued to deliberate Washington's ideas, reflected on why Washington took such positions, and even leaned toward some of Washington's stances. As scholars have argued, the relationship between Washington and Du Bois and their positions on black education must be viewed more "holistically in the historical and ideological contexts of the period."[101] Though many black educators implemented industrial education, especially as they secured northern philanthropic funds and southern white support, others developed classical liberal education, sometimes in the same schools with industrial education. The dichotomy between industrial education and classical liberal education needs to be rendered more complex, with considerations of how each curriculum influenced and intersected in the development of black primary and secondary public, private, and higher education institutions.

In the rural South, where most African Americans lived, this dichotomy played out significantly in how white southerners and northern philanthropists sought to control black education as a means to benefit the economy and to control African Americans as second-class citizens.[102] Although northern philanthropists may have been thought of as altruistic in their contributions, James Anderson argued, "The philanthropists were not a group of antiracist, democratic northerners challenging southern racism by goodwill, tact, and hard work. Rather, white superiority seems to have been one of the few things upon which virtually all of the northern philanthropists and white southerners agreed."[103]

Two organizations had enormous influence on the development of southern black education. A group, primarily of young adult male white southerners, formed the Southern Education Board, and Robert C. Ogden led the General Education Board (GEB). Ogden had helped to start Hampton Institute in 1868 and fundamentally believed in industrial training. By 1906, Ogden held presidencies of five organizations: the Conference for Education in the South, the Southern Education Board, the GEB, Hampton's board of trustees, and Tuskegee Institute's board of trustees. Such roles allowed him to have influence over a number of individuals and to promote industrial training. Others involved, including George Foster Peabody, William H. Baldwin, and James Hardy Dillard, invested in the role of the black worker to substantiate the "urban-industrial nation" built on sharecropping in the South and the continued importance of cotton to that national economy.

Northern philanthropists developed other organizations—the Peabody Fund, the Slater Fund, the Anna T. Jeanes Foundation, and the Phelps-Stokes Fund—and African American communities supplemented these organizations' contributions through what Anderson described as a "double taxation." As white southerners used white and black tax dollars to disproportionately support white schools over black schools, African Americans often contributed additional monies to black schools. Although the double taxation, in the form of cash, land, and labor—often by many living in poverty—may have been an "accommodation to the oppressive nature of southern society," it also showed blacks' commitment to education and their belief in education as a tool for improving their communities.[104]

In urban areas like Atlanta, African Americans' activism was essential as they used petition campaigns and strategic voting to gain more educational facilities in the late nineteenth century. Blacks exchanged their votes for democratic concerns (e.g., prohibition) to gain schools and to have black teachers employed in the schools. Despite these gains, Atlanta leaders rarely made improvements to the schools, and they hired black teachers to reduce the school board's costs.[105] By the early twentieth century, public elementary schools in Atlanta and other urban areas, including Savannah and Charleston, were often overcrowded. In Atlanta in 1903, there were twenty white schools and two hundred white teachers for 14,465 white pupils compared to five black schools and forty-nine black teachers for 8,118 black pupils.[106] If all had been equal, then there should have been ten black schools and one hundred black teachers. Schools operated on double sessions, but many students still could not attend school because there was simply not enough space. Although the institution of the white political primary in 1892 had diminished black voting, African Americans still relied on the power of their vote because white city leaders would often break their campaign promises to improve black education. In 1917, the local NAACP learned about the passage of a bond that required support from two-thirds of all registered voters. The NAACP launched a massive voter registration and called for black citizens not to vote for the bond because it did not provide improvements to black education; the bond failed.[107] Many whites thought the very idea of a black public high school was absurd. However, black citizens used the power of their vote to deny school bonds until the city leaders approved the building of a black high school.[108] In 1924, Booker T. Washington High School, the first black public high school, opened. However, unlike its counterpart white high schools, city leaders only provided a structure that included classrooms. There were no additional facilities for athletic or other extracurricular activities.

Although gradual, schooling for younger black children increasingly became a reality in the first half of the twentieth century, because of African Americans' continued agency and activism. For example, the percentage of black children attending school more than doubled from 36 percent in 1900 to 78 percent in 1940. In comparison, 55 percent of white children attended school in 1900, and by 1940, 79 percent of white children attended school.[109] Yet, the percentage of black students enrolled in high school remained low compared to the overall black population, the overall population, and the growing overall rates of high school attendance and graduation. For example, in 1940, 23 percent of black youth were in enrolled public secondary schools; this percentage was even lower—at less than 18 percent—for Alabama, Arkansas, Georgia, Louisiana, Mississippi, and South Carolina.[110]

The shortage of public schools led to blacks' reliance on segregated black private schools, especially in the late nineteenth and early twentieth centuries. In the early twentieth century, the importance of private schools was evident. By 1916, of the 20,872 African Americans who attended public and private schools, 11,130 were in private schools. In Georgia, like other deep southern states, private schools were essential. For example, "of the 2,278 Negro pupils in secondary schools in Georgia in 1913, 2,119 were in the thirty-two private schools."[111] Some private schools operated independently of church denominations, but many were supported by denominations such as the Methodist Episcopal Church, the Northern Congregational Church (or the AMA), Presbyterian Church North, Southern Presbyterian Church, Protestant Episcopal Church, the ABHMS, Colored Baptists in America, African Methodist Episcopal Church (AME), Colored Methodist Episcopal Church, Catholics, and Seventh Day Adventists. Schools like Allen Normal School, Boggs Academy, and Dorchester Academy offered boarding components. They were members of a larger network of black boarding schools including well-known schools: Palmer Institute in North Carolina, Avery Normal Institute in South Carolina, Piney Woods and Utica Normal and Training Institute in Mississippi, and Snow Hill Institute in Alabama.

As in other settings, philanthropic and missionary endeavors brought interracial and intraracial battles over control and curricular direction in private schools. At normal schools, northern philanthropists tried to implement the Hampton-Tuskegee model of industrial education, but most schools associated with religious denominations and private schools independent of religion had four-year courses of study. Yet, some private schools were explicitly established as offshoots of the Hampton-Tuskegee model. William Edwards, founder of Snow Hill Institute in Alabama and a graduate of Tuskegee, sought to replicate his education. Edwards met opposition from local parents and his AME church, which wanted him to operate a denominational school. Despite offering teacher training, "the heart of Snow Hill Institute was its emphasis on agricultural and manual training."[112] Other schools such as the Palmer Institute, begun in 1902 by Charlotte Hawkins Brown, initially included both liberal arts and industrial training; the latter was in part because of the continued appeal of industrial training to white benefactors. "By 1922, the Palmer Institute became the only rural high school in Guilford County to earn academic accreditation. The nine-month high school year included courses in English, math, physics, chemistry, French, Latin, history, and civics. Domestic science and agricultural and industrial subjects rounded out the offerings."[113] In the 1930s, for funding purposes, Palmer came under the auspices of the AMA. However, "after her uncompromising rule led the AMA to disown Palmer in 1934, Brown rejuvenated the school as an independent academic finishing school that increasingly drew middle- and upper-class students from across the United States."[114]

Over time, with the support of black southerners, tax dollars, and philanthropic funds, southern school boards established black public schools in urban and rural areas, which in large part displaced black private schools. By 1930, black student enrollment in small private normal and county training schools declined. Often, county training schools were subsumed under the public system, and teacher candidates were more likely to attend four-year colleges because higher levels of education were required for teachers. During the 1929-30 school year, only two private teacher-preparation institutions existed.[115] Denominations also decreased their support of private schools. In 1943, schools supported by the AMA were no longer operating as private schools. For example, Ballard Normal School, an AMA school, had come under control of the Board of Education of Bibb County.[116] In total, by 1950, the number of black private schools in Georgia were reduced from seventy-eight to twenty-one.[117] Although the number of private schools decreased, they were important to the fabric of black educational opportunity in the South that the first black students inherited.

Primary and secondary public and private black schools were accompanied by the development of historically black colleges and universities (HBCUs) which also reflected the ideological tensions and provided additional opportunities for schooling at all levels. Birthed during and immediately after Reconstruction, many HBCUs advanced liberal arts instruction. Leaders of HBCUs promoted the liberal arts curriculum even when they included industrial education, and they did this despite ideological challenges from northern philanthropists and their southern white allies who called for more industrial education because it was believed to be the proper education for southern blacks.

Because four million newly freed African Americans sought education at all levels, HBCUs developed as their pupils did. Elementary and secondary education divisions were prominent in HBCUs from their earliest years. Atlanta University, established in 1869, included a grammar school, a preparatory department or high school, and a normal school. In 1881, the grammar school provided a curriculum of "reading, spelling, grammar, geography with map drawing, United States history, elementary geometry, botany and physiology, writing, inventive and freehand drawing, vocal music, and gymnastics."[118] The preparatory department featured a classical curriculum, and the normal department trained school teachers.[119] Upon its discontinuation in 1894, "the grammar school students represented an average of 61 percent of the total enrollment."[120] Ten years later, the Oglethorpe Practice School was established as both a kindergarten and training site for teachers.[121] By the 1899-1900 school year, enrollment at Atlanta University, Clark, Atlanta Baptist Seminary, Spelman Seminary, and Morris Brown was largely in the lower grades.[122]

As these institutions took root and grew, they heavily influenced the black middle class, including some black families of the first black students to desegregate Westminster. For example, the AUC was emblematic of the influence of AMA on the development of the black middle class in Atlanta in the latter part of the nineteenth century.[123] The influence of the ABHMS is further evidenced in the cultural and social mores of those who attended Spelman. Evelyn Brooks Higginbotham wrote, "Without doubt, the Talented Tenth reproduced and disseminated the reigning values of middle-class Protestant America, but it nevertheless expressed a race consciousness that united black men and women in a struggle for racial dignity and self-determination."[124]

Prior to attending Westminster, Michael McBay, Malcolm Ryder, Jannard Wade, Wanda Ward, and others would be nurtured and influenced by a complex southern black educational system. What they inherited and experienced was birthed in the education of the enslaved and their yearning for additional knowledge and new literacy in the United States, though reconciling with that new knowledge and literacy was not always even. Black education in the South was further developed for a century after the Civil War because of African Americans' continued initiative, advocacy, and willingness to contribute time, treasure, and talent to their educational institutions and experiences. As black institutions were denied public resources by white local and state leaders, black institutions became sites of ideological battles among those also contributing to black education: black educational leaders, northern missionaries, northern industrial philanthropists, and southern industrial reformers. The first black students to desegregate Westminster would experience how black educators sought to educate the whole child and also served as mediators between the school and community. As Vanessa Siddle Walker described, black educators both provided institutional caring, which "combines personal relationships and supportive school structures," and advocated for the well-being of their students and schools.[125] The first black students of Westminster would bring all of this with them, consciously and unconsciously.

DURING THE EARLY TO MID-1950S, Pressly oversaw Westminster's growth undergirded by independent school leaders' concerns over public image, a regional debate about accreditation standards, a state context seeking to evade imminent desegregation, and a city's preoccupation with its positive image on race relations and its economic prosperity as civil rights activities increased in frequency and intensity. Pressly and other school leaders made Westminster distinct in its marketing, fundraising, and academic offerings, by building a new campus, and by significantly increasing the number of students enrolled at the school. In some respects, the school provided a haven for white students, similar to that of the segregationist academies that emerged in opposition to desegregation. A school with a complex and contradictory racial climate was coming of age.

The very students who would desegregate Westminster were also coming of age in largely segregated black communities, and they inherited the segregated black educational world created behind the veil of Jim Crow. They would come of age as more blacks challenged the segregation of schools, including historically white elite private schools, and higher education institutions in the midst of the civil rights movement. Because of how school desegregation would unfold in Atlanta, black parents, who also had inherited and advanced the African American faith in education, faced difficult decisions. While segregated black private schools had been created out of necessity, how black parents contended with the realities of public school desegregation would present them another set of dilemmas and challenges in the mid- to latter twentieth century as they chose schools for their children.

In the coming years, Westminster's leaders would be forced to consider desegregation. Members of the Westminster board would assert their own concerns regarding the school's position in the wake of public school desegregation, and students would challenge one another on racial issues and their willingness to accept integration. Westminster, similar to much of the South, would move with cautious deliberation in deciding to desegregate. As independent school leaders would further blur the lines of public and private as they positioned their schools in a changing U.S. society, Pressly would continue to manage and negotiate Westminster's local, state, and national contexts.

CHAPTER TWO
Contending with Change and Challenges

The late 1950s and early 1960s brought significant change as elite private schools contended even more with changes in public schools, federal intervention into education, and larger questions about access and opportunity. Following the national publicity surrounding Little Rock's Central High School, and the treatment of the Little Rock Nine, leaders of other southern communities, including those of Atlanta, became much more deliberate about how school desegregation occurred in their cities and states; in essence, these leaders sided with "all deliberate speed."

Although desegregation occurred in some public facilities in Atlanta, state law prevented the desegregation of public schools. In January 1958, twenty-eight black parents, led by Vivian Calhoun, tested these laws and Atlanta's pragmatic desegregation politics by suing the Atlanta school board in *Calhoun v. Latimer* for black student admission to white schools and an end to segregation in Atlanta Public Schools (APS). Subsequently, white flight from APS rose. William Pressly, president of Westminster, recollected, "The school agreed to test every student who applied, letting parents know that classes were absolutely filled but that their children would be tested anyway to see if they were eligible. It wasn't easy to turn them away without igniting hard feelings."[1] Pressly later contended in the 1960s that "the school had never capitalized on racial controversies by taking in 'refugees' from the public schools," but enrollment had grown and educational facilities had expanded.[2]

By 1958, Westminster's enrollment of 1,050 students was four times its initial enrollment of 240. Additionally, the school employed 115 faculty and staff members as compared to the original 18. The operating budget had grown from $75,000 to $652,000, and rather than being housed on four acres in four small buildings, the Westminster campus had moved to its current location in North Atlanta and occupied 180 acres. The campus consisted of three large classroom buildings, the president's home, a small music building, two field houses, three basketball courts, one gymnastics room, one dance studio, a twenty-seven-acre playing field, eleven regulation fields, tennis courts, and a track.[3]

As Westminster grew, pragmatic desegregation politics continued in Atlanta. Mayor William B. Hartsfield reiterated, "We're a city too busy to hate. Atlanta does not cling to the past. People who swear on the old Southern traditions don't know what the hell they are. I think of boll weevils and hook worms."[4] In January 1961, Charlayne Hunter-Gault and Hamilton Holmes confronted Georgia's segregation policies as they applied for admission to the University of Georgia, and the state legislature remained committed to segregation until the legislators could no longer accept the ramifications of how their policies might affect the university where their sons and daughters went to college. With the desegregation of the University of Georgia and the repeal of Georgia state segregation laws, nine black students desegregated APS that fall. By 1962, Mayor Hartsfield's vision for Atlanta as the heart of the New South would be solidified and further developed by incoming mayor Ivan Allen Jr., whose children attended Westminster and whose wife served on the board of trustees.

Although some black students desegregated APS, most Atlanta schools remained segregated in the early 1960s. Independent schools occupied an important space in the southern landscape as white parents continued to support them, as enrollment numbers grew, and as more whites established segregationist academies after *Brown*. Yet as more students attended historically white elite private schools, school leaders deliberated the growing federal role in schooling, including in the private sector. They debated the role of federal aid to elite private schools, and they became more aware of the possibility of losing their federal tax exemption if private schools remained all white. At the same time, black parents, including civil rights leaders such as the Kings, Abernathys, and Youngs inquired about admissions policies for their children at Atlanta's leading private schools on the north side, including Trinity, Lovett, and Westminster.

Outside of the South, some independent school leaders focused even more on the recruitment of black students with the development of additional recruitment and scholarship programs. Pressly remained a national independent school leader as the national organizational structure changed. These developments affected school cultures and added to what the first desegregation generation would inherit as they transitioned from segregated to desegregated schools. As during the early 1950s, Westminster school culture included racist traditions, but white students discussed and debated more deeply contemporary racial issues.

The following pages delineate how private schools became even more central to the era and the questions that arose about race. Elite private school leaders, such as Pressly, continued to negotiate change and challenges. The blurring of public and private lines deepened as historically white private school leaders grappled with the realities of public school desegregation, the rise of segregationist academies, increased recruitment of black students, and inquiries into southern schools' admissions policies by local and national civil rights activists and leaders. In total, during the late 1950s and early 1960s, independent schools like Westminster examined their policies and their beliefs about black students and African Americans more broadly.

Contemplations during a Public School Dilemma

Westminster prepared for the ramifications of *Calhoun v. Latimer*, the case calling for the desegregation of APS. In November 1958, Westminster board members decided to appoint a committee on Westminster's relationship to the public school dilemma. Dr. Vernon Broyles, chairman of the Westminster board, during a board meeting suggested that "the Trustees should be formulating an adopted policy of the school in the event the public schools in Atlanta are closed under the Supreme Court ruling." Upon the board's agreement, "Dr. Broyles appointed Dr. Roland Frye to serve as Chairman of a Committee to study this problem and to formulate a statement of policy for consideration by the Board."[5] Recently elected to the Westminster board of trustees in the spring of 1958, Dr. Frye, an Emory professor of English, was also an active member of Help Our Public Education, Inc. (HOPE).[6] White parents, mothers in particular, established HOPE in an effort to keep public schools open despite the Georgia legislature calling for their closure upon desegregation.[7] Joining Frye on this Westminster board committee were Welborn Cody, the school attorney, Dr. P. D. Miller, Louise Allen, and James Porter.

In December 1958, as part of his first report, Frye stated "that he felt no formal statement of policy was necessary but that the Board is in general agreement that the school should not change in size or character due to pressures resulting from the public school dilemma." The board also agreed to help "organize and advise with other private school groups."[8] The adoption of this committee signaled that Westminster leaders were aware of what could occur in Atlanta, including the enforcement of state laws that called for the closure of any desegregated public school. The changing legal policies concerning the education of white and black students had informed Westminster's position locally. As one solution to the admissions problems facing the school, the board decided to raise the testing fee from $8.50 to $10.00. The board presumably believed that fewer individuals would be able to afford the fee or would be unwilling to pay a higher fee and thus not apply.[9]

Frye's second report came just a month later at the January 1959 board meeting, during which he "reviewed the various problems which Westminster would face in the event that the public schools should be closed. He urged all members of the Board to give thought and consideration to these problems."[10] Frye's report did not include details on the various problems identified by Frye's committee, but an article published on April 3, 1959, offered insight into Frye's position on public schools. In a meeting before the Atlanta Jaycees, Frye "maintained that private schools 'simply cannot do the job of educating all children,'" citing the costs of private schools as one justification. While another speaker before the group advocated resistance to desegregation, Frye stated "that it is 'a poor and perverted expression of love for the South to deny children free education.'"[11]

Admissions policies remained on the board's agenda in January of 1959. According to the board minutes, "Dr. Pressly stated that due to the extremely large number of applications for the coming year, the school's enrollment would be closed as of January 27, when testing of applicants for admission begins." The board came to another agreement—not to admit "new students to the senior class, except under unusual circumstances."[12] Within a very short period, Westminster leaders had prepared for the possibility of APS closing.

Judge Frank A. Hooper, in June of 1959, decided in favor of the black Atlantan plaintiffs; he ruled that the "Atlanta Board of Education had indeed operated a racially segregated school system and such a practice violated the Fourteenth Amendment."[13] Hooper ordered the Atlanta school board to craft and submit a desegregation plan for implementation in January 1960. Despite the plan's gradual desegregation process, the black plaintiffs tolerated it "in order to force the Georgia General Assembly to accept responsibility for closing the public schools."[14] Advocates for desegregation included black Atlantans and white individuals and groups such as Ralph McGill, who was also a Westminster parent, and HOPE. Yet the desegregation plan still openly and outwardly defied state law.

In the midst of Westminster responding to potential school closures in Atlanta, Pressly remained chair of the National Council of Independent Schools' (NCIS) executive committee. During the late 1950s, independent school leaders considered federal legislation and the effects of desegregation on the growth of independent schools. NCIS monitored federal legislation and took into account the National Defense Education Act of 1958

(NDEA), which Congress passed following the Soviet Union's launch of Sputnik in 1957. The launching of Sputnik pushed educational and policy leaders to address quickly what they considered deficits in U.S. education in the areas of math, science, and foreign languages. Independent schools were not exempt from the U.S. government's indictment, nor the resources that policymakers made available.[15] Later that year in NCIS's November *Report*, the front page featured a "Special Memorandum on Legislation" with briefs detailing parts of NDEA most applicable to independent schools, including Titles III, V, and VI. Title III referred to the loans to schools, and Title V concerned testing of students in nonpublic schools; these tests were identical to those used in public school systems that had no program of standardized testing. Title VI allowed for teachers and counselors, including those of nonpublic schools, to participate in counseling and guidance institutes and language institutes free of charge.

At the same time that NCIS monitored federal involvement in improving U.S. schools, NCIS leaders contended with the realities of southern public school desegregation. As whites continued to establish segregationist academies, NCIS leaders fielded inquiries that came their way. By March of 1959, individuals in Virginia desiring to begin private schools had sent inquiries to NCIS.[16] The Southern Association of Independent Schools (SAIS) had issued a statement about segregationist academies in late 1958 that included the support of public schools and the need to keep them open because closing them would not be beneficial to the South. SAIS also disavowed "the attempts of any individuals or groups to make financial profit out of the present emergency by the opening of substandard private schools." Although SAIS took this rather strong stance, NCIS shied away from a complete condemnation of any new private schools. NCIS stated that it could not be assumed that all new schools would be started for these reasons but that if groups were establishing schools to avoid desegregation, that independent school associations would need to be mindful of such intentions when reviewing membership applications.[17]

One does not know how well SAIS publicized its statement or the measures the organization would take to determine which schools were started for profit or to avoid desegregation. Nor did this statement include a position on existing schools that had not admitted black students. Ironically, the next *Report*, in June 1959, included an announcement about the development of a "How to Do It" manual for organizing a new school. Part of the statement read: "It should probably be emphasized that the manual will be presented not from the point of view of urging or encouraging groups to start a new independent school but from that of giving assistance to groups which have determined that they wish to do so, and need guidance and information to help them decide whether it is practical, and if so how to proceed."[18] Rather than take a stance against those schools established to maintain segregation practices, NCIS leaders walked a tightrope as they provided guidance in support of new private schools across the country.

The growth of private schools was a national topic of discussion. Following an administrators conference at Teachers College, Columbia University, in the summer of 1959, William W. Brickman, editor of *School and Society*, wrote an editorial in which he attributed the growth of private schools to racial desegregation as well as the "improved economic situation of families and some dissatisfaction with the public schools." Brickman specifically noted the rise of private religious schools in northern states; he also defended parents' rights to choose schools best for their children, and he suggested that public schools might be enhanced because of the growing number of private schools. In Brickman's estimation, "Fair competition can contribute toward the raising of the standards of public education. The democratic way in education is neither monolithic nor monopolistic. Fortunately, the national motto still remains *e pluribus unum*."[19]

As the role of private schools in the United States took on new meaning, Judge Hooper's decision in *Calhoun v. Latimer* forced Georgia politicians to consider school desegregation. By May of 1960, a limited number of black students had desegregated only 749 out of 7,016 school districts in the seventeen southern and border states that had been legally segregated. By that fall, other southern cities such as New Orleans and Richmond joined this limited group.[20] The civil rights movement, having gained momentum in the mid- to late 1950s, advanced with student protests emanating from the lunch counters of Greensboro, North Carolina, in 1960. In an attempt to gain more time by delaying the repeal of Georgia laws, Governor Ernest Vandiver in 1960 established the Sibley Commission led by John Sibley, the same businessman that Pressly had consulted in the spring of 1951 before accepting McCain's offer to lead Westminster.[21] Vandiver charged the commission with developing a state desegregation plan while still maintaining some form of resistance. During March 1960, the same month that black Americans—in particular, college students from the Atlanta University Center (AUC)—began sit-ins at Atlanta lunch counters, the commission held hearings in each of Georgia's ten congressional districts. Despite the preference for absolute segregation by 60 percent of the 1,600 witnesses, the majority of the commission members recommended "that the state abandon massive resistance and adopt a more practical position" that still ensured a high level of legal segregation. Conversely, "a sizable minority of the commission disagreed and submitted its own report, calling for the continuation of massive resistance."[22] Following the release of the Sibley report in April 1960, the state leaders remained divided on the issue of desegregation, and Westminster leaders continued to make decisions regarding the number of students to admit. For example, in the December 1960 board meeting, board members decided to offer admission tests for only kindergarten and sixth and eighth grades for the following school year. Having agreed not to grow the school, school administrators seemed to have put this policy in place to limit which people could apply.

On January 6, 1961, when Judge William T. Bootle ordered the University of Georgia to admit Hunter-Gault and Holmes, the General Assembly attempted to avoid Bootle's decision. Following a campus riot on January 11, Bootle ordered the readmission of Hunter-Gault and Holmes and "enjoined Vandiver from cutting off state funds to the University of Georgia" on January 12.[23] On January 18, Vandiver asked the legislature to repeal laws that would close desegregated public schools for two reasons. First, the General Assembly was prohibited from denying funds to the university. Second, because of their professional and personal interests, assembly members opted not to close the university. By the end of the month, the legislature passed three bills: "the first to suspend massive resistance laws and guarantee a grants-in-aid and pupil placement plan, the second to allow for local option, and the third to turn control of schools over to their local school boards."[24]

Simultaneously, the question of tax exemption for private educational institutions, which would become pivotal in discussions about race and K-12 private schooling in the latter part of the decade, was already surfacing in higher education. At Emory University in Atlanta, board chairman Henry Bowden formed a committee to review Emory's admissions policy relative to black students.[25] Similar to the leaders of the city of Atlanta who compromised on issues of race in order to sustain Atlanta's prosperity, Emory leaders followed the same agenda. Deciding to admit black students could be costly because schools like Emory received state tax exemption by maintaining an all-white student body.[26] The Emory board chose not to act during the spring of 1961 as it mulled over the possibility of desegregation and the Georgia tax-exemption law. When the board did not issue a statement, "faculty and students reacted with dismay," and the board promised a decision by November.[27]

As higher education administrators changed and contemplated admissions policies, city leaders and local citizens prepared for the desegregation of APS, and Westminster leaders continued to weigh their school's position on desegregation. Westminster also began receiving pressure to desegregate, in part, by the Greater Atlanta Council on Human Relations (GACHR), a branch of the Georgia Council on Human Relations. GACHR's purpose was to improve all areas of life in Atlanta, to encourage cooperation and advancement among different racial groups, and to join forces at the local and state levels to accomplish their goals. Most of GACHR's efforts were in the public arena, including the desegregation of public services (e.g., transportation and healthcare), facilities (e.g., lunch counters), and the arts (e.g., the Atlanta Symphony Orchestra); higher education; and black and white churches working together. GACHR included private primary and secondary schools on their agenda, and GACHR formed a committee focused on private school desegregation that would inquire about the admissions policies at Westminster and other local private schools.[28]

In the spring of 1961, the Westminster board adopted positions relevant to aid offered by the federal government for the establishment of private schools. In April, the Westminster board decided against accepting any federal loans from the government to independent elementary and secondary schools for building purposes. Additionally, "it was seconded and passed that Dr. Pressly should inform the National Council of Independent Schools that Westminster is not interested in federal loans and that the Westminster Board of Trustees hopes the Council will not pursue passage of such legislation."[29]

The board's position on federal aid was indicative of NCIS's close watch on the NDEA monies available to private schools and the role of the federal government in education. In 1960 and 1961 *Reports*, NCIS continued to inform readers on the NDEA amendments. NCIS went on record in support of amendments to Title II, V, and VI. These amendments ensured that private school teachers would receive loan forgiveness and be able to attend guidance and counseling institutes and foreign language institutes free of charge like public school teachers.[30] NCIS polled school leaders for their opinions on such amendments and one hundred responses were summarized in a report.[31] In the April 1961 *Report*, larger concerns about federal involvement in education and the flurry of activity under the Kennedy administration were outlined. Some leaders supported the Kennedy administration's efforts to extend federal monies to schools, but there were differences of opinion about specific allocations for public and nonpublic schools, especially concerning teacher salaries.[32] NCIS agreed that responses to the administration's proposals were too diverse among school leaders for NCIS to issue a collective position. That NCIS members engaged in discussion about these topics displays how private school leaders remained aware of what was happening with federal policy and the effects of such policy on their schools.

Westminster: A Decade after Its Founding

Westminster approached its ten-year anniversary during the very years in which African Americans legally challenged segregation in the public education sector in Atlanta and Georgia, and independent school leaders paid more attention to segregationist academies and the relationship between the federal government and education. As Westminster developed, the slave auction fundraisers continued and the performances of black entertainers received even more coverage in the school newspapers.[33] How students covered events in their school newspapers indicated what was important to the newspaper staff as students attempted to report on noteworthy events and moments in school life.

In writing about the black entertainers, students' comments showed their familiarity with the performers and their music. In October 1958, Dwike Mitchell and Willie Ruff, a black jazz duo, were featured on the front page of the *Mark Sheet*; they had performed for an assembly, and the student writer noted, "'Fugue for Lulu,' an original by the duo, followed. This bit of musical abracadabra illustrated graphically the influence of Bach and his contemporaries of the 17th and 18th century on modern jazz. . . . Mitchell's use of the twelve-tone scale in 'Old Man River,' coupled with Ruff's dissonant bowings on the bass, made this number outstanding."[34] When Mitchell and Ruff returned to the stage for an encore presentation, "bits of Brahms, Chopin, and Lizst [sic] were deftly blended with a really knock-down-drag-out jazz beat that sent the Westminster jazz aficionados back to their 4th period classes in a cool, but happy mood." The author noted that Mitchell and Ruff were classically trained at Juilliard and Yale, but "the basic feeling for genuine jazz was completely apparent." The reporter lauded the Mitchell and Ruff performance as "the most successful musical program ever presented."

In less than a year, the Midnighters' performances during Westminster's Jazz Weekend in January of 1959 received even more coverage than the Mitchell and Ruff performance. Again front page news, three pictures accompanied an article titled "Midnighters Entertain at Two Dances and Jam Session during Big Jazz Weekend." As reported, the Midnighters, a black music group, played in front of a captivated audience. The article described their performance as fabulous, as the group "emerged from the dressing room and began their song and dance revel which gradually built up to a massive assault on the piano and the nerves of the audience." Although the group repeated some songs "because of the expurgation of several suggestive pieces," "songs like 'The Twist,' 'Work With Me Annie,' and 'Daddy's Little Baby,' gave the enraptured boppers many moments of joy."[35] Black bands continued to perform at Westminster the next school year. "The Drifters," an all-black group that performed at Westminster's Jazz Weekend, was pictured in the April 1960 edition of the *Mark Sheet*.[36] Additionally "Noted R&B Expert Comments on Bo Diddley" appeared on the front page of the February 1961 edition.[37] Although white students participated in racist traditions, they, like many other white Americans, liked the music performed by black musicians. Such affinity certainly did not absolve their fondness for the Old South or how other school events indicated a potential lack of consciousness concerning racism.

Students also addressed the major issues of the day. Young men, more than young women, wrote very directly about issues of race and desegregation. Yet, in the October 1958 edition of the *Westminster Chimes*, the newspaper produced by the girls' school, a student wrote an editorial entitled "Any Disturbance Affects Students throughout US." The writer initially asked, "Little Rock, Clinton, Norfolk: names in the news, places we may never see. How can their affairs affect us?" The writer continued by stating that parents from these locations had been calling Westminster regarding admission for their daughters.

Though the student did not reveal her source for knowing this information, her article corresponded with Westminster turning away 1,800 applicants for the 1958 school year. She additionally addressed public school closings from a white student's perspective by noting, "Their daughters are filing applications for college, without even knowing whether they will be able to finish their senior year of high school." The writer also retold the story of a former Westminster student attending a school in a different state. The former student was not attending the "best" school in her new city, and the school operated on double shifts. With this, the writer concluded by challenging Westminster students not to take their education for granted in light of the educational disturbances around the country.[38] Three additional articles in the *Westminster Chimes* in the October 1960 and

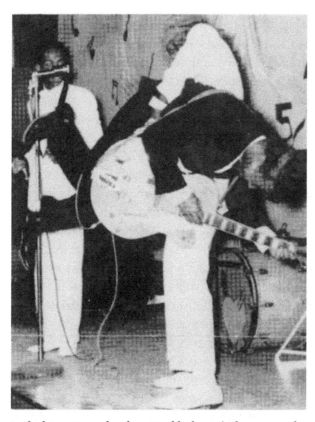

In the late 1950s and early 1960s, black musical groups such
as the Midnighters often performed at Westminster dances
and events. Newspaper accounts indicate how much the
students enjoyed their music. In the early 1960s, Pressly
banned this group and others from performing on campus,
and students debated the reasons for their dismissal in the
school paper. In time, other black performers such as
Graham Jackson appeared on campus. Source: "Midnighters
Entertain at Two Dances and Jam Session during Big Jazz
Weekend," *Mark Sheet*, February 13, 1959, 1, RG 21.05,
Beck Archives-Westminster.

February 1961 editions highlighted young women's opinions on national issues, but the authors did not discuss race explicitly. The articles covered students' thoughts on the 1960 presidential election between Kennedy and
Nixon, a call for students to think nationally, and advocacy for more student opportunities to voice their opinions on local, national, and international situations.[39] The girls appeared to choose topics that covered

broad political and social changes, but they, unlike the young men, did not see race as central to those political and social changes.

In the *Mark Sheet*, young men more readily focused on racial issues of the day. A month after the young woman's editorial in fall 1958, a young man wrote about the public schools. The author first noted the desegregation suit against APS. To him the result of the case was obvious: "The Atlanta Public School System will be forced to admit Negroes." He also pointed out, however, that because the state legislation called for the closing of public schools if desegregated "that most of Atlanta's students might not be able to enter school next September." The student urged that a city vote on desegregation be considered, and he called for individuals to pressure the state legislature to overturn their laws. The writer highlighted the effects of public school closings in other locations and called for Westminster students to recognize the privileged position that they occupied. He suggested that Westminster students would only be indirectly affected by public school closings: "We can voice our opinions with more force than can those who are actually going to be deprived of the chance to learn. While their pleas may be interpreted as only personal anger, we can speak out for the maintenance of the public school system for the sake for the principle alone. This cannot help but have great influence on the minds of thinking Atlantans."[40]

This editorial touched on a variety of topics including the need for Atlantans to speak out against the state legislation plan that stipulated the closing of public schools if the courts ordered desegregation. The desegregation of public facilities, begun in the 1950s, the fear of losing Atlanta's economic position, and the agency of black Americans had fueled the development of the Northside-Black alliance. The student writer suggested that others speak out "on principle alone." He did not elaborate on this principle, yet one possibility could have been upholding the *Brown* decision despite the opposition of the Georgia state legislature. A year later in December of 1959, an editorial in the *Mark Sheet* titled "The Problem of Tolerance" provided additional insight into how Westminster students conceptualized changes in society as the author attempted to make a distinction between tolerance of ideas and tolerance of others.[41]

John Pendergrast was one such Westminster student. His mother, Mrs. Nan Pendergrast, was an active member of GACHR, and so John came by his concern for equity honestly. John and his six siblings all attended Westminster for the seventh through twelfth grades after completing the elementary grades in public schools. Because of her stance on segregation,

Nan stated that sending her children to Westminster was "tough." She continued, "I thought about it. For one thing, as you can see, we live right next door. This is actually my 100th year of connection to Westminster. . . . I went to Washington Seminary and my mother went to Washington Seminary, class of 1909. The thing was I did not feel happy about Westminster, but the public schools were no better; it was not a question of making a choice." Preparation for college was important to Nan and her husband, Britt Pendergrast. According to Nan Pendergrast, "At the time it seemed to me terribly important to send them to the best colleges, and they were not in the South."[42] In fact, having taken advanced placement courses at Westminster, some Pendergrast children were able to graduate college in three years, thereby eliminating the cost of one year's tuition. How the Pendergrasts reconciled sending their children to Westminster provides insight into one reason why some white Atlantans chose Westminster. Westminster had become known for its academic rigor and college preparation, although aspects of the school culture countered efforts by Nan Pendergrast and other white moderates and liberals.

Nan Pendergrast's activism influenced her children. In February of 1960 the state of Georgia upheld its antidesegregation policies despite Judge Hooper's 1959 decision concerning APS, and that month John wrote an editorial titled "Separate but Equal?" In "Separate but Equal?" John Pendergrast stated that the integrationist needs to counter the "supremacist" who believes that "there is an unbreachable gap between the races and that each race should be allowed its natural place, the Whites above and the Negroes below." He said that this countering needed to occur with "a bewildering array of statistics proving conclusively that Negroes given the same opportunities have done as well as Whites." Pendergrast questioned the defense of "tradition" as a rationale for continuing separate but equal. In stating that integration needs to be accepted, Pendergrast wrote, "The truth is that more Negroes are born each minute than can be deported in a week. We are going to have to live with the Negroes like it or not. Though the supremacist will still not be convinced, integrating schools and facilities will provide equality under the law for blacks."[43]

John Pendergrast addressed the inferior status attached to black Americans. He acknowledged that "no amount of statistics is going to convince the White supremacist that he is no better than the average Negro," and that change will not come overnight, "but it will take the Negroes' supposed inferiority off the books." Yet underlying this editorial's tone was the notion that regardless of what people may think or want (i.e., deporting Negroes), whites will have to live with blacks. Pendergrast concluded by stating that with integration, blacks will have "a chance to fight for equal opportunities. They will no longer be stifled, and the White supremacist can rest his brain from the exertions of trying to twist logic away from the truth."[44]

As Westminster's leadership navigated the school's position on racial matters on the cusp of the school's tenth anniversary, the school newspapers shed light on a school environment that continued to promote traditions such as the slave auction fundraiser and performances by black entertainers. Articles in Westminster's school newspapers suggest what some white students thought about race. Some students took very clear stances against segregation and notions of black inferiority, and at this time, took positions that Pressly, their school leader, did not as he continued to grow the school. Young white men who were coming of age during a vastly changing political and social era displayed engagement with issues of the day while participating in events that also suggested understandings of racial subjugation. This complex and contradictory school environment would be sustained in the years prior to black student enrollment.

Confronting Racial Reality and Public School Desegregation

In the spring of 1961, black students wishing to transfer to segregated public white schools faced "unnecessarily complicated, arbitrary, and capricious requirements within a very limited period of time."[45] Transfer procedures were made public on April 24, 1961, and applications were made available from May 1 to May 15. Students wanting to transfer had to demonstrate prior academic achievement, certain psychological dispositions, and good morals and physical health. Their applications were reviewed in light of what their admission might mean for faculty, staff, and students at their new schools.[46] The admissions criteria developed by the board of education echoed similar pupil placement plans across the South including in New Orleans, Richmond, and Memphis.[47] To the black community in Atlanta, it was obvious that "the board had created barriers intended to limit the number of transfers and to discourage applications."[48] With sixty persons from the National Association for the Advancement of Colored People (NAACP) and GACHR assisting prospective applicants and their parents, 300 black students secured applications and 136 applied for transfers.[49] Of those students who applied, the board granted sixteen interviews and chose ten to desegregate Grady, Murphy, Brown, and Northside High Schools. As the beginning of the school year approached, ongoing racial tensions persisted as evidenced by continued sit-ins, but Atlanta's white leadership maintained the mantra of the "city too busy to hate."[50]

During the summer of 1961, the white community prepared for desegregation with the assistance of OASIS—Organizations Assisting Schools in September. The organizations and city leaders, including Mayor Hartsfield, were determined that what happened elsewhere (i.e., in Little Rock and the University of Georgia) would not occur in Atlanta in order to preserve its viability as a booming economic center. As McGrath wrote: "OASIS did not criticize the concept of pupil placement, rather the organization stressed the importance of peaceful implementation. Unlike HOPE, which made a conscious decision to exclude blacks, OASIS consisted of fifty-three civic, professional, and religious organizations representing black and white constituencies."[51] Interested in promoting positive public relations, OASIS took certain steps. OASIS leaders invited President Kennedy to be a keynote speaker at an event highlighting Atlanta schools, developed a code of ethics that was distributed to local radio stations, published a pamphlet entitled "Background: A Handbook for Reporters Covering the Desegregation of Atlanta Public Schools," and "use[d] their influence with young people to encourage mature and respectful behavior when school opened in the Fall."[52] OASIS and school officials met with white parents and students prior to the opening of school, while GACHR held meetings for the black students transferring to segregated white public schools. During these meetings the black students met some of their white classmates. GACHR also organized the only meeting among school officials, black students, and their parents. Perhaps indicative of Westminster's complex position in the greater community as Atlanta sought positive public relations, Westminster students participated in some of these preparation meetings.[53]

On August 30, 1961, all of the preparations culminated as escorts in undercover cars drove nine black students—out of a total student population of 110,000—to their respective Atlanta public schools.[54] With the police poised to react to any disturbances, the students desegregated Grady, Murphy, Northside, and Brown High Schools without major protests. Attendance was normal at each school with police arresting five individuals.[55] But the experiences of the black students were anything but positive. White teachers and principals stimulated the negative responses of their white students as white teachers and principals designated particular areas where black students could sit. Martha Ann Holmes and Rosalyn Walton, black students at Murphy, ate lunch by themselves, and white students, like their counterparts in Clinton, Tennessee, and elsewhere, subjected the black students to verbal and physical attacks.[56] As aptly noted by Kruse, "Token integration was often just a new form of segregation."[57] Yet, the desegregation of APS did cause Westminster leaders to consider race more directly.

GACHR had formed a committee on private school desegregation in January 1961, but GACHR did not inform the Westminster board and administration about the committee. During a September 1961 board meeting, "Dr. Broyles expressed the belief that the Board should have a policy on integration in order that Dr. Pressly will have a stated policy to be used, if that occasion should arise. Such a policy need not to be announced to the public." The Committee on Race was assembled "to study this subject"; the committee consisted of Dr. McCain, who served as chair, Mr. Hal Smith, and Mrs. Thomas Hines."[58] Ironically, the day before Broyles made this proposal, GACHR had decided to "inquire of all private schools and county schools" their future plans regarding desegregation.[59]

Again in October, the Westminster board was "opposed to any sort of federal aid to non-public schools," this time in response to an NCIS survey of schools regarding this issue and others.[60] Yet, the majority of the members voted in support of an "income tax deduction allowable to parents paying tuition to private schools."[61] Measures concerning tax deduction or credit, according to the April 1961 *Report*, had "been introduced in every legislative session for the past several years and several of them have already appeared in this session . . . the history of the proposals has been that despite considerable and varied backing, they have run up against flat opposition from those responsible for government finance both in the administrative and legislative branches."[62] One can assume that Westminster's support of tax credits and refusal of federal aid paralleled overall sentiment by independent schools toward political and social changes.

As the desegregation of APS occurred and Westminster leaders once again considered how to position the school, students wrote about desegregation and race and even raised questions about the possibility of Westminster's desegregation. On the other hand, the climate of Westminster continued to be shaped by racist traditions as well as student interest in the performance of black bands (and their subsequent ban by the school administration).[63]

In October of 1961, the editor of the *Mark Sheet* wrote a short piece on the desegregation of APS in which he discussed the South's ability to do what is "right." With the election of Mayor Ivan Allen Jr., which "demonstrated Atlanta is ruled by law and wisdom," and with the seemingly peaceful desegregation of APS, the author wrote, "No matter what our personal feelings are we must realize that disobedience to the law can only bring anarchy and complete disorder." He was grateful that Atlanta was not another Little Rock, and the editor called on the Westminster administration: "Let us hope that our administration will never deny an applicant admission to Westminster because of race, creed, or color."[64] This quote sparked the first discussion in the school newspapers regarding Westminster's desegregation. Though determining whether students had knowledge of the formation of the board's Committee on Race is difficult, this article and others appeared concomitant with actions concerning desegregation at Westminster.

Previous newspaper coverage had indicated how much students enjoyed the performances by black musicians, but in November of 1961, Pressly announced at the Parents' Council meeting the school's decision to ban black bands from performing at school dances.[65] This policy might have indicated Pressly's concern about a generational shift occurring in the South during the mid-twentieth century. As Pete Daniel noted, "Many adults saw rock 'n' roll's fast beat, obscure lyrics, frantic performances, unorthodox wardrobe, and hectic dancing as lewd, lowdown, transgressive."[66] Some whites "contemptuously referred to rhythm and blues and rock 'n' roll as 'nigger music.'" Further, how the music drew in white women and girls raised long-standing fears. As indicated by Daniel's examples, white female college students flocked to dance parties where black bands performed. The combination of political changes, music, and other societal entities created a transformative power that presumably Westminster administrators and parents dreaded.

Student responses to the school's banning of black bands, though only from young men, provided a forum for discussion about prejudice and discrimination. In "Prejudice?," an October 1961 editorial, Ralph McGill Jr., son of Atlanta Constitution editor Ralph McGill, wrote, "As everyone knows, Westminster is a Christian school, founded on Christian ideas. Prejudice is not one of them. Nevertheless, there appears to be evidence of prejudice in a ruling handed down by the school." While the young McGill cited that the reason for the ban on Negro bands resulted from "a number of unfortunate incidents," he declared that banning all Negro bands "for the misconduct of a few" was wrong. Further, he charged that the ban was related to race: "The character of a performer determines his actions, not the color of his skin. Musicians should be chosen solely for quality."[67]

In direct response to McGill's editorial, the newspaper staff printed a second editorial with the same title of the editorial in the November 1961 edition. The author argued that the decision was not based on prejudice but rather on "a standard of comparison." Further, "if many of the Negro bands have been found to be lacking in dignity, and if the nature of their music has been judged inferior to that of most white bands, then they should not be invited back. The ruling is one of taste, not of prejudice." In making this argument, this student challenged McGill to look at the setting. In this student's opinion, "it is of questionable tolerance for one to sit in the confines of a school such as Westminster and expound the principles of racial equality, since ours is strictly a selective school."[68]

In another editorial in the same edition, a student discussed the meaning of discrimination. He defined discrimination as "the act of making a distinction or observing a difference." He argued that individuals discriminate every day when choosing which clothes to wear and that Westminster administrators discriminate against students based on IQ scores. The author agreed that the administration did discriminate in banning bands, but the decision was "not based on blind prejudice but analyzed fact." Such facts cited included the conditions in which black bands arrived at dances and the need for the school administrators to correct the behavior and song selection of black performers. As the writer contended, "with white bands this has never been necessary."[69] Finally, "Criticism," a third editorial in November, challenged students to consider the type of criticism that they level upon the faculty and administration, but the "Negro band" and "twist" controversies had sparked the editorial.[70]

The banning of black bands had ignited conversations at Westminster about the definitions of prejudice and discrimination.[71] At the heart of these issues was race, thus indicating a school climate in which some students, at least in the boys' division, examined decisions important to the student body and did so with some sophistication. Students illuminated the complexities of attending a school that clearly had appealed to students and parents despite its celebration of the Old South and the continuation of racist traditions and because it was a school in which some moderate and liberal positions could be espoused in the school newspaper. Through the newspaper articles, white students demonstrated a level of consciousness about societal inequities and how African Americans' identity had been negatively constructed in U.S. society. That the students might both participate in activities with racist connotations and write about race and racism with such sophistication exhibits the contradictions of prejudice, the inconsistencies in their own decisions, and how they, like many others, negotiated societal norms and pushed to change those norms.

Increased Inquiries, Civil Rights Action, and National Efforts

Civil rights activists, while focused on public accommodations, tested admissions policies at historically white elite private schools. In March of 1962, the following was reported in GACHR's *School News*: "In a response to a telephone inquiry, a spokesman in the admissions office at the Westminster Schools said that applications from negro students will be processed like any other applications, which in many cases of course means getting a place on a waiting list."[72] GACHR's monitoring of Westminster's policies continued that May. Eliza Paschall, executive director of GACHR, wrote to Pressly regarding black citizens being forced to sit in the Westminster balcony during the baccalaureate service at the end of the school year. She indicated that GACHR expected Westminster to be a leader in human relations and that GACHR members hoped this report had been false.[73] Though Pressly did not address this inquiry in writing, discrimination charges by Paschall seem plausible considering Pressly's announcement during an April 1962 Parents' Council meeting. During this meeting, Pressly dispelled the notion the board of trustees had decided to admit black students. Further he asked that parents correct this notion if they heard it.[74]

Pressly's request to end rumors regarding the admission of black students suggested an avoidance of desegregation, despite black Atlantans having inquired about Westminster's policies that year. In his 1962 annual report to the board, Pressly wrote the following: "During the year, at least four controversial issues have arisen in independent school education." The fourth issue listed by Pressly was the question of desegregation. He noted that four black students had been tested for admission. Two potential high school students did not qualify for admission because their IQ scores were less than 110, and they had scored very low on the admission test. Two black boys also sat for the admission test. According to Pressly, one, like the girls, scored very low, but one of the boys exceeded expectations. However, the grade for which he was tested was already full.[75]

When asked how Pressly felt about desegregation, Nan Pendergrast stated that he often remarked, "'We'd let them in but they couldn't possibly do the work.'"[76] In the first decade of Westminster, Pressly had not initiated conversations about the desegregation of Westminster, although he was surely aware of other schools such as Sidwell Friends in Washington, D.C., opening their admissions to all students. Pressly ascribed to beliefs that black children were not prepared to succeed at schools like Westminster, although Pressly lived and worked in a city with several historically black colleges and universities with faculty and staff having earned degrees throughout the nation and with black K-12 teachers most likely having earned advanced degrees outside of southern states because they were not allowed to attend historically white institutions in the South.[77] Although the grade to which he applied was full, the second black boy's test results had shown that black students could academically achieve at Westminster, and perhaps that is why his mother had him take the test despite knowing that his potential grade was full. That these students took admission tests also increased pressure on Westminster following the GACHR inquiries. Because of Pressly's national prominence, he was conscious of the national climate regarding desegregation, both in general and within independent schools as questions concerning Westminster's admissions policies and that of other local Atlanta schools would only increase.

Pressly remained a national leader as the organizational structure of independent schools changed when NCIS and the Independent Schools Education Board (ISEB, formerly SEB) merged to form the National Association of Independent Schools (NAIS) in 1962. The directors of the newly formed NAIS sought to continue the work of both organizations with ISEB's focus on academics and curriculum and NCIS's focus on administration. The expressed purposes of NAIS were "to assist, strengthen, and promote the interests of independent schools of the United States and similar schools elsewhere and to aid them to serve effectively the free society from which they derive their independence."[78] Pressly was a founding NAIS board member, and per bylaw requirement, he was also a member of the School Administration Committee.

In tandem with the development of NAIS, black students desegregated parochial schools in Atlanta, and the desegregation of APS moved slowly. During the 1962–63 school year, "there were six additional desegregated high schools; the number of black students in all of the schools had risen to only forty-four, while 10,945 whites attended multiracial classes."[79] The NAACP lawyers returned to federal court arguing that APS remained segregated and called for a more accelerated desegregation plan. Judge Hooper and the Fifth Circuit denied the motions, and upheld gradual desegregation. The court decision did stipulate that test scores and personality interviews were not to be used to discriminate against black students in placing them in white schools.[80]

The issue of tax exemption for higher education institutions continued to be critical for decision making about admissions policies. Following the desegregation of APS, Emory University's board of trustees announced an open admissions policy in the fall of 1961, but they would only enact the policy when tax-exempt status was not threatened. The following spring, "after receiving the application at the Dental School from a qualified black applicant, Emory filed suit on March 12, 1962, carefully arguing that the tax exemption was valid but the racial restriction within it was not." Though the district court did not decide in favor of Emory, the Georgia Supreme Court did in October 1962. Later that fall, a part-time black graduate student enrolled at Emory. Ideally board chairman Henry Bowden wanted Emory to "remain segregated," and he resented "pressure from either the government or private donors who threaten to cut" funds if Emory did not "integrate." He further concluded that it was clear that the federal government was "deeply embedded in private as well as public education." He stated, "We are of the opinion that in the not too distant future we will find Congress acting to cut off Federal funds from institutions which by charter or rules prohibit negroes from attending."[81] The implications of federal government involvement threatened the research enterprise of Emory and, in turn, its ability to grow as a major research institution. Bowden also received inquiries from foundations and accrediting agencies regarding the university's position on desegregation. As independent school leaders considered how to respond during this era, such changes at Emory and other higher education institutions gesture to the growing concern about tax-exempt status for private institutions and, more broadly, how the federal government affected public and private institutions.

Outside of school desegregation, the civil rights movement continued to unfold in Atlanta in the summer of 1962 when the NAACP held its annual convention in Atlanta. Despite school and lunch counter desegregation, hotels remained segregated. The NAACP tried several tactics to change these policies, including picketing and filing a lawsuit, *Reed v. Sarno*. The ruling in the case was "that policies of a private business could not be construed as 'state action.' If a businessman wanted to discriminate in his choice of customers, he had that right."[82] That spring, the NAACP launched a campaign for a municipal public accommodations law, but even moderate businessmen would not budge. For example, "John Sibley, who had guided Georgia through its school desegregation crisis, shuddered at the thought of businessmen compelled to serve black customers against their will."[83]

In the spring of 1963, civil rights leaders tested admissions policies at Atlanta's elite private schools. GACHR inquired again about Westminster's policy on desegregation and encouraged the desegregation of other local private schools.[84] A coalition of black parents formed under the leadership of Dr. Staughton Lynd, a professor at Spelman College. Lynd contacted Edyth Ross, the wife of Dr. Hubert Ross, a professor of anthropology and sociology, and Juanita Abernathy, Coretta Scott King, and Jean Young, the wives of Southern Christian Leadership Conference (SCLC) leaders Reverend Ralph Abernathy, Dr. Martin Luther King Jr., and Andrew Young.[85] Paschall would support the families as they sought admission to Trinity, Lovett, and Westminster, leading private schools on Atlanta's north side.

When Ralph and Juanita Abernathy made an application for their daughter to Trinity, the chairman of the board asked for the application to be withdrawn. The chairman stated that if black children were tested and admitted, Trinity would lose much parental and congregational support and face an economic crisis. The Abernathys, however, continued the application process although Juanita Abernathy "knew immediately her child could not pass the test that was being administered to her."[86] Trinity school leaders did not admit the Abernathys' daughter, but the Abnernathys continued to inquire about Trinity's policies. They contacted Reverend Allison Williams, minister of Trinity Church and a member of GACHR. Williams investigated the admissions matter and countered the position of Trinity's board chair by gaining support from members of Trinity Church and Trinity School who supported desegregation. Because of the support Williams received from the Trinity church and school communities, desegregation became a possibility. Later, during the spring of 1963, under the urging of the Abernathys, Jean and Andrew Young had their daughters tested for admission at Trinity, and the school's admissions staff readily accepted them for the fall of 1963.

As the Abernathys and Youngs inquired about admission at Trinity, the Kings sought admission for Martin Luther King III at the Lovett School. Like Westminster, the Lovett School flourished as a result of public school desegregation. Lovett headmaster Vernon Kelley shared with a reporter, "'In all candor, the segregation-desegregation struggle gives impetus to the development of private schools.'"[87] Though the Lovett School had no formal policy on segregation, the Episcopal Diocese and Bishop Randolph Claiborne had taken a stand against all forms of discrimination. In the spring of 1963, however, the Episcopal Church was forced to confront Lovett's position on race.

With the encouragement of the Reverend John Morris, an Episcopal priest whose children attended Lovett, and with the belief that Lovett was open to all children, Martin Luther and Coretta Scott King submitted an application for Martin III in January of 1963. Upon receipt of King's application, Billy Sterne, successor to John Sibley at Trust Company of Georgia and chairman of the Lovett admissions committee, called Cecil Alexander to a meeting. Alexander, a Lovett board member, was an Atlanta architect who was a committee member on the city's only interracial committee, and he sat on the Atlanta Citizens Advisory Committee on Urban Renewal. During this meeting and in subsequent meetings, the Lovett board, upon advice of the admissions committee, decided not to accept Martin Luther King III.

After having received notification from Reverend James McDowell, headmaster at Lovett, about the Lovett board's decision, the Kings issued a statement: "Our sole purpose in making application to the Lovett School for our son, Martin III, was a sincere attempt to secure for him the best possible secondary education. This was not meant to be any sort of a test case, though we do desire for our son the experience of integrated schooling."[88] Because of the decision not to admit King, Alexander, a prominent white businessman with unique connections to the black community, resigned from the Lovett board. Furthermore, the board severed the school's relationship with the Episcopal Church.

Out of the group supported by Paschall and Lynd, the Ross family would challenge Westminster. Pressly dissuaded Hubert and Edyth Ross from having their daughter vie for eighth-grade admission to Westminster, as recounted in a letter from Paschall. At the time, their daughter was attending the Oglethorpe School, and her father did not want to send her to a "Negro high school" nor "send her away from home." One day prior to the scheduled admission test on February 9, the Rosses met with Pressly, and he told them the following: "The policy of the school up until either June, 1962 or Dec. 1962 was to accept *for testing* any student, but there had never been any clear policy by the trustees as to what they would do about a qualified Negro student who applied for Westminster." Yet, Pressly did not appear optimistic about the board's decision if the Ross child qualified academically for admission to Westminster. Pressly then suggested that the Rosses consider schools outside of Georgia such as Miss Porter's and Deerfield Academy. Pressly offered to "help them in trying to get her in one of these places." The Rosses, however, learned that Pressly had previously offered the same help to other black families seeking admission at Westminster. Realizing the end result, the Rosses opted for their daughter not to sit for the admission test. Paschall wrote, "He [Dr. Ross] said he and his wife are not interested in doing anything to lessen Westminster's 'position'—he thinks it is good for the community to have such a school—but he is perfectly willing for his experience to be used in any way that might be helpful." Paschall pondered what GACHR should do about the situation—"a letter to Broyles asking for the policy? A tip to the papers? Nothing???"[89] The media gave very limited coverage to this Westminster situation. As Gannon noted: "McGill's reference to Westminster's "shameful" behavior in the October 1963 *Diocese* interview is the only public coverage of integration at Westminster. Perhaps this was due to the power of the Westminster board of trustees in Atlanta, the lack of a media worthy name like King associated with the story, or to the fact that a private school defending its version of private rights was not deemed newsworthy."[90] All three reasons postulated by Gannon are valid, yet Pressly's 1962 report to the board also indicated another reason—Westminster had already maneuvered to evade applications by black students.

As desegregation became a reality for some independent schools in the South, independent school leaders outside of the South began to launch an effort to recruit black students from across the nation to independent schools. In February 1963, twenty-one representatives from independent boarding schools met.[91] The group "banded together to expand a program which had formerly been in operation as part of the overall activity of the National Scholarship Service and Fund for Negro Students [NSSFNS]."[92] The program operated independently of NSSFNS under the title the Independent Schools Talent Search Program (ISTSP) through a "substantial grant" from the Merrill Trust. In addition, each of the sixteen participating schools contributed "one dollar per boarding student" enrolled in their schools.[93]

Late spring and summer also brought watershed moments in the civil rights movement that would influence how NAIS leaders continued to develop their national agenda regarding the recruitment and retention of black students. In May 1963, more violence unfolded during civil rights demonstrations in Birmingham, Alabama. White police officers arrested a large number of demonstrators, including youth and Martin Luther King Jr., but marchers continued to advocate for civil rights. In turn, Birmingham police violently used dogs and high-pressure water hoses against the demonstrators. Because of these events, President John Kennedy knew that the federal government would have to intervene, although he had been very reluctant to do so for fear of alienating white southern Democrats. On June 11, 1963, President Kennedy made his plea to the nation for civil rights legislation, including, first and foremost, legislation for equal accommodations in all public facilities. That same day the first black students had registered at the University of Alabama. But that night, violence struck again when Byron de la Beckwith murdered Medgar Evers, NAACP field secretary, in the driveway of his home in Jackson, Mississippi, shortly after midnight.

On June 19, 1963, just eight days after Kennedy's plea for civil rights and Evers's death, independent school leaders, including NAIS president Cary Potter, attended a meeting of over two hundred educational representatives at the White House. President Kennedy had "called on [the educators] for suggestions and advice as well as for their cooperation in furthering equality of opportunity in education for Negroes and other minority groups, emphasizing particularly the need for local activity of a variety of sorts, and the role which he hoped educational leaders would take in their respective communities."[94] As national leaders of historically white institutions deliberated their next steps, Atlanta's segregationists refused to support civil rights legislation. President Kennedy, however, needed white southern support, and he called upon Mayor Ivan Allen, whose wife continued to serve on the Westminster board, to testify on behalf of what would become the Civil Rights Act of 1964. Allen feared that supporting civil rights legislation would hamper his political career, but a phone call from President Kennedy and the support of white and black business and civic leaders convinced Allen to testify. During his July testimony, Allen urged Congress to act. He believed that not acting "'would amount to an endorsement of private businesses setting up an entirely new status of discrimination throughout the Nation. Cities like Atlanta,' he warned, 'might slip backward.'"[95] The summer of 1963 culminated with the March on Washington for Jobs and Freedom and King championing civil rights. Martin III, just a few months prior, had been denied admission at one of Atlanta's leading private schools.

THE ISSUE OF DESEGREGATION and questions of prejudice and discrimination were apparent at Westminster. Between 1958 and 1961, the board had adopted two committees dedicated to looking at Westminster's position in relationship to public schools and to desegregation. Yet conversations that transpired in these committee meetings were not revealed in official board minutes nor were board members' varying positions on desegregation. Additionally, board members had decided on more than one occasion not to accept the assistance of the federal government. By 1963, as the first black students to attend Westminster were being educated primarily in segregated black schools, civil rights activism had captured the nation's attention, including that of independent school leaders. Historically white independent school leaders sought more black students through such efforts as the ISTSP. Conversely, black parents, such as those in Atlanta, had begun advocating for the inclusion of their children into white private schools, including Westminster, and they had received support from local activists. Like the first ten years of the school's existence, racist traditions continued to be part of the school culture, but student writers also addressed political and social changes that indicated changing racial attitudes.

In the next few years, the constellation of factors converged and catalyzed Westminster's decision to desegregate. The civil rights movement and public school desegregation had set the era's tenor. There would be additional internal and external inquiries into Westminster's policies as questions about federal tax-exemption policies continued to swirl. Pressly, although aware of developing national efforts to increase the number of black students attending historically white elite private schools, had sought to keep Westminster's student body all white as he negotiated multiple constituents and as he contemplated his own beliefs about African Americans' capabilities. By the mid-1960s, however, Westminster became part of the national trend to recruit and admit African American students. These shifting positions signify how independent school leaders responded and acted during a highly strained, dangerous era in which African Americans and others lost their lives as they advanced calls for equality and civil rights. Historically white elite private schools or independent schools wanted to show that they fell on the side of not accepting these public displays of racism, and their schools came to reflect larger societal, political, and social change, although black students had to find their way through an uneven school culture. Because of Pressly's national position, how Westminster leaders positioned the school was not without knowledge of developing national policies and practices concerning the recruitment of black students to independent schools.

CHAPTER THREE

The Blurring of Public and Private

The ongoing civil rights movements and tragedies in the fall of 1963 brought to the fore the reality of state-sanctioned and interpersonal racism that permeated American life and history, and this reality set the tenor for changes at Westminster during the mid-1960s. As the semester progressed, Westminster leaders discussed admissions testing. During the October 1963 Westminster board meeting, Dr. Broyles stated that the period for admissions testing was fast approaching and that the board might want to discuss the testing policy.[1] This statement could be indicative of how Westminster leaders thought about the harsh realities of racism and inequality in the United States. The admission of black students to neighboring independent schools surely had raised internal questions within the Westminster community about its exclusionary policies and how those policies might have to change.

The student newspaper continued to be a vehicle for students to discuss the most pressing issues and events of the day. In the November 1963 edition of the new *Westminster Bi-Line*, a joint paper between the boys' and girls' schools, a student urged that others adopt a Christian attitude in response to members of the Ku Klux Klan and the bombing of the Sixteenth Street Baptist Church in Birmingham, Alabama.[2] The September church bombing had killed four black girls—Addie Mae Collins, Carol Denise McNair, Carole Robertson, and Cynthia Wesley. The Westminster student wrote, "We did not prevent the bombing of this church, but we should and could have. We can at least help to rebuild it through funds and words of love. In this way we might also endeavor to realize these people's belief to man's kindness and his desire for brotherhood."[3] These comments showed Westminster students' acknowledgment of the world around them and the tragedies that were occurring during the civil rights movement. That November, the nation mourned the assassination of President John F. Kennedy. A month later, in the December 1963 edition of the *Bi-Line*, a student challenged his fellow students to act on the side of righteousness and justice and to quell evil by "improving educational opportunities and living conditions for those less fortunate than we."[4]

As the nation grappled with tragedies, the realities of racism, and resistance to the civil rights movement, David Mallery, then director of studies for the National Association of Independent Schools' (NAIS) Committee on Research, noted that independent schools were being tested "from within, by faculty, students, board members, parents, and administrators and from without, by community forces, by national events, and by the moral climate of the nation itself."[5] Some independent school leaders responded by advancing their efforts to recruit black students although their articulations of such efforts echoed at times the dominant deficit, racist discourses of the era. This was evident in articles in the *Independent School Bulletin* (*ISB*) and publications such as Mallery's *Negro Students in Independent Schools*. Mallery, a former English teacher at Germantown Friends School in Philadelphia, Pennsylvania, used the publication to provide advice for headmasters and boards of trustees for recruiting and retaining African American students.[6] *Negro Students* briefly mentioned the admission inquiries into Atlanta's independent schools in the spring of 1963, but in general the national publications paid less attention to southern independent schools.[7]

In Atlanta, school desegregation remained gradual. When school began in the fall of 1963, black students still attended mostly segregated black public schools. Only 144 African American students were enrolled in ten formerly all-white public schools.[8] Following the well-known split of the Lovett School from the Episcopal Church and the denial of admission to Martin Luther King III, the Atlanta Speech School and the Trinity School enrolled black students for the first time. At Trinity, with the admission of Andrea and Lisa Young, daughters of Andrew and Jean Young, parents withdrew 61 out of 247 white students from Trinity and 250 out of 2,000 members left Trinity Church. However, Trinity also benefited from desegregation. With the aid of Ralph McGill, Trinity received a $15,000 grant to help improve the academics of newly admitted students.[9]

Race relations remained fragile. Restaurants that had been temporarily desegregated reverted back to segregated spaces. A coalition of groups formed to address the issues. In October of 1963, the Committee on Appeal for Human Rights and local chapters of the National Association for the Advancement of Colored People (NAACP), Southern Christian Leadership Conference (SCLC), and Student Nonviolent Coordinating Committee (SNCC) comprised the Atlanta Summit Leadership Conference. This coalition of groups announced its plan for Atlanta desegregation under the title "Action for Democracy." Lestor Maddox and a group of fellow segregationists responded by forming the People's Association for Selective Shopping.[10] These schooling and city conditions underscored continued inquiries into

Westminster's policies. At the end of 1963, Eliza Paschall wrote to Pressly, "I noticed in the Sunday paper an announcement that Westminster is now accepting applications for admission to certain grades. This brings up my perennial question about applications from Negroes. Do you accept them and if so, do you consider them on the same basis as applications from white students?"[11] A response from Pressly is not apparent, but the inquiries would continue.

For the next three years, the blurring of public and private continued because of the constellation of factors emanating from the civil rights movement; continued inquiries into Westminster's admissions policies; independent schools' focus on race and black students more broadly that would garner private and federal monies; and potential changes to federal tax-exemption policies. Pressly carefully managed how this constellation of factors converged and affected Westminster as the school's politics reflected that of Atlanta's pragmatic desegregation politics. He was judicious and organized in his communication with different Westminster constituents as the board adopted an open admissions policy and as he spoke about the academic ability of black students. Westminster's desegregation plans drew on examples from other independent schools across the nation while also differing from them. Westminster sought black students for the first time, and the first admitted black students came from working- and middle-class families. They were educated in segregated black schools and had been bequeathed an African American tradition of the importance of schooling. The black students prepared to enter an all-white school that adhered to segregationist practices of the era. The Westminster that awaited them had an environment that included racist traditions and a segment of white students who raised important, nuanced questions about the issues of the time.

A Constellation of Factors Influences Westminster's Decision

In 1964, civil rights remained at the forefront of city life, and the Greater Atlanta Council on Human Relations (GACHR) continued reporting on Westminster. Student-led sit-ins were occurring throughout the city; however, "unhappy with the pace of change, students turned to aggressive direct action techniques to combat private discrimination," which would not only cause tension with moderate whites but also older, moderate, and pragmatic African Americans.[12] One standoff, in January 1964, escalated at Atlanta-based Leb's Restaurant. After the police refused to intervene, owner Charles

Lebedin locked the doors to the restaurant and barred the restrooms, leaving inside forty students led by John Lewis of SNCC. According to Kruse, "as the hours passed, the students abandoned their nonviolent ways. They smashed drinking glasses to the floor, overturned coffee urns, and flipped a few brown-and-yellow leather booths upside down. With the restroom doors still locked, some demonstrators relieved themselves on the floor."[13] Following this occurrence, white city leaders, such as former Mayor Hartsfield, became more "suspicious of black activists," and in time black activists "realized that local actions—whether protests in the streets, lawsuits in the courts, or negotiations in city hall—would never secure the victory they sought."[14] That same month, as a follow-up to its December inquiry, GACHR announced the following: "Recent announcements of admission tests for Westminster in the daily press prompted inquiries about racial policies. Dr. William Pressly, President, said that there is a committee of the trustees working on the matter, but the school *does not now accept applications from* Negro students. It does administer tests for admission to other schools and colleges to Negros as well as white students at its testing center."[15] Westminster's policy of not accepting black students was becoming more public, but the announcement about the testing of black students was a first. This acknowledgment may have been Pressly's way of implying that some black students had taken admission tests at Westminster.

In March, Paschall continued to question Westminster. In a letter to Max Taylor, the new director of the Westminster summer camp, she asked about admission to Westminster's summer camp because of GACHR's effort to maintain a list of opportunities available to all. Paschall asked, "We would appreciate your informing us if you will accept applications from Negroes at the Westminster Summer Camp."[16] Again, there was no response to Paschall's letter, but this letter was the last direct communication from Paschall and GACHR to Westminster regarding admissions policies.

One indication of GACHR's decline in inquiring about Westminster is gleaned from a confidential memo from Paschall to GACHR board members following the passage of the Civil Rights Bill. In the section concerning how the council should proceed with education, the last question asked was— "Is it important to us that Westminster still does not take applications from Negroes?"[17] The following school year, Paschall took a leave of absence, and GACHR did not ask further about Westminster's policies. Westminster leaders did receive a query from one of their most well-known parents.

Rabbi Jacob M. Rothschild asked about Westminster's exclusionary practices. Rothschild, a long-time member of GACHR and a Westminster parent, served as rabbi of The Temple, Atlanta's oldest synagogue, which had been bombed in the fall of 1958.[18] Despite having paid tuition for his children to attend Westminster, Rothschild declined in April 1964 to make a pledge to the school's annual fund. He credited the school for his children's education, and he noted, "The social ethic of Judaism and Christianity is certainly not disparate and their knowledge of a faith other than their own will only serve to make them better Americans and better Jews." Rothschild concluded his letter with the following explanation as to why he could not support the school's annual fund: "However, as a rabbi and even more important as a religious person I find it impossible to accept—precisely because Westminster is a school which prides itself upon being Christian—its unwillingness to educate qualified children of any race. To allow private schools which are under religious sponsorship to become the last bastion of segregated education seems to me to be contradictory, untenable, and indefensible."[19] Rothschild's letter raised significant implications because it challenged Westminster's policies. What is not known is if there were additional letters sent by other parents or the effect of Rothschild's letter on the board's deliberations. Rothschild's letter may have had little influence since he and others advocating for racial justice continued to enroll their children at Westminster. Still, this letter, combined with the previous inquiries, indicated that there was discontent with Westminster's policies.

Across the region, public school desegregation moved at a slow pace, and private schools became escape routes for whites. For example, following the desegregation of New Orleans Public Schools in 1960, "Louisiana's private schools thrived on state money allotted to students who attended them. In 1964-65, the number reached a high of 10,777 white recipients in New Orleans alone."[20] Further, "Ten years after the U.S. Supreme Court declared racial segregation in America's public schools unconstitutional, 873 black students out of a citywide black enrollment of 64,893 were attending schools with white students in New Orleans."[21] Simultaneously, independent school leaders focused new programs on the recruitment of black students to independent schools.

In the summer of 1964, as Congress passed the Civil Rights Act and as President Johnson signed it into law, the Independent Schools Talent Search Program (ISTSP), initiated in February 1963, continued alongside the start of Dartmouth's A Better Chance (ABC) program, sponsored by the Rockefeller Foundation. Dartmouth College offered "in its ABC program, an opportunity for intensive study to 50 boys from disadvantaged groups, primarily in the New England area."[22] Most of the boys were identified through ISTSP and admitted to New England boarding schools. According to the "Two Year Report" on ISTSP, the program served as "a summer transitional program to help disadvantaged students make the academic and social adjustment to the independent schools."[23]

Over the next year, independent schools' increasing focus on African American students and looming changes to federal tax policies created a constellation of factors for change. At Westminster, the 1964-65 school year began with Pressly raising the federal tax-exemption status issue by reiterating "Federal Judge Elbert Tuttle's statement that the courts would ultimately remove [the school's] tax exemption" if Westminster did not soon desegregate. With this inevitable fate, Pressly and Broyles gathered the board for an informal meeting in October 1964. As Pressly recalled, the positions of the members ranged from "Let's integrate right now" to "I haven't decided yet" to "Let's never integrate—I couldn't live with it."[24] No formal vote was taken, but three members of the board were clearly in favor of integration: McCain, Reverend Allison Williams (of Trinity), and Billy Beers (who had served on the Lovett School board the previous year when Lovett denied Martin Luther King III admission).[25]

In January 1965, Pressly wrote a lengthy letter to the faculty regarding various curriculum matters, standards for students, and reminders to teachers (e.g., teaching load, writing for *ISB*, having professional teaching certificates). Pressly also mentioned the reading requirements at St. Augustine, an African American Catholic School in New Orleans. He questioned, "Do our eighth graders match the negro boys at St. Augustine in reading twenty-five books a year?"[26] In making this comparison, Pressly showed his familiarity with St. Augustine's curriculum and possibly the achievement of black students in segregated schools. Just a few years prior, Pressly had gently dissuaded the Rosses from seeking admission for their black daughter. A black applicant also had done well on the admission test but had not been admitted. But now Pressly sensed that Westminster's admissions policy would need to change, and he began to suggest that he now believed that there were black children who could achieve at Westminster.

Just as Pressly was anticipating a change in Westminster's policy, a host of changes during the next few months contributed to how independent school leaders further blurred public and private. NAIS leaders continued to pay close attention to legislation such as the National Defense Education Act (NDEA), tax reform that could limit charitable donations to independent schools, and tax credits for parents paying tuition to independent schools.[27] According to NAIS's February 1965 *Report*, long-awaited amendments to

NDEA with respect to private school teachers had finally passed.[28] Beginning in May 1965, NAIS's legislative concerns included the Elementary and Secondary Education Act (ESEA), which with the Civil Rights Act allowed the federal government to hold southern school districts accountable for public school desegregation by threatening to deny districts funding if they did not comply. According to the *Report*, the purpose of ESEA was "to provide aid for school systems with substantial numbers of children from low-income families, and the bulk of the financial aid will go for that purpose."[29] There also appeared to be provisions for independent schools and their students, including books through Title II and provisions for supplementary educational centers via Title III. NAIS also encouraged independent school leaders to communicate with the chief educational officer of their individual states to familiarize themselves with ESEA.[30]

Though NAIS monitored such legislation, President Cary Potter was leery of increased federal government presence in education, but he also resolved for independent schools to be a part of the conversation. After attending the White House Conference on Education in 1965, Potter noted the centrality of education in everyday American life and the national focus education had garnered.[31] In the increasingly changing political climate, Potter challenged independent school leaders, despite only being a fraction of the country's educational system, to be aware of their schools' unique offerings. Potter contended, "The qualities of independence, diversity, imagination, and commitment which have characterized the best independent schools of the past should serve equally well in the rapidly changing times in which we find ourselves."[32]

In May of 1965, NAIS accepted the Office of Economic Opportunity's support of the ABC program. This funding allowed for an additional one hundred students, bringing the total number of students in the ABC program to two hundred. A new ABC program for girls began at Mount Holyoke, also supported by the Rockefeller Foundation, during the summer of 1965. By the fall of 1965, sixty schools were participating in the program, and close cooperation continued with the Dartmouth ABC program, which "served as the principal recruiting agent."[33] Forty-nine boys enrolled in twenty-six participating schools of ISTSP after completing the ABC program; twenty additional students enrolled directly in participating schools. The Danforth Foundation, General Electric Foundation, and the Charles F. Kettering Foundation also supported ISTSP. The funding made available to ISTSP indicated the role of foundations in financing the educational opportunities of black Americans in independent schools in the mid-twentieth century, a continuation of the influence of philanthropic giving on black educational opportunity.[34] For NAIS this was quite positive. As noted in the February 1965 *Report*, "Despite strong efforts by schools themselves, and wide commitment on the part of school heads to the objective of 'broadening the base,' results are slow in coming, especially in the face of a continued general increase in costs of normal operation."[35]

Alongside the growth of programs such as ISTSP there was also an increased emphasis on black students and educational enrichment programs in *ISB*, with a focus on the disadvantaged. Noblesse oblige was a running theme in the articles. Wanda Speede-Franklin, former director of minority affairs for NAIS, posited that noblesse oblige was another imperative that influenced the recruitment of black students to independent schools in the 1960s. According to Speede-Franklin, this term "suggests that the privileged class is morally obligated to alleviate conditions of poverty through charitable gestures toward the poor and so-called disadvantaged."[36] In April 1965, *ISB* included a short article on an educational conference at Williston Academy. A conference theme was "encouraging and finding a place for the Negro student." One headmaster discussed a program in which white students tutored black students as a suggestion for closing "the cultural and educational gap" between black and white students. This headmaster summarized that the program provided a "ray of light that shows them things are going to get better."[37] Black students were seemingly perceived as individuals who needed help. The article mentioned very little about the positive attributes black students brought to these schools.

As NAIS gave more attention to black students, its organizational efforts would reflect both a perceived pathology about black Americans and the need for change because of racism. In 1965, Daniel Patrick Moynihan outlined his perspective on "a new crisis in race relations" in "The Negro Family: The Case for National Action."[38] Moynihan contended that the urgent problem in the United States was the instability of the Negro American family, in particular those families of lower-class status. He also argued that this tangle of pathology that encapsulated black families was perpetuated on its own accord without white assistance. Although a black middle class was growing, Moynihan asserted that those individuals remained susceptible to the tangle of pathology "that affects their world," because of housing segregation that causes middle-class blacks to live in close proximity to lower-class blacks. Moynihan wrote that the middle class "are therefore constantly exposed to the pathology of the disturbed group and constantly in danger of being drawn into it."[39]

Concurrently, there were changes in Atlanta. In spring of 1965, the U.S. District Court ruled on the 1963 NAACP appeal that challenged gradual public school desegregation. The court ordered the complete desegregation of Atlanta schools by the 1967–68 school year. Further, Atlantans celebrated the awarding of the Nobel Peace Prize to Martin Luther King Jr. that same spring, and Jean Young, wife of Andrew Young, was appointed to the board of Trinity School. Although the Westminster board met that spring and decided to table the vote on desegregation, increasingly, the timing and setting were apparent for the Westminster board to make a decision about considering all applicants regardless of race.

Pragmatic School Desegregation Politics

By the fall of 1965, black students had desegregated all public school grades in Atlanta, and the number of black students in Atlanta Public Schools (APS) (61,344) had begun to outnumber white students (52,894). Additionally, "enrollments at all of the black high schools exceeded capacity by as much as 240 percent, while six of the all-white or majority white high schools had vacant classroom seats."[40] Still "only 6% of African American students attended schools with whites statewide."[41] Though Atlanta's city leaders had attempted to maintain an image of racial harmony, segregation and inequality persisted in the education of black students. A letter to the editor in the *Westminster Bi-Line*, published three days before the October 1965 board meeting, illustrated the internal conversation. The student contended that with integration, "the school would perform definite service for the community and the students." He further wrote, "The Negro students would benefit greatly from the first-rate education the school gives. The [current Westminster] student would then be better prepared to accept responsibility of leadership." In the second part of the letter, the student discussed how both white and black students would benefit from integration by "studying with each other; learn[ing] the other's problems, worries and dreams." Moreover, "the mutual understanding derived in this would be of incalculable benefit in a world full of hate."[42] Notions of who benefited from desegregation abounded in the 1960s. Often the onus was on black students to attend formerly all-white schools, but it was not lost on some whites about what they would gain from increased interactions with African Americans.

The question of tax-exemption status continued to be a concern as the Westminster board further deliberated desegregation. In October of 1965, "the Internal Revenue Service suspended action on all applications from private segregated schools for tax-exempt status."[43] This decision came after the 1964 decision in *Griffin v. County School Board of Prince Edward County*, a case initiated following the closing of public schools in Prince Edward County, Virginia, from 1959 to 1964, during which time a set of private schools was established for white children. In *Griffin*, "the Court held that the closing of public schools by the county school board and the board's support of private segregated schools constituted a violation of the fourteenth amendment."[44] On October 14, while a formal Westminster board meeting was held, no significant minutes were taken; those taken were as follows: "The meeting consisted of open discussion of matters of current importance to the schools. The discussion was informal and no action was taken. It was decided that the Board should meet again in the evening next month."[45]

Sixteen years after its founding, the external inquiries, internal dilemmas, and national and local changes coalesced and compelled change. On November 11, the board met and a member motioned to "make no distinctions on admitting applicants."[46] While Westminster's admissions policy had never included a direct statement about not admitting black students, this exclusion gave the board leeway to make a distinction between being "desegregated" and "integrated," and Westminster opted for the term "desegregated."[47] *Desegregation*, by definition, means to end a policy of racial segregation, while *integration* means the mixing of people from different backgrounds. By choosing the term *desegregated*, the board apparently acknowledged that the school had been segregated by choice and that it was ending that practice and changing policy.

From this meeting, Pressly issued a letter to parents indicating the change in school policy. The letter stated, "I want you to know that the Board of Trustees, after careful consideration, has decided that, beginning with the academic year, 1966-1967, the Westminster Schools will test for admission and consider the applications of any and all candidates." The letter concluded by asking for continued cooperation. Though Pressly signed the letter, Mrs. James N. Frazier, Arthur Howell, and William Parker, members of the Committee on Race, had composed the statement.[48] As school leaders, Pressly and Broyles, board chair, had recognized in the late 1950s that private schools were part and parcel of resistance strategies to public school desegregation and that Westminster leadership needed to address these matters. They first established the 1958 Committee on the Public School Dilemma and then the 1961 Committee on Race. What it meant to have black students at Westminster had been a topic of discussion for some time, and the push and pull of factors at all levels led them to this 1965 decision. By having the Committee on Race write the letter to parents, Pressly sought support from others and could potentially rely on them in case of questions about the policy change.

Westminster was the first nonsectarian institute in the South to announce an open admissions policy, and from Pressly's perspective, the Westminster community accepted the board's decision to desegregate.[49] Later, Pressly wrote, "At last, Westminster stood on the verge of no longer being regarded by many as a 'social club.'"[50] Pressly noted that out of approximately 150 letters and telephone calls, "only 10 expressed dismay," and he stated that no children were withdrawn from Westminster because of the decision to consider all applicants, although an Atlanta businessman and a mother of a Westminster student questioned Pressly at church.[51]

Despite that, the decision to desegregate Westminster was not unanimous, but disagreement among the trustees was not revealed in public. Similar to how Atlanta leaders sought to preserve the city's image during the desegregation of public spaces, Pressly sought the same for Westminster. How Pressly communicated with different Westminster constituents was important for advancing the school. He and others timed the delivery of the news by sending parents the letter on Friday morning, and then by giving letters to faculty members Friday afternoon. Pressly informed the press Saturday morning, and a news story was published the next day. Pressly noted, "I declined to say how many had opposed the decision, so a reporter wouldn't portray a 'fight' among the Trustees."[52] In "Westminster Board Sets Desegregation," the article published in the *Atlanta Constitution* on Sunday, November 14, 1965, disagreement was not discussed. Reporter Wayne Kelley included the following statement from Pressly: "'The board has had the matter of desegregation under consideration for more than a year,' Dr. Pressly said Saturday. 'The trustees were under no pressure and there was complete agreement,' he added." Additionally, when asked to comment on any opposition to the decision, Pressly stated, "I don't think that is important."[53]

Kelley reported that Pressly indicated that "more than 20 of the 24 members of the board of trustees attended the session Thursday," though the board meeting minutes listed fourteen trustees present and nine absentees. The reason for the discrepancy is not known, but it was markedly important to Pressly, as it had been with other leaders in Atlanta and other desegregation processes, to present an image of cooperation on the change in admissions policy; this approach was thought to prevent white parents and students from leaving Westminster. In Pressly's memoir, he stated that one absent member, Pollard Thurman, "telephoned to say he'd be absent on the 11th but would mail in his vote in favor of admitting black students."[54] Neither the minutes nor Pressly's memoir account for others' positions, except for the resignation of Verdery Boyd, who did not approve of black and white students attending school together.[55]

Thus, disagreement did exist within the Westminster community; yet, a mass exodus of students did not occur. Several reasons may suggest why this may have been the case. First, the decision to desegregate was supported by the six principals of the school. In the December minutes of the board's meeting, their support was expressed: "Your recent decision effecting a change in admissions policy is welcomed by those of us in administrative positions within the school."[56] By having the support of the principals, Pressly and others could move forward with the operation of the school, and the principals could be brokers or liaisons between Pressly and the board and any parents and students who might have had concerns. Their support also contributed to showing the larger community that multiple stakeholders were on board with the decision. Second, Pressly seemingly avoided the same publicity that the Lovett School had garnered in the spring of 1963. Not wanting a similar response, Pressly appeared to have acted in ways that would guarantee an image of solidarity regarding desegregation. As a local and national independent school leader, Pressly knew of the potential ramifications to the board's decision. He managed this policy change deliberately so as not to disrupt the growth and development of Westminster as a nationally recognized independent school. Third, Pressly recognized the importance of funding for the school. Over the last fifteen years, Pressly had garnered the financial support of many, and he knew that continued fundraising would be important to Westminster. Accordingly, he remained in communication with business conservatives such as Robert Woodruff of Coca-Cola, who had been a close adviser to Mayor Hartsfield during the 1950s and 1960s as Atlanta positioned itself in the larger civil rights movement. Following Westminster's decision to desegregate, Pressly wrote to Woodruff. In the short letter, Pressly reassured Woodruff that faculty and students supported the decision which inevitably Pressly thought would help counter any negative responses including from funding sources.[57] Yet how white students pondered micro and racial issues reflected the mixed welcome that black students would ultimately receive at Westminster in the fall of 1967.

There was some indication of the optimism and support of white students in having black classmates. In one December 1965 article, the news staff reprinted the letter that Pressly had sent to parents. The article also quoted Pressly as directly stating (unlike the letter) that Westminster would continue "to apply its high standards for admission, though now race will not be one of the factors considered." Again, it was reiterated that "the trustees were under no pressure and there was complete agreement."[58] The editors of the *Bi-Line* also expressed their approval by stating that the decision had been necessary if Westminster was "to grow further as an outstanding preparatory school," for such policies had been in place at outstanding preparatory schools in the Northeast. Similar to the student letter in the October paper, the students shared what desegregation would mean for their educational experiences: "We are free to discard the sheltered, artificial atmosphere of studying only with members of our race. New freshness in viewpoint from Negro students will help us to see a better concept of social conditions and problems, free from the distortion of small prejudice."[59] In conclusion, the editors urged that the decision be adopted in the middle and lower schools, though there was no indication otherwise that the decision did not apply to all grades; they also thanked those who had supported desegregation when the idea was resisted.

In contrast, white students also showed resistance to how African Americans exerted agency during the era. In "Senior Students Examine Birch, Bigotry, and Tolerance," two students argued that Americans must realize the power of communists, who the students believed had infiltrated the civil rights movement. The authors wrote, "The Negro and white supporters of the civil rights movement have been duped and stirred to revolt by a few hard-core communists." They challenged those who had not been duped "to realize the evil forces and evil purposes behind this pretense of humanitarianism." By doing so, "the whole horrible fraud would fall to pieces in three months." Again, the students compared the "good patriotic, and idealistic Americans" with the extremists, who are referred to as "a bunch of nuts." The students further claimed that Westminster students "are generally tolerant," but that they need to "constantly guard against a rigidity in our 'tolerance.'" Although the students shared their opinions about the threat of communism, they called for an engagement of the other side for "it would be very easy to fall back upon the security of our 'authority.'"[60]

The December editorial, "Minority Scapegoat Idea Needs to Be Cast Aside," likewise posited a warning to students regarding black Americans.[61] The writer stated that minorities have been scapegoats for the majority. He wrote, "We who have been imbued with a simple delineation, based on color, between good and bad, friend and foe, are finding difficulty in purging this simple method of separation from our minds." The writer then told two stories about experiences in Monroe, Georgia, on a golf course, with the first occurring a few years prior and the second only a few weeks before the writing of the editorial. During the first story, the writer shared the following about what a white man said after seeing a "blood-spattered" black boy: "A bunch of animals, that's all they are. Those niggers stay in fights ninety percent of the time. Hell, I know my son's got to go to school with them soon; that really isn't so bad—they play hooky most of the time anyway. I just don't want any outsiders coming in and stirring 'em up. Why jeez, you look at those animals, they always carry a stick. . . . They'll start swinging the sticks and somebody will get killed." In the second story, the student described an exchange with a caddy wearing SCLC Project SCOPE buttons. At first the caddy asked the student what he thought of the civil rights movement; the student responded by asking the caddy the same question. The caddy stated, "Well, if we didn't pay taxes it'd be different. But we deserve all the rights everybody else has. But the main thing is an education. That's the main thing right now. I got to get an education first off." The author's final words on the matter were that outside agitators had come and "riled up all the niggers about nothing." He further wrote, "Yes, and even that small caddy was swinging a stick at me. It wasn't wooden, however. It was constructed of an idea, and that is the most dangerous kind." Although on one hand, some white students welcomed the idea of attending school with black students, other white students seemed to issue a warning about being aware of black people and their ideas. Such opinions would inform the climate that the black students would navigate, how black students would be received based on their actions and ideas, and how black students would ultimately speak to race relations at Westminster.

How white students wrote about notions of blackness in the *Bi-Line* echoed the sentiments articulated in a six-part *ISB* feature, "The Responsibility of the Independent School," published in December of 1965. For example, in "The Education of the Disadvantaged," Thomas M. Mikula, a mathematics instructor at Phillips Academy in Andover, Massachusetts, argued that independent schools should play a greater role with the underprivileged "who for so long have lived under what must be considered less than a second-class citizenship."[62] But Mikula characterized black students and their parents as hopeless and unmotivated. He contended that help from independent schools must be extended and that independent schools should seek "Negro and other culturally deprived but capable students."[63] While increasing the number of black students in independent schools, the independent school could then offer white students a more realistic learning environment reflective of the larger society. It would provide a better formal education for the capable student coming from a culturally deprived community. Mikula hardly acknowledged the achievement of black students in segregated schools and black students' potential contributions to independent schools.

In a second article, "Community Service," Edward Blair discussed a tutoring program in Baltimore; most of the faculty from the program taught at the Park School, an independent school in Brooklandville, Maryland. Courses were offered in a variety of subjects including English, remedial reading, ancient history, remedial arithmetic, algebra I and II, and foreign languages. The students also participated in a discussion group and enjoyed talking about "teen-age standards of ethics and morality, politics and the Negro's opportunities in politics, education, and integration." From Blair's perspective, this was one of the most enjoyable parts of the program. Undergirding the effort were the believed perceptions about segregated education for black students. Blair wrote, "A segregated school provides little incentive for the Negro child, and it does not give him a tangible basis for cultural comparison. We were, therefore, dealing with culturally, economically, and academically 'disadvantaged' children, a problem which manifested itself in different ways."[64] He discussed the students' lateness, attributed to both other duties and lack of concern for timeliness, and lack of patience. Blair did conclude by making suggestions, including the need for additional teachers so that students would receive more individual attention and the need for more community organizations to be involved.[65] One could read Blair's perspective as one with good intentions, but it is one heavily influenced by stereotypes about black education and students. Like Mikula, Blair did not consider the assets of black schools in spite of segregation. Moreover, he lacked a nuanced approach to understanding educational possibilities of black students and the larger sociocultural context sustained by inequality.

During the next year, as Westminster attempted to create a welcoming environment for black students, the school climate reflected these larger societal norms around race. As a southern independent school, Westminster had the latitude to progress gradually with desegregation, and it offered an exemplary academic program while maintaining vestiges in its culture of the Old South and racism. School leaders set the academic admissions standards that black students had to meet, and black parents needed to be in a position to afford the tuition. Pressly, as a national figure in NAIS, presumably knew that Westminster needed to distinguish itself from segregationist academies established after *Brown* as independent schools nationally heightened their recruitment of black students. In the year prior to desegregation, he continued to maintain Westminster's image while students engaged in community service and discussions about the political changes of the era. Even as Westminster attempted to create a welcoming environment for black students, the school climate reflected the larger societal norms around race.

The Preparation Year

In the 1966-67 school year, for the first time, NAIS surveyed its membership about black students; 740 out of 780 schools responded. Four hundred sixty-two schools reported enrolling 3,720 black students during the 1966-67 school year; half of the schools enrolled their first black students after 1960, again an indication of independent schools responding to the social and political climate and agency of African Americans to create change in the United States. According to the survey, "This is approximately 3.2% of the student population in the schools with Negro students, and about 1.5% of the total student population in all NAIS member schools." Schools seeking black students (i.e., ninety-five schools with "open enrollment" that did not have plans to recruit black students) continued to report difficulty in finding qualified applicants and establishing communication networks with black individuals in their communities. The survey also revealed that only 149 black teachers worked in independent schools and that nearly half the black students received scholarships. In the Southeast, 15 of 99 schools reported having enrolled black students with 42 of 99 indicating "No Negroes, no plans to take them." Across independent schools, 130 out of 239 schools reported having five or more, but less than ten black students. The conclusion to the report discussed "tokenism"—"whether the enrollment of one or two Negro children is more than just a matter of avoiding criticism."[66]

As public school desegregation progressed gradually and independent schools began to monitor enrollment of black students, whites established more segregationist academies. David Nevin noted that "in 1969 before *Alexander*, the Southern Regional Council called attention to the phenomenon and estimated that some 300,000 southern youngsters were in private

TABLE 1 Number of schools enrolling Negroes

	Number of Schools	Percentage of the Total
Negroes enrolled this year	462	62.4%
Negroes enrolled, but not *this year*	35	4.7%
Want to enroll them, but unsuccessful as yet	56	7.6%
None yet, but plan to enroll them	23	3.1%
None yet, "open enrollment," but not seeking	95	12.8%
No Negroes, no plans to take them	69	9.3%
	740	100%

Note: Numbers are presented here as they are given in the original source. As in the original source, numbers do not always combine to the printed total.
Source: Reprinted from National Association of Independent Schools, Summary Report on Enrollment of Negro Students, March 1967, RG 26.01, box 21, Special Collections, Pressly, Dr. William L., Beck Archives-Westminster.

schools that were segregated in practice."[67] The Westminster board remained very much aware of these growing numbers. For example, in the April 1967 board meeting, the following was reported: "The Committee from the Georgia Association of Independent Schools, working on legislation to formulate minimum standards for independent schools, is still working on a proposed bill which would be acceptable to the many types of schools involved."[68]

Also, Westminster leaders decided again not to accept federal aid. In the May 1967 board meeting, board member W. Stell Huie presented "a study of 1) available federal aid to Westminster; 2) the needs of Westminster; 3) the experience of similar institutions participating in federal programs; 4) additional burdens participation might place upon Westminster; and 5) conclusions reached by the Committee." The committee noted that the funds available would not necessarily address Westminster's most pressing needs, including construction and debt retirements. With respect to similar institutions, the committee maintained that the most any school participating had received was $2,500 for library funds "with the exception of scholarships to Negro students." Some of the nonparticipating schools that the committee contacted had not adopted integration policies, and "others, having adopted such policy, have not yet determined to sign the compliance forms required for federal participation." One of the burdens noted was the "continuous supervision regarding the appropriateness of each

TABLE 2 Enrollment of Negro students in southeastern independent schools

	Number of Schools	Percentage of the Total
Negroes enrolled this year	15	15.1%
Negroes enrolled, but not *this year*	1	1.1%
Want to enroll them, but unsuccessful as yet	6	6.1%
None yet, but plan to enroll them	7	7.1%
None yet, "open enrollment," but not seeking	25	27.2%
No Negroes, no plans to take them	42	42.4%
	99	100%

Note: Numbers are presented here as they are given in the original source. As in the original source, numbers do not always combine to the printed total.
Source: Reprinted from National Association of Independent Schools, Summary Report on Enrollment of Negro Students, March 1967, RG 26.01, box 21, Special Collections, Pressly, Dr. William L., Beck Archives-Westminster.

expenditure of such federal funds."[69] Thus, the committee's recommendation considered all of these factors, and they declined federal funds. Committee members did not believe that declining funds would interfere with the school's new admissions policy and its compliance with Title VI of the 1964 Civil Rights Act.

After the November 1965 announcement, Westminster prepared to desegregate. Although some independent schools had desegregated in the South, national publications did not necessarily offer an exact template for the desegregation of an elite private K-12 school in the capital of the New South that was both a day and boarding school. However, the school appeared to follow the advice offered in Mallery's 1963 publication, *Negro Students in Independent Schools*, as well as some of the methods and procedures of schools that had already desegregated. *Negro Students in Independent Schools* provided advice and consideration of race relations and educational opportunity from heads of schools as well as from Dr. Robert Coles, noted African American psychiatrist; Robert Weaver, administrator for the U.S. Housing and Home Finance Agency; and Richard Plaut, president of the National Scholarship Service and Fund for Negro Students (NSSFNS). The publication addressed why independent schools needed to desegregate and the possibilities for helping black and white students by desegregating, by maintaining academic standards, and by admitting more than one a

TABLE 3 Enrollment of Negro students in individual schools

No. of Students	No. of Schools
100 or more	2
50 or more	8
20 or more	27
15 or more	25
10 or more	47
5 or more	130
	239

Source: Reprinted from National Association of Independent Schools,
Summary Report on Enrollment of Negro Students, March 1967,
RG 26.01, box 21, Special Collections, Pressly, Dr. William L.,
Beck Archives-Westminster.

student at a time. The commentary reflected the larger discourse of the era when discussing the culturally deprived. As schools began to desegregate, Mallery encouraged school leaders to prepare and to pay close attention to their school climate. Quoting Plaut, Mallery included the following: "'Be sure the climate is right and that the trustees, faculty, and students are prepared. All three of these elements are important. It's not just a matter of having them consenting. They must have understanding of and sensitivity to the problems which may arise. The whole adventure is part of the educational process—it's really an informal course in human relations.'"[70]

While Westminster did not enroll black students for the 1966-67 school year, it did enroll its first black student in the school's summer program of 1966: Jeannie Hawkins. Understanding the larger racial climate of Atlanta, Pressly had promised to notify parents if desegregation were to occur at the school.[71] Because Jeannie's identity, however, was unknown until she arrived that summer, Pressly opted not to notify parents at the last minute, and Jeannie was not allowed to live in the dorms. Jeannie did remain at the camp and lived in the home of Westminster's elementary school principal, Chris Stevenson, and his wife, Chessie.[72]

Westminster's climate continued to support both annual traditions with negative racial implications and more heightened racial discussions, as students were "prepared" for desegregation. Pressly recalled, "Westminster primed its students for the day when blacks would study, socialize, and play on athletic teams with them. In 1966-67, Westminster's last school year with an all-white student body, we insisted that blacks shouldn't be singled out and that everyone should stress similarities, not differences. Everyone should make sure, we said, that no black student eats lunch alone or attends social functions without company."[73] Yet, Hill Martin, a 1972 white alumnus, did not "remember hearing any social responsible voice from the faculty, administrators or parents stand up and outline the wisdom of the decision," as students contemplated the decision.[74] Even if white students were being "prepared" for desegregation, the school continued to reflect its white southern mores that harkened to a white southern way of life, built on the institution of slavery and the exploitation and inhumane treatment of those enslaved. In 1967, the Old South was celebrated at the Junior-Senior Ball, with no apparent sense of how offensive that might be to black students. Prior to the dance, students were told the following: "To set the mood for this gala occasion, the foyer and front lawn will be decorated as a southern plantation. Dress will be formal; gentlemen may wear either old Confederate uniforms or tuxedos."[75] These celebrations of the South's right to secede from the Union in order to maintain slavery were apparently normal at Westminster. If the same dance were to occur the following year, would black male students also be expected to wear old Confederate uniforms or tuxedos?

School newspaper articles concerning issues of race, politics, and social change also provided indicators of the environment that black students would enter at Westminster. In February 1966, Bill Rothschild, son of Rabbi Rothschild, wrote an article titled "Julian Bond Issue: Beyond the Joke," a reference to the attempt of the Georgia state representatives not to seat Julian Bond because of his endorsement of SNCC in opposition to the Vietnam War. Rothschild reported on Bond's tactics in front of the Georgia House of Representatives, a group of "politicians who for 100 years have preached open defiance of federal laws and sections of the Constitution of the United States witch-hunt a man who exercises the same prerogative for a cause **unpopular** with their constituents" (emphasis in original). Further, SNCC, "a band of overly disgruntled, self-acclaimed second class citizens, foresees an opportunity to embarrass the hallowed congressional halls of Georgia as racist, and exploits the war in Viet Nam to do so." He then contended that the House committee that ousted Bond did not deal with "constitutional issues," but argued "one man, one vote—as the cause of such radicals getting elected in the first place." That, nonetheless, was the exact freedom for which the United States was supposedly fighting; so while Rothschild seemed to disagree with Bond because of how "unpopular and illogical those dissentions [sic] may be," he seemed also to be saying that it was Bond's right to dissent.[76]

Similar to national independent school trends, the news staff gave attention to urban issues, often with underlying stereotypes of black pathology. In "Unless Conditions Are Improved Violence in Ghettos Will Continue," the writer discussed the need for long-range solutions as well as immediate encouragement.[77] He assessed that the uprisings were natural occurrences, for "where a minority group is continually oppressed it will rise up. No one is saying that this violence is good, only that it is a natural result of adverse economic and social conditions." He characterized the hopeless by providing an example of Atlanta: "One needs to only visit the Merritts Avenue Section near North Avenue and Peachtree Street to see the magnitude of the problem. There, households are comprised of women and children; fathers exist only in the biological sense. Children are everywhere, ill-clothed, ill-fed, and ill-housed. Most have never seen the inside of a schoolroom; many have never even seen Peachtree Street, a few blocks away." Students' comments on neighborhood social conditions reflected how they had not really interacted with the people living in those neighborhoods and how the underlying ethos of the era concerning black pathology influenced some students. Moreover, students had not been educated about the multiplicity of black realities and the relationships among race, class, and systemic inequality.

His editorial continued: the "black community" could not take care of its own, for those who have left are not looking to return. He called for the local, state, and federal government to enforce truancy laws and fund food, clothing, and education. He then stated that "responsible civil rights and anti-poverty programs" were necessary to counter violence. The threat of violence was apparent, and this editorial characterized racial minorities as victims: "Negroes, Puerto Ricans, and other minority groups will be the pawns for anyone offering the 'easy' solution of violence only as long as equal political and economic opportunities are denied." Yet the author did conclude by warning whites about their own racist attitudes and actions and the need for "accelerated efforts . . . in the direction of political and social equality and economic opportunity."[78]

When a Westminster student reported on Head Start in the school newspaper in "Project Head Start Gives Challenge to Student," student consciousness of service was apparent. The purpose of Head Start was explained as helping "underprivileged children develop fully enough so that when they enter first grade at six they will meet with success." There was no explanation as to why children were underprivileged, nor did the author seek to answer whether or not a child saw himself as "growing up fighting for his life in a slum of downtown Atlanta." The student also solicited volunteers, and it was explained that "no salary is paid for service of this kind, and few volunteers feel the need for any. They know what they are doing is important, and they receive full payment for their efforts from those they help."[79] That fall, three students reported on their experiences with Head Start. The article recounted what was believed that the children learned and experienced: "They learned how to brush their teeth and keep clean" and were "taught the pleasure of learning and the necessity for listening and following directions in a class." The student, however, did not discuss what the girls found "enlightening and rewarding" about the experience.[80]

Students also seemed to engage one another in the issues of the day. In November 1966, an article reported on a Westminster student poll that included twenty-five questions pertaining to political candidates, policies related to U.S. involvement in Vietnam, foreign aid, public school policies, prayer in school, and Johnson's poverty program. The majority of students polled said they disagreed with Julian Bond being seated in the General Assembly, agreed with the U.S. policies in Vietnam, agreed that the federal guidelines for public schools were unconstitutional, and felt that "Johnson's poverty program is a give something for nothing program."[81] These poll results showed some students' political and ideological alignment—a lack of concern for remedying the long history of racism and structural inequality in the United States. Students also gave attention to the fall 1966 campaigns, including the gubernatorial race between Bo Callaway, the Republican Party nominee, and Lester Maddox, the Democratic Party nominee and avid segregationist. The majority of Westminster students polled favored Callaway, but the continued stronghold of Dixiecrats or southern Democrats proved to be quite powerful.[82] The close race between Callaway and Maddox had to be decided by the Georgia General Assembly. With a democratic majority legislature, Maddox, who campaigned on states' rights, was elected governor.

Westminster students discussed political and social change, which meant that they were attentive to matters outside of Westminster. For those students writing in the school newspaper, they knew that the society into which they were born would not be the same when they graduated high school and enrolled in college. Their analyses sometimes adhered to denigrating notions of black life in America and Atlanta which was indicative of their school climate and the era. White students did not seem to fully understand that black residents understood their conditions and protested. For example, with the onset of the Black Power movement, more urban grassroots organizing by SNCC occurred in locations such as Vine City, "a rigidly segregated poor and working-class Black neighborhood," where Westminster students would perform community service in the coming years.[83] As social unrest occurred, especially among poor and working-class African Americans feeling neglected and subjected to racism, neighborhood protests took place in Summerhill and Dixie Hills during the summers of 1966 and 1967. The protests, according to historian Winston Grady-Willis, "challenged the hegemony of the biracial Atlanta regime in ways that no previous occurrence had."[84]

As students continued to use the school newspaper to analyze topics of the day, including both progressive and regressive oppositional examinations, Pressly began to speak more about race and desegregation. In February 1967, Pressly gave a speech at the headmasters' meeting entitled "Valedictory" in which he spoke of Georgia's political regression with the election of Maddox. Pressly contended, "In Georgia, we don't live among the ruins of antiquity, we live in present ruin . . . engendered by ancient wrong." Pressly, however, did state what made him proud: "We are proud of our liberal Governors, Ernest Vandiver and Carl Sanders; proud of our young Congressman, Charles Weltner; proud of our integrated restaurants, hotels, hospitals, schools; proudest of our educated, sane Negro leadership." Pressly, similar to the student newspaper article from 1965, also questioned and denigrated the role of outside agitators: "Then came Stokely Carmichael and SNCC, inciting a riot, defying our humanitarian Mayor, Ivan Allen—the friend of the Negro, who had strained old friendships to go to Washington to plead for the passage of the Civil Rights Act. Stokely Carmichael screaming Black Power, loud enough to raise the dead—the dead issues." As the speech continued, Pressly, in contrast to how he attempted to maintain Westminster's image in 1965, noted the effects of Westminster's adoption of an open admissions policy. According to Pressly, "Admittedly, the wreckage is also a bit personal. Early, for independent schools in the South, Westminster announced a policy of integration. In the backlash, a Board member resigned, two others became suddenly too busy to lend a hand, several rich men removed Westminster from their wills, funds no longer flowed freely our way. I began to wonder—the school, too, among the ruins?"[85]

In a different venue, however, Pressly publicly praised Westminster's efforts to desegregate in a spring 1967 article for *University*, Princeton's quarterly magazine. In "Meanwhile Georgia's Schools Are Getting Better," Pressly attempted to counter the negative images of Georgia's political tensions.

Pressly discussed the academic rigor of independent schools, accreditation requirements, freedom of independent schools, and curricular emphasis and offerings. Pressly noted the morality behind the decision to desegregate, Westminster's lead in desegregating, and the slow pace of desegregation. Pressly also considered how students and faculty were supportive of the board's decision and the difficulty in finding qualified black applicants. He concluded by stating that with increased knowledge of Westminster's open admissions policy, more qualified students were applying to the school.[86]

No black students entered the school full time until the fall of 1967; perhaps Pressly was referring to Jeannie Hawkins and any daytime summer school students. Additionally, Pressly cited that one student who had sought admission scored at a reading level of fourth grade and a math level of second grade: "As we are not a remedial school, we of course could not admit him."[87] Therefore, one might wonder if Pressly and other Westminster leaders would adhere to advice that would be given to independent school leaders regarding disadvantaged students or those deemed culturally deprived. Pressly suggested that the onus of desegregation came from school leaders; he did not discuss the various pressures, external and internal, that had pushed Westminster leaders to adopt an open admissions policy.

Westminster board meeting minutes indicated how discussions of race and serving the disadvantaged became a part of the board's deliberations. In response to a 1967 talk at the NAIS Annual Conference by Harold Howe, then U.S. commissioner of education, Pressly suggested to the Westminster board that tuition for Westminster's summer program be subsidized for thirty underprivileged children. In "The Need for Entangling Alliances," Howe challenged independent schools to be more outward and visible with respect to state and national conversations on education. He also pressed schools to enroll disadvantaged students, without lowering their academic standards, but also giving these students the time and space to catch up to other students. Howe called for independent school leaders to think differently about the term "culturally disadvantaged" by considering how a disadvantaged child could educate a more privileged child.[88] According to Westminster board minutes, "Some of the Trustees questioned the advisability of such a project for fear that some of our own students who need special help would be neglected. Many questions were asked and opinions expressed regarding curriculum, grades, etc., especially in regard to the Middle School."[89] While others would articulate a concern about what the presence of black students did for white students, Howe's speech pointed to how schools should have conceived of their white students' privilege and the lessons that others could teach them, not just what the privileged could teach to others.

Finding the Fearless Firsts

For the 1966-67 school year, three black students had applied but scored low on the admissions test. Some faculty argued for their admission despite the low test scores, but Pressly did not feel that this was in the best interest of the students. "When the administrators decided not to accept the first three black applicants, rejecting them rather than crucifying them academically, some members of the boys' faculty felt we were against integration and 'standing in the schoolhouse door like Governor Wallace,'" Pressly recollected.[90] By not admitting students because of low test scores, Pressly echoed the sentiment of school heads in previous years as they perhaps tried to assuage any resistance from white parents who might have felt that standards would be lowered with the admission of black students. In 1949, Mira B. Wilson had noted that Northfield Academy only admitted African American females who met the "academic entrance requirements without question."[91] The 1956 Sidwell Friends' nondiscriminatory policy stated, "No departure from the school's present academic standards will be made."[92] Westminster's position on the applicants for fall 1966 also reflected the debate about what constituted qualified black applicants in Mallery's *Negro Students in Independent Schools*. Janice Porter, a former staff member with NSSFNS who had worked with their independent school program, was noted as saying, "It's nice if a Negro student is a little more than average in the school in his academic competence. But he shouldn't always have to be the prize person." After discussing that some schools were disappointed when their black students did not excel all-around inside and outside the classroom, she stated, "I think a headmaster has to be self-conscious about what it is he really wants in his students—and for his students—including his Negro students."[93] A school leader argued that schools take chances with admissions in general, "and if a possibly promising Negro student appears, even with relatively poor educational background and test scores, here is a time to gamble."[94] Yet for the 1966-67 school year, Westminster did not take that chance, and Westminster needed to attract more African American applicants.

John D. Verdery, headmaster of the Wooster School in Danbury, Connecticut, was clear in his advice for recruiting black students: "From a practical standpoint the institution that wants Negroes must at first ask them to come. If it has none, it is really quite fair to say that it simply does not want them."[95] By the late 1960s, independent schools were recruiting black students on their own as well as enlisting the help of black parents, community members, and organizations such as the Urban League, and programs such as NSSFNS, ISTSP, and ABC. The private and public investment in African American students that morphed just two years previously led to more independent school administrators' efforts to diversify their student bodies.[96] Independent schools became involved in joint efforts such as Boston's Educational Research Program, New York's Project Broad Jump, Detroit's Horizons–Upward Bound Program, and Hartford's Supplementary Program for Hartford in Education Reinforcement and Enrichment; such programs "were designed more to enrich public schools than to lure black students from them."[97] Although Upward Bound programs were primarily held during the summer on college campuses, some programs were held elsewhere. For example, the Detroit Upward Bound program, also sponsored by the Ford Foundation, was held at the Cranbrook School, an independent school.[98] Other recruitment and scholarship programs included the Black Student Fund in the Greater Washington, D.C., area; and Prep for Prep of New York.

The Stouffer Foundation was an additional vehicle for identifying qualified black applicants for independent schools. Anne Forsyth, the founder, was the daughter of Anne C. Stouffer and granddaughter of R. J. Reynolds, owner of R. J. Reynolds Tobacco Company in Winston-Salem, North Carolina. Forsyth used trust money left by her mother to seed the foundation.[99] Forsyth, a white woman, believed that the program would aid black students, and rationalized starting the program because of the benefits to both black and white students:

It occurred to me that the white Southern boys who went to equivalent schools in the South probably comprised 80 percent of our leaders in the South, and I felt that if we could pick out really smart kids and show these (white) boys that they (blacks) aren't just basketball players or football players or musicians, but that they are bright, with good attitudes and willingness to learn, in the end I felt it would be a far more enriching program for whites than for blacks. I felt that if we could change the minds, of say, 85 percent of those (white) boys and stop them from being bigots and help them see black people as they are—fellow human beings—we would have done a great thing. I wasn't just doing something for blacks, I was also helping whites.[100]

Admitting recipients of the Stouffer Foundation scholarships ensured Westminster officials that the black students were academically prepared as the applicants were interviewed and tested. The Stouffer Foundation's initial list of southern independent schools, in particular boarding schools, spanned from Virginia to Texas; these schools presumably had either changed their admissions policy or were willing to consider admitting black students. John Ehle, then a consultant to the Stouffer Foundation, and Douglas Lewis, then headmaster of the Summit School in Winston-Salem, North Carolina, traveled throughout the South meeting with potential black young men, because at this time only young men were eligible for Stouffer Scholarships. Ehle and Lewis looked for students, sometimes identified by local screening committees, who had personal qualities and a level of academic achievement that they considered suitable for independent schools.[101]

The Stouffer Foundation awarded scholarships to Michael McBay and Jannard Wade, two of the first black students to desegregate Westminster. Michael McBay experienced the priceless inheritance of black belief in the power of education first through his parents who worked at the Atlanta University Center (AUC). Dr. Henry McBay was on the faculty at Morehouse College in the chemistry department, and Dr. Shirley Mathis McBay was then a mathematics professor and administrator at Spelman College.[102] The family, which included Michael's younger brother Ron, who began attending Westminster in 1968, were living in Urban Villa, an "almost entirely black, middle class" neighborhood in the West End of Atlanta. While most of the kids in Urban Villa attended Walter White Elementary School, Michael McBay was attending Oglethorpe Elementary School, a school close to the AUC, when he applied to the Stouffer Foundation and to attend Westminster.

As part of his experiences in black segregated public schools, McBay knew the care of black teachers. He had skipped ahead a grade, from first to second, and was supported by a "wonderful" first-grade teacher named Mrs. Montgomery. According to McBay, "she had a strong impact on my life even taking such an interest in my development that she personally drove both Ron and me to Sunday school."[103] Still, McBay faced early mild physical abuse and ostracism because, in his words, he was "not being Black enough for most of the other kids in general." McBay, despite this harassment, was prepared academically through "the combination of extreme emphasis on early scholastic training and academic performance at home as well as the curriculum and quality of teachers at Oglethorpe."[104]

McBay was an ideal candidate for the Stouffer Foundation with an IQ of 162. He also scored 10 plus in five out of nine categories on the Metropolitan Achievement Test, the standardized test used by the Stouffer Foundation to determine students' academic abilities. Ehle wrote that McBay "is a likeable young man, abundantly personable and assured, who enjoyed talking with us about his books, his experiences and his hobbies, which include drawing. He draws comic strips representing science-fiction ideas, and certain happenings of his school and neighborhood—these he publishes on occasion in the school newspaper or in a neighborhood newspaper which he distributes to the mailboxes of his friends."[105] Ehle discussed McBay's desire to be a "vertebrate paleontologist" and that the school subjects most interesting to him "revolve around science, so does his reading, so do his imaginings and ambitions." Because of his aptitude and fortitude, Ehle and the Stouffer Foundation chose Michael as a full-scholarship recipient from a pool of two hundred.

In addition to the availability of scholarship funds through the Stouffer Foundation, parental choice and support were also key factors for the first black students choosing to apply and attend Westminster. The parents of the first black students at Westminster, whose professions included teacher, professor, and nursing assistant, chose it primarily because of its academic standards. The process of desegregation in APS began to hamper black schools as some schools were overcrowded and had to offer double sessions as a result. Black parents, some of whom had earned degrees from HBCUs and from historically white institutions of higher education, appeared to survey the educational landscape in Atlanta. These parents considered how to provide an education for their children that would offer academic rigor and resources that would best prepare their children for higher education. The parents, however, also recognized and faced the quandary of what it meant socially and psychologically to send their children to schools like Westminster. White independent school leaders recognized this dilemma too. Verdery stated, "It took us some years to face honestly the simple fact that Negro parents, like other parents, are not eager to place their children in an environment in which they have reason to believe they are not really wanted."[106] Both sides clearly understood that historically white elite private schools could not necessarily provide the holistic caring and support that black children needed and wanted to survive, but black parents weighing multiple variables chose these schools for their children.

Jannard Wade, who also received a Stouffer Foundation scholarship, believed that his mother's beliefs about educational opportunity influenced his enrollment at Westminster.[107] Wade, like Michael McBay, had formally educated parents who accentuated the importance of education. His father, Fred Douglas Wade, graduated from Morehouse College in 1951 and completed graduate work in education, and social and political science at Atlanta University.[108] He worked as a nursing assistant at the Veterans' Administration Hospital in Atlanta. Wade's mother, Willie Eva Brown Wade, graduated from Paine College in 1955 and completed graduate study in the field of library science, also at Atlanta University.[109] She worked as a teacher and later as a librarian for the Atlanta Board of Education.[110] Wade lived in a small apartment house on Division Street in the Simpson/Ashby Streets neighborhood in Atlanta until third or fourth grade. By fifth or sixth grade, Wade and his parents had moved to Collier Heights, a middle-class black neighborhood located about four miles west of Division Street.[111]

Wade was attending A. F. Herndon Elementary School, a segregated black school, when he applied to Westminster.[112] He too experienced what he considered "a good school" and "a solid school" with adequate facilities, "good discipline," and "pretty good" teachers who "cared about the students." In particular, Mr. D. P. Burch, a sixth-grade teacher, wanted to encourage his promise and that of others. He stated that Burch "took us to see 'The Sound of Music.' He took me and Wanda [Ward], and maybe a couple of others. He said we had promise and he wanted to do something special for us. That was kind of neat." Despite Wade's success at Herndon, his parents believed that he was not being challenged enough and that an environment like Westminster could enhance his education.[113] Wade believed that his mother, who worked in the school system, "knew that the private schools were a lot better, had a lot more to offer, would broaden my horizons, be more challenging." He also thought that she "wanted to show that, again, we can compete with anybody, the students that grew up in our neighborhood, given the right tools and guidance."[114]

In addition to parents seeking out educational opportunities, black teachers, also aware of their students' academic potential, recognized the possible academic opportunities at Westminster, and conversations between parents and teachers influenced Dawn Clark and Wanda Ward to attend Westminster for the fall of 1967. Dawn Clark, who would be the youngest black student to desegregate Westminster in 1967 when she entered fourth grade, grew up in West Atlanta in the Peyton Forest area in a family of black educators. Her mother, Dr. Johnnie Clark, was a professor in the School of Business at Atlanta University, and she would later become dean. Dawn's godfather, Dr. John Middleton, was president of Morris

Brown College and pastor of Allen Temple African Methodist Episcopal (AME) Church, which she and her family attended. Her godmother, Merlissie Middleton, was also a professor at Morris Brown. Dawn attended M. Agnes Jones Elementary School in Atlanta, and she excelled because of her preparation at home. Clark recalled, "I went to first grade knowing how to read, write, add, and subtract. Only thing I did not know how to do was to multiply and divide."[115] Because her mathematical and literacy skills exceeded those of most other children entering first grade, Clark was not being challenged academically. According to Dr. Clark, her daughters' teachers suggested private schooling as an option "because [Dawn] was becoming disenchanted, and a problem in school because she did not have enough to do . . . so [her father and I] began to look around and in the process ended up at Westminster."

Wanda Ward learned about Westminster from Burch, who was sixth-grade teacher to Ward and fellow student Jannard Wade at A. F. Herndon Elementary School in Atlanta. The role of private education had been a part of Ward's family because her mother, Elaine Jackson, and her siblings had attended the Oglethorpe Elementary Laboratory School (Oglethorpe later became a public school). Wanda's mother also graduated from Booker T. Washington, the first black public high school in Atlanta, located in the AUC neighborhood. Ward's grandmother, Renita Pace Phillips, had attended the AUC and, with her husband, was instrumental in raising Ward.[116] While growing up, Ward's mother taught in Head Start programs, and her grandmother taught in the Vinings neighborhood in Cobb County. Jackson described how her mother commuted each day to Vinings from 1938 to 1972 and that she had "a very good rapport with the whites in Cobb County, and most blacks." Phillips, Jackson's father and Ward's grandfather, worked in a downtown hotel for forty-six years. Ward poignantly described the ethos that emanated from her family: "So here I had the epitome of the educator married to the traditional black male provider who worked in a hotel, but who also understood and was committed to the value of education. They sent their kids to college, and all this kind of stuff, some of whom finished and some of whom didn't. So in that regard, I think we were typical of what would have been regarded at that time as middle class blacks."[117]

Burch, the same sixth-grade teacher who had taken Wade and Ward to *The Sound of Music*, identified Ward's excellent performance at Herndon. In a letter to Wanda's mother, he wrote, "In all the content areas, Wanda has excelled to such an extent that I wanted to share with you this joyous, satisfying feeling that comes from working with your daughter. Certainly the grades that she has been receiving could not alone tell the entire story; she has exhibited the ability, wisdom, and personality of a mature student, and at such a tender age, this is a rare compliment of which she is more than worthy."[118] Because of Wade, Burch knew of Westminster's open enrollment policy and of the Stouffer Foundation. Yet, the Stouffer Foundation only recruited young men. Nonetheless, Burch recommended Westminster to Ward as she recollected, "It was the sixth grade teacher, although I was in the seventh grade by this time, who contacted my mother and indicated that he was aware that there was this private school that was now recruiting, I guess city-wide, black kids to attend. And he felt compelled to let my mother know that he was aware that one of my close friends, who was a black boy, had been recommended to apply or attend Westminster by the school administrators."[119] Further Ward remembered, "And so had [Mr. Burch] not shown that independence of thought, we wouldn't have even known this social experiment was underway. And so because of that, my mother agreed and was very committed to allowing me . . . to be considered. That's how I wound up at Westminster in the eighth grade."[120]

THE FIRST BLACK STUDENTS became aware of Westminster in different ways. They had experienced the best of segregated black schooling, including the care ethic of black teachers and rigorous curriculum they offered. In the mid-1960s, gradual desegregation and white flight resulted in overcrowded conditions in segregated black schools. Westminster, a school that helped to launch the Advanced Placement Program, had grown into an important academic institution in Atlanta. African American parents and teachers like Burch recognized the potential academic preparation students would receive at Westminster, and they also recognized the import of claiming access to such opportunities.

As black students prepared to enter Westminster, many educational institutions confronted their histories and contemporary realities of racism, and historically white elite private schools were not exempt. Westminster's open admissions policy that came to fruition, Pressly's desire to maintain a positive image of Westminster, and the school's climate contributed to a contradictory and complex school culture. How Westminster positioned itself during this time was informed by what was happening nationally. Increasingly, as independent school leaders sought to separate themselves from post-*Brown* segregationist academies, they developed programs to recruit African American students to independent schools.

Everyday life, however, at independent schools reflected the pull of institutional racism and the push of progressive action that defined the initial years of desegregation. Parts of Westminster's first black students' experiences would echo that of their counterparts in independent schools elsewhere, such as those recruited through ABC to attend independent schools. For example, the black students recruited through ABC have reported interpersonal racism.[121] Community was also important to ABC students, but for the first black students at Westminster, both for the day and boarding students, community took on a particular unique role. Community was defined as both their own black communities in which they were raised and continued to live, but the black community at Westminster, including the black workers and themselves. The black students' communities had high hopes for their success, and the students relied on their multiple communities and previous experiences as they began to navigate Westminster.

CHAPTER FOUR

The Fearless Firsts

In his letter to William Pressly about Michael McBay's interview for the Stouffer Foundation Scholarship, John Ehle wrote, "[Mr. Douglas Lewis, the headmaster of Summit School in Winston-Salem and I] talked with Michael about a few irritations he just might encounter while attending a school which had not previously admitted Negro students. He was unruffled by such prospects."[1] However, Michael McBay experienced more than just "a few irritations" when he began at Westminster in fall 1967. His white peers subjected him to verbal abuse and physical attacks, similar to what Michael's counterparts experienced when desegregating other educational institutions. McBay recalled: "No one could have prepared me for the psychological scarring I was about to receive. The very first day of class—8th grade—I walked in—the 'dominant' white males (about 8 of them or so—many on the football team) immediately surrounded me ('How nice!' I naively thought, 'They are welcoming me to class!'). Then they proceeded to humiliate, hit, push, shove, punch, and 'haze' me into hysterics such that I ran to the bathroom to hide and cry."[2] Ron McBay, Michael's younger brother, who would begin attending Westminster in the fall of 1968, also recalled the harassment Michael experienced:

> During that [first] year, I vividly recall that my brother was having a
> difficult time at Westminster. The kids picked on him. . . . One thing
> I specifically recall was that it was the season of the 17-year locusts
> (cicadas). When they emerged from the ground, they shed the outer
> casing of their exoskeleton, leaving a hollowed out hard mold of this
> bug lying around in the grass. The white kids would put these shells in
> my brother's hair, finding it funny that [they] would get caught up in
> the naps of his afro and he couldn't get [them] out of his hair easily.[3]

Although Michael was open to the possibility of attending Westminster, white students quickly subjected him to harassment. Michael and other black students were to benefit from the experience and white students were to benefit as well, but programs like Stouffer and schools like Westminster did not fully anticipate and prepare accordingly for the depth of interpersonal and institutional racism that black students would negotiate.

Michael and the other fearless firsts entered a world with which they were not familiar, and their presence was resisted by some. They attended a school with nearly 1500 white students.[4] Some of the fearless firsts were financially supported by their families, and others were supported by their families and the Stouffer Foundation. They attended a school that cost $875 for day students in seventh through twelfth grades and $2,500 for boarding students. Such costs were out of reach for most Americans because the average U.S. salary combined for white men and women who worked year round was $6,535 and for nonwhite men and women was $4,355.[5] The first black students entered a world in which it was customary upon high school graduation for Westminster alumni to enroll in colleges and universities such as the University of Georgia, Vanderbilt University, the University of North Carolina-Chapel Hill, Emory University, Duke University, Washington and Lee, Sweet Briar, Yale University, and Princeton University; some of these institutions had just desegregated or had begun enrolling more black students.[6] Westminster graduates were attending schools deemed the best in the nation, and they pursued careers in business, medicine, law, education, and the ministry.[7] In time the first black students would attend some of these same institutions of higher learning and pursue similar careers.

What occurred at Westminster as the fearless firsts desegregated the school was part of broader, sustained fights for equitable black educational opportunity and against perpetual underlying beliefs about black inferiority. Although monetary benefits were tied to the Civil Rights Act and the Elementary and Secondary Education Act (ESEA), legal battles continued over school desegregation. One tactic for implementing public school desegregation had been the use of freedom of choice plans in which blacks (and whites) could opt to attend public schools. In *Green v. County School Board of New Kent County* (1968), the Supreme Court found freedom of choice plans unconstitutional because "such plans placed the burden of integration on blacks, who were reluctant to transfer in the face of intimidation." The court ruled "that schools must dismantle segregated dual (or segregated) systems 'root and branch.'" A year later in *Alexander v. Holmes County [Mississippi] Board of Education* (1969), the Supreme Court ordered that schools be desegregated and that districts subsequently maintain unitary schools.[8] With these Supreme Court decisions, more southern school districts desegregated. As a result, segregationist academies became more commonplace, and whites continued to leave city centers for suburban areas.

At the same time that battles over school desegregation remained, the "Equality of Educational Opportunity" report or the "Coleman Report," originally released on July 1, 1966, had come to influence national educational policy. In this report, sociologist James Coleman argued that schools had less effect on student achievement in comparison to a child's background. At first the report did not gain national traction, but in 1968, Daniel Patrick Moynihan, who had risen to national prominence because of his role in the federal government and his discussion about the pathology of black individuals, wrote "a laudatory review in the *Harvard Educational Review*" about the Coleman Report. The Coleman Report then became central to educational policy discussions, and Coleman became a fixture in the Nixon administration.[9] The Coleman Report had contributed to the pervasive deficit theory "that students (particularly of low-income, racial/ethnic minority background) fail in school (e.g., perform poorly on standardized tests) because such students and their families have internal defects or deficits, that thwart the learning process."[10] Such theories influenced how educational leaders, both public *and* private, thought of African American students and the factors that contributed to any potential academic success.

Concurrently, everyday citizens would test the continuation of federal tax exemption for private institutions with discriminatory admissions policies, and independent school leaders responded. If the federal government was calling for equity in public schools and higher education, then it would have to account for granting financial incentives to private institutions that openly discriminated. Public and private blurred with questions of federal tax-exemption status, and national independent school leaders paid even more attention to recruiting black students and to race relations. In 1967, the National Association of Independent Schools (NAIS) established the Minority Affairs Committee, of which William Pressly was a member. In 1968, NAIS issued an open admissions policy that called for open admissions in all schools, but there were no consequences for those that that did not implement these policies. In 1969, NAIS hired William Dandridge, the first NAIS director of minority affairs. In total, during the first three years of black students attending Westminster, the number of black students attending independent schools nationally more than doubled. The national changes among independent schools, including the increased policies, publications, initiatives, and the further development of recruitment and scholarship programs, however, could not interrupt the institutional and interpersonal racism that African Americans experienced in independent schools, including in the newly desegregated private schools in the South.

I posit that two main themes characterize the initial years of desegregation at Westminster. First, Westminster, like other southern schools admitting black students for the first time, did not have an exact template to follow. Westminster, at times, institutionally prepared for desegregation, thereby anticipating how it might uphold its institutional commitments. At other times, school leaders did not take these steps, and school officials seemed to be more reactive than proactive. How independent schools addressed race, made policy changes, and added personnel to address minority issues most likely captured the attention of many administrators, faculty, and additional staff at Westminster, especially because of Pressly's continued leadership on the national level. Further, advocates and activists continued to push U.S. society to understand inequality and racism as the nation mourned and reacted to the assassination of Dr. Martin Luther King Jr. Societal changes, coupled with increased attention to black students by NAIS, perhaps implicitly encouraged those who positively acknowledged the first black students' presence, assisted in their matriculation, and alleviated unfavorable conditions.

Second, the first black students to attend schools like Westminster, because they were not in the national spotlight, did not realize how courageous they were to attend historically white elite private schools each day. On any given day, black students could experience interpersonal racism that was both overt and subtle. While there would be more visible appreciation for black culture and life in the Westminster community, white students' community service in black neighborhoods at times reflected an ethos of the era which characterized black Americans as disadvantaged and inferior. Though it was not their responsibility, the fearless firsts used the contents of their backpacks to the fullest extent to navigate courageously this institutional culture that was birthed in vestiges of the Old South and that remained contradictory and complex. Through academic achievement, extracurricular activities, and support from their communities and from particular white and black individuals at Westminster, they journeyed on a new terrain, chartered new pathways on that terrain for others to follow, and made those pathways more easily navigable for those who came behind them.

The Fearless Firsts Journey on New Terrain

What Michael McBay experienced indicated that Westminster was not prepared to nurture its first black students. In the fall of 1967, McBay,

Dawn Clark, Jannard Wade, Wanda Ward, and three other students—Bill Billings, Janice Kemp, and Isaac Clark—arrived at their new campus. Yet, it is not entirely evident that Westminster took great measures to engage its white day school students and their parents about the enrollment of the new black students, and there do not appear to be any additional communications beyond the 1965 letter announcing the change in admissions policies. Such inaction marked how Westminster approached desegregation. In the previous year, Westminster leaders believed that they had prepared white students for desegregation. The admissions team had also admitted qualified black students who presumably did not fear attending a historically white elite school and who were prepared academically, emotionally, and socially. Therefore, perhaps Westminster faculty and staff assumed that no additional measures needed to be taken to ensure that black students would be positively welcomed, but additional measures did need to be taken because of what the black students would experience. Further, Westminster's institutional culture remained mostly ambivalent around major issues even though there was a cadre of politically conscious white students.

Michael was not the only black student to experience racial harassment during the first year; Dawn Clark, the youngest of the first black students, did as well. During the summer of 1967, Clark attended Westminster's summer program, which presumably would have helped her transition to Westminster. Clark remembered the summer program as fun, exciting, and full of new learning opportunities.[11] No racial incidents occurred during the summer program, perhaps because Jeannie Hawkins attended during the previous summer. Her presence paved the way for more black students to attend and prepared the program administrators for black students. When Clark arrived at Westminster in the fall, she knew other students who had attended the summer program. Yet, much conversation ensued about Clark attending the school full time; "I did not understand what the deal was, why all of a sudden there were all these adults getting involved and having heated conversations about me going someplace I had just been. You know I did not understand it."[12]

White students made Clark's first year quite difficult. Clark remembered being bullied and harassed, having her head dunked in the water fountain, being tripped, having the word *nigger* written on her desk, and having her dress sashes taken by other students. One student, larger than most of the other students, chased, sat, and rolled on her after school, and a student with a disability used his walking crutches to trip her. Additionally, Clark's hair "was a constant source of criticism and ridicule."[13] Clark's white classmates did not choose her for the one opening in the Girl Scout troop at Westminster, but she joined a newly formed troop with Joia Johnson and Janice Edwards, black girls who would begin attending Westminster soon after the first year of desegregation. Clark also recalled "being invited to a birthday party that was supposed to be a swimming birthday party [and] . . . they just changed the day. . . . And then I remember also being invited over to a sleep-over and we actually went and knocked on the door, and they would not open the door."[14] Clark believed the swimming party was changed to a different date because some white parents did not want their children in the same swimming pool with her.

Because of these incidents, Clark felt compelled to respond, and she answered physically at least twice to the harassment. Once, she jumped on the student who had "rolled on" on her, and she hit one student who had been mean to her. Some white parents questioned the administration about Clark's attendance at Westminster, but Clark's parents insisted that she be left alone. Although school leadership had not publicly indicated that they were prepared for dealing with racial harassment, they did react. Clark recalled that Chris Stevenson, the same administrator who had housed Jeannie Hawkins the previous summer, "made it really clear that I was not going anywhere and that this harassment in class needed to stop and that the teachers needed to be accountable for it, and they [the teachers] needed to tell their children how to behave."[15] Stevenson's words were important to Clark and her parents, because as an administrator he stood up for Clark and acknowledged that Westminster's white teachers had a responsibility to stop such harassment.

Despite Stevenson's words, adjusting to Westminster was not easy as black students encountered a puzzling institutional culture with Old South vestiges. The slave auction fundraiser, as part of the boys' school Annual Christmas Fund Drive, continued. Yet, students increasingly, as compared to previous newspapers and yearbooks, lauded black Americans, including those who worked on campus.[16] While black students were new to the school, African Americans had been working at the school, most likely since its inception. Students thanked Stanley, who was pictured behind a school bus steering wheel, and C. E. Lovelace, Pressly's long-time assistant. The students showed appreciation to Willie Harris, an athletic trainer and former college and semipro football player, with students claiming that his spirit "typifies Westminster athletics."[17]

Of all, national tragedy most highlighted Westminster's ambivalence toward the country's race relations, though there was a faction of students who cared deeply about the society around them. On April 4, after Dr. Martin Luther King Jr. was assassinated in Memphis, Tennessee, outrage erupted across the nation. Historian Peniel Joseph estimated that "125 cities in twenty-nine states experienced racial unrest, and an estimated $45 million in property damage was reported. The human cost included thirty-nine dead and three thousand, five hundred injured."[18] King's death also influenced the advocacy and activism of youth and young adults as they continued to resist what they deemed as inequitable schooling conditions at all levels. Historian Ibram Rogers (now Ibram Kendi) has suggested that "through his death, King dramatically appealed to the moral conscience of white Americans, particularly those in the academy, as dozens, probably hundreds of institutions succumbed to students' requests, or often on their own accord, established scholarships, recruiting initiatives, race committees, and other memorials in King's honor."[19] Student requests and protests, often undergirded by students writing "Black Manifestos," led to the establishment of ethnic studies programs and African American studies programs and increased resources for black students. For example, in March 1969, Emory University's Black Student Alliance gave university president Sanford Atwood a "Manifesto," outlining specific demands. After not receiving a satisfactory response, African American students interrupted the Sunday worship service on campus on May 25, 1969, led a demonstration in support of the African American workers on campus, and organized a rally. Atwood tried to secure an injunction, but the "student and faculty senates passed a joint resolution calling for an end to campus racism and nullification of the restraining order. Atwood, who had followed black student protests across the country, announced the university's intention to implement a Black Studies program."[20]

Yet at Westminster, in the immediate and more distant days after King's assassination, there was no collective gathering nor even widespread conversation, according to the first black students, but King's death had reverberating effects on them. Jannard Wade, who was personally devastated, recalled how scary a time it was and his worry about the aftermath becoming volatile, especially in the South.[21] Although he felt that most students at Westminster respected King, he did remember that there were "a couple of knuckleheads that brought up the fact that they thought that he was a Communist or something like that. But those people, you just kind of considered the source and moved on."[22] Wanda Ward described King's death as a "deep demarcation" that showed how the nation "hadn't lived up to its creed" or "to its potential." Ward remembered that many people were sad.

She, however, did not speak to a lot of classmates about King's assassination, and not a lot of her classmates spoke to her about it. Ward vividly remembered those who did talk about King as "the more politically conscious and they were angry. They were deeply, deeply angry and hurt because it was such a loss to the nation."[23] Westminster had not directly addressed King's assassination, but in the immediate days after, some students showed their concern. Despite the school culture, the first black students would remain at Westminster.

During the first year of desegregation, interpersonal racism had been evident and the institutional culture remained mixed in its position and acknowledgment of its white southern vestiges. The black students who had matriculated to Westminster had been well-equipped in their black neighborhoods and schools so that they could begin to find their way in this new environment. For example, Wade played on the eighth-grade football and basketball teams, and Ward played on the junior high girls' basketball team and served on the junior high service council.[24] New black students applied to Westminster and were admitted, and they would have to begin their period of adjustment as they endured the realities of Westminster. At the same time, the national independent school world continued to embrace, although cautiously, their commitment to black students.

More Fearless Firsts, but Continued Troubles

As the first students of 1967 continued to find their way at Westminster, Ron McBay, Malcolm Ryder, and three other black students (in total, four boys and one girl), joined the original seven at Westminster for the 1968-69 school year. One student enrolled in kindergarten; the others, including Ron and Malcolm, were in the fifth to the ninth grades. Family, prior schooling in segregated black schools, and community experiences were also important to the new black students to Westminster.

Though his older brother Michael had experienced difficulties, Ron McBay was still excited about the possibility of attending Westminster, a school that he knew as "the best in town." He recalled, "As much as I clearly remember knowing how unhappy he was going there, it was going to be my turn to attend Westminster the next year; but I also remember clearly being excited about the opportunity to go. I was looking forward to it greatly." McBay excelled academically from an early age. Even before starting elementary school, McBay knew his multiplication tables, but he did not like receiving any attention for being an advanced student. Like his older brother Michael, Ron attended Oglethorpe where he described receiving "a good education" and where other "very good students" attended school. Ron, who was self-conscious about his academic aptitude, did not like the idea of skipping the first grade because he missed his friends and felt isolated.[25] Because McBay skipped grades, he was always a year younger than his classmates and a year behind in physical development, which he considered "bad for sports, bad for social development."[26] He carried these feelings about his stature with him to Westminster, and they would affect how he experienced the school.

Ron, like Dawn Clark the previous summer, participated in Westminster's summer program, which shaped his first impressions of Westminster. Before the summer program, McBay had one white classmate and would see his white neighbors, a Jewish family, only in passing. So for him, having always been in all-black environments, his "sense [of] 'normal, average' skin tone was totally out the window in this new environment." McBay noted, "The literal brightness of the skin of white people was a big shock to me." He "clearly remember[ed] thinking, 'Wow. They really are WHITE!'"[27] Westminster's wealth also shocked McBay as it had some of the black students the previous year. In his words, "the large campus was, frankly, a more posh environment for 1,200 K-through-12 students than the entire set of campuses for 12,000 students at the AUC schools. That was obvious right away."[28] Ron was making sense of race and class at a young age. He had begun to contemplate what it meant to be white in America and what it meant to attend a school that exuded more wealth than the historically black college campuses on which he spent time as the son of professors. How he would make sense of race, class, and himself were important to his development and initial Westminster experiences.

In his first year, Ron McBay, who joined Dawn Clark in the fifth grade, felt the cultural weight of institutional racism, and he experienced interpersonal racism. At the same time, he came to understand himself. As Ron attended Westminster each day, he could not help but think of what had happened to Michael the year before; knowing so intimately what happened to his brother had both helped to prepare him for Westminster and put him on edge. For example, in his fifth-grade homeroom, Ron and the other students would play a game called "G-H-O-S-T." For this game, students sat in a circle and called out letters to spell a word. According to McBay, "When it's your turn, if you say a letter that completes a word ("C"-"A"-"T"), then you're out; but all the letters said (including yours) must be the beginning of a real word, or else you're also out." McBay described sitting in the fifth spot, and the letters before his turn were "T"-"E"-"T"-"R." So he could either spell "TETRA" (the name of a fish) or say another letter and be challenged to come up with a word other than TETRA. "So in my mind, my thoughts immediately go to the kinds of things that happened to my brother," stated Ron. "So to me, this was 'Let's get rid of the black kid right away.' So I panic and run out of the room crying, run down the hall into the bathroom, and hide in one of the stalls." A student followed Ron and asked why he left the room crying when they were just playing a game. For Ron, "the genuine innocence of this kid really got to me—he had absolutely no idea that I thought some racial incident had just occurred. Suddenly, I felt bad even thinking such a thing about these people."[29] Ron was understandably thinking through a racial lens as a black child coming of age in the late 1960s whose brother had been racially harassed just the year before. This incident led him to question that instinct moving forward, but additional occurrences, his own self-development, and his smaller stature only reinforced what it meant to be a young black man at Westminster.

Other incidents spoke to the vestiges of white southern culture and how the school culture remained very much the same in the second year of school desegregation. Ron McBay remembered being interviewed by a television crew about singing "Dixie" in a school assembly; as a ten-year-old, Ron did not believe that he was making any kind of political statement. In his opinion, this response was not liked by the camera crew. Ron also remembered doing well on a test in fifth grade and that the Daughters of the American Revolution (DAR) commended those who did well. He recollected "the teacher saying that if the D. A. R. had realized I was black they probably would have rescinded the certificate, 'but we won't tell them.'"[30]

Another situation involved his mother. By the end of fifth grade, Ron excelled in reading comprehension. Over the summer, all the students were to read and write book reports, but he did not complete the assignment nor had he told his mother about the assignment. When school resumed, his reading comprehension skills had significantly decreased. During a meeting about the issue, Ron's teacher blamed Dr. McBay for her son not doing his summer work. According to Ron, "My mom . . . misinterpreted the situation and thought this white lady was simply saying her black son 'couldn't read.' So my mom was offended over what she perceived as a racial incident." Always, a quiet child, Ron said that he "might speak up once to try and clarify the situation between the two of them, but after that—once the adults don't listen to what a kid is saying, I bowed out of it and just let them argue when neither one understood where the other was coming from."[31] In part, this situation showed a young black boy acting like any other young person, but because of race and racism, his mother thought the worst.

Ron McBay felt accepted as the only black boy in the fifth grade, but his candid, descriptive memories point to how race and self-concept are intertwined. Having thought of himself as small in stature since skipping the first grade, his self-concept affected how he understood himself and his interactions with others. During his early years at Westminster, however, Ron was inspired by the Jackson Five, in large part because of Michael Jackson, the younger brother and "star" of the group. Michael's presence and performances encouraged Ron. He stated, "All of a sudden, the world was no longer telling me that I have to be this ignorant joke character; instead, I could be this mesmerizing performer."[32]

In addition, Michael McBay's experiences during the first year of desegregation were on Pressly's mind as Ron settled into Westminster. Ron recalled that one afternoon Pressly approached him and asked how he was doing. After giving a generic "I'm fine," Pressly responded with, "No. I know what kind of things they did to your brother. If anything like that has happened to you, I want you to tell me."[33] Though Pressly's comment to Ron could not and would not interrupt the interpersonal racism and harassment experienced by the first black students, the inquiry indicated that Pressly wanted to be made aware of those issues. Pressly may have had multiple reasons for wanting to know about any incidents. As a national leader of NAIS, he presumably wanted to make desegregation work at Westminster. He also most likely did not want the experiences of black students to worsen as he and others continued to recruit and enroll more black students.

Malcolm Ryder, the first black male boarding student and a Stouffer Foundation scholarship recipient, also began in the fall of 1968. Malcolm's background was similar to other first black students at Westminster. His parents, Noah Francis and Georgia Atkins-Ryder, had worked at Norfolk State College, a historically black higher education institution where they established and grew the music program.[34] His experiences in the black community were also of importance. In addition to his church community at Bank Street Memorial Baptist Church, Ryder enjoyed being around artists and intellectuals. He recalled, "We [my sisters and I] were constantly seeing them performing and building things with each other. So the idea that you're in a community and the community takes care of itself, it wasn't just an idea to us. That was pretty much all we knew. As children, growing up, that's just the way life was. We actually had to leave home to find out that there was some other way of getting things done."[35] Growing up knowing everyone was important to Malcolm and being around a variety of adults helped to both ground him and to foreshadow possibilities for himself and others. Understanding these possibilities fortified the high expectations that his parents had for his sisters and him. When Malcolm was eight, Noah Ryder became ill and died two years later. Following Noah Ryder's death, Georgia Ryder took it upon herself to provide for Malcolm and his two sisters. When Malcolm was about twelve, his mother began to pursue her doctoral degree at New York University, and during her first year there, Malcolm and his sisters lived with their respective godparents.

As the first black students desegregated Westminster, Malcolm attended a newly built, desegregated public school in Virginia. Lake Taylor, in his words, was "well run" with small classes. As Malcolm stated, "they just moved your group around from one teacher to another. So I made some new friends, and I had white friends for the first time, but not a lot of them."[36] In comparison to his earlier neighborhood schools, Lake Taylor's standards were higher, but Ryder was very cognizant that the greater availability of resources helped students to meet the expectations.[37]

An honor-roll student, Malcolm was emotionally detached while attending Lake Taylor, in part because he considered it a transitional year. Ryder had expected to move to New York City the following year and had already begun emotionally withdrawing from Norfolk when a different opportunity presented itself. Georgia Ryder, wanting Malcolm to be challenged academically, learned of the Stouffer Foundation from the Goss family, who were fellow church members and family friends. During the previous year, the Stouffer Foundation had awarded a scholarship to Wade Goss, who was close in age to Malcolm. His mother, Jocelyn Goss, a teacher and career educator, was very good friends with Georgia Ryder and suggested the Stouffer program to her.

Malcolm impressed the Stouffer Foundation. Douglas Lewis of the Stouffer Foundation described Ryder as "a wispy, quiet, gentle fellow who hopes, at the moment to be an astronaut. 'I think it's different and fascinating—the idea that we can break away from the earth and actually travel in space.'" Ryder was viewed as "handling his present school challenges (including the problem of being one of twenty Negroes in a 1600-student junior high." Lewis commented that Ryder, while subdued and serious in the interview, was "apparently well-liked and respected, having been vice president of his student council in sixth grade, president of the council in seventh grade (both in an all-Negro school), and nearly won the election to the council this year in his new school." Lewis did take note of a recent fight between Ryder and a "foul-mouthed acquaintance who was messing up the yard. Apparently, Ryder was fighting defensively, and for a cause."[38] But the fight did not detract from Malcolm's ability to impress the interviewers. A second interviewer commented, "It would be difficult to find a more suitable candidate for a scholarship than Malcolm Ryder. He is a superior person. He will be a challenge to the preparatory school which receives him, and he will contribute significantly in many areas of work and life at that school."

After the Stouffer Foundation administrators granted a scholarship to Malcolm, he visited Westminster and became excited about the possibilities of going away to school. For Ryder, "[Westminster] felt like a college rather than a high school. It communicated opportunity to me. Dr. Pressly also arrived to personally meet me and my mother. We talked just outside of the main hall in the bright sunshine. He said he'd heard about me for a while and was excited that I was coming to study and play music at WM. So overall it initially felt like the place was being given to me."[39]

With the new school year approaching, Malcolm took steps to prepare for Westminster. As a requirement of the Stouffer Foundation, Ryder and the other nineteen recipients attended Duke University's A Better Chance (ABC) Program, a program philosophically committed to "assisting the student with the transition from public to private schools."[40] The daily schedule included classes in English, mathematics, and reading, study hall, cultural activities, and athletics. The classes were not of the remedial level but were intended to enhance and further "the individual's particular needs and capacities, from the fundamentals to esoteric points of excellence." The students also watched movies, including *On the Waterfront*, *The Guns of Navarone*, *Macbeth*, *Living Desert*, and *Ulysses*; staged and performed the play *Stalag 17*; visited the University of North Carolina-Chapel Hill; and enjoyed a weekend sailing and camping trip.[41] The Southern Regional Council, a biracial organization established in 1944 committed to solving the problems of the South, also sponsored an orientation for the Stouffer Foundation. The orientation provided the students the opportunity to meet Vernon Jordan, then a lawyer and civil rights activist who directed the Voter Education Project, and other black leaders to discuss "the opportunities and problems they had or would soon encounter as Negro students in previously all-white preparatory schools in the South." Thirty-seven young men attended the retreat; in addition to Ryder and his cohort, some of those who had received the Stouffer Foundation scholarship the year before also attended.[42]

On one hand, the summer program prepared Malcolm in a different way than his fellow black students at Westminster. Malcolm was afforded an opportunity to connect with other young black men headed to historically white elite boarding schools in the South. The summer curriculum helped to shore up their academic preparation and provided hands-on experience with the academic culture that they might encounter in independent schools. On the other hand, the summer experience also provided a false sense of reality. Ryder recollected that the summer program made it "very clear with us about the fact that we were going to institutions where black people were few and far between." Because the summer program was only for new black students attending historically white elite private schools, they did not experience the reality of their new schools until they arrived at them. As Malcolm noted: "So I knew intellectually that when we get to Westminster there would be me and maybe a couple of others, and a bunch of white kids, but it just didn't really strike home that I'd be living alone with whites in a single building—that I would be living there, not just going to school there."[43]

Prior to Malcolm's arrival for the second year of desegregation, Pressly did take a public step in spring 1968 to prepare white students and parents, which was in line with advice provided in Mallery's *Negro Students in Independent Schools*. Pressly notified Westminster parents of Ryder's admission in May 1968. In a letter, Pressly described Ryder as "a boy with very high academic achievement and with much talent in the fields of Art and Music." Pressly continued by stating, "Our policy of admitting students without regard to race has brought us some remarkably fine boys and girls in our day school. We are all pleased with the ease with which they have fitted into the student body, and I am sure Malcolm will fit easily into the dormitory, receiving much from the group and giving much to the group."[44] Pressly sent this letter a little over a month after King's assassination. He acknowledged how black students were adjusting to Westminster, and this letter seemed to be the first official indication of how Westminster was attempting to make it an environment in which black students could succeed.

Pressly's letter, however, did not stop Ryder from experiencing racial harassment, and the summer program had not prepared black students for these moments. One day Malcolm arrived to find his part of the bedroom that he shared with three other students vandalized: "Not long after school started, I came home from classes one day and—so I had three roommates. We were in one of these rooms that's got a divider that's where your closets and things are, so basically there's two of you on one side of this divider and two of you on the other side. So it's basically four bedrooms.

Malcolm Ryder, the first black student to live in the boys' dormitory beginning in the fall of 1968, is pictured here with Janice Kemp, one of three black girls who desegregated Westminster in 1967. Janice was on the honor roll and involved in school activities but left Westminster following ninth grade. Malcolm, who endured racial harassment in the dormitory as a ninth grader, remained at Westminster and excelled inside and outside the classroom. Source: *Lynx* (Yearbook), 1969, 2, RG 21.03, Beck Archives-Westminster.

So I walk into our room after class and my part of it was totally destroyed and the other three are pristine. So it's very clearly targeted vandalism." Malcolm returned to his dorm room another day to find a hunting knife sticking out of his closet door. Then there was the time he found that his notebooks, "the spiral bound kind—had been opened and filled, just page after page of about threats and insults, 'Go home, nigger.'" The incidents caused fear and affected Ryder emotionally. He remembered "that's where it went from being weird to being scary because you never know. It just kind of threw me into being very kind of self-protective and wary, and it kind of shut me down." But he was "rescued" by an older white student who also lived in the dorm. "When he took me under his wing virtually all of this stuff stopped," stated Ryder. "He was a white guy, and I think it just kind sent of a message to everyone who needed to get it."[45] Ryder had been isolated in the dormitory, and these incidents were allowed to happen. Fortunately, an older white male student stepped up to stop what was happening; his response showed other white students that one could object to such harassment. The remainder of the year was more tranquil for Malcolm, but he had already felt the pangs of racism which would stay with him.

The second year of desegregation at Westminster had brought two firsts—a pair of black siblings and a black boarding student, and both Ron McBay and Malcolm Ryder, like Michael McBay, had to make sense of the racial harassment they experienced. Perhaps because of what occurred the previous year or because a boarding component provided a different experience for students, Pressly had taken a step to prepare those white students who boarded and their parents, but the racial harassment continued. That some white students challenged their fellow classmates was an important step in the Westminster community. Clearly the presence of black students was having an impact, and the role of white allies would be important in the coming years.

Progress and Resistance

As Ryder endured these challenges while boarding in the ninth grade, the black students living at home in Atlanta had begun to find their niches in school life, both in academics and extracurricular activities. Michael McBay was listed among sixteen other students on the freshman honor roll.[46] Wanda Ward and Janice Kemp were both on the freshman honor roll, the junior varsity basketball team, and members of the Quest Club, a discussion group open to all freshmen and sophomore girls. Ward was also on the varsity basketball team, which had a successful season of fourteen wins and four losses.[47]

The first black students were not only adjusting to life at Westminster but also faced their own personal challenges as developing young people. When Jannard Wade's mother passed during his ninth-grade year, he was devastated. To make sense of his loss, he made a conscious effort to delve more into school life, which turned out to be a very positive move as he involved himself in new opportunities. Jannard tried anything and everything. He was the first black student to play soccer. He fondly remembered why he tried out for the team: "They thought I was going out for basketball because I was black, so I went out for soccer. Coach Sims, the soccer team [coach], . . . recruited me."[48] Wade became a standout player and was recognized in the yearbook: "The first year boys were led by Alan Simons, John Wilson, Tyler Spratlin, and youthful future greats Jannard Wade, Scott Pendergrast, and Charlie McCoy."[49]

Although athletics were a great outlet for Jannard, he too experienced racism. A football coach once remarked after practice, "Now if we work like a bunch of niggers, we'll win the State Championship." Though the coach may have thought the remark would motivate his players, the remark scared Wade. He was the only black player on the field, and the only other black person was Willie Harris, the team bus driver and trainer. According to Wade, the coach and his son apologized and the coach "was later fired for [the remark]."[50] His firing indicated that in some instances Westminster took steps to quell racism. Wade also faced racism on the field. Against Fitzgerald in the first round of the playoffs for the state championship, Wade said, "I was cursed out, called names the whole game. The referee wouldn't call the plays. If I did something, he'd say I'm out of bounds, or whatever. . . . But that just made us more determined to kick their butts, and we did. But it was kind of scary because South Georgia and Atlanta are two different animals, even today."[51]

During the second year of desegregation as black students experienced both trauma and engaged more in student life, the larger school culture remained paradoxical. The slave auction fundraiser continued; one yearbook picture even showed students stomping on another student with the caption reading, "slaves quickly learn humility from their masters."[52] Again, the slave auction fundraiser revealed how white students at Westminster understood the relationship between slaves and masters and how slaves were subjected to their masters' will. Previous references echoing how whites auctioned off slaves of African descent denoted white students' conceptions of slavery as rooted in the U.S. institution of slavery, thereby gesturing to their understanding of U.S. history and the historical relationship among whites, blacks, and slavery. Some faculty and staff did support black students and acknowledged black life and culture. During the September 1968 Faculty Public Relations Committee meeting, some members expressed a desire to highlight the achievement of black students.[53] In October, Dr. William Borders, an African American pastor of Wheat Street Baptist Church and civil rights activist, spoke during Religious Emphasis Week; a year later, his granddaughter Lisa Borders enrolled at Westminster.[54]

Black workers continued to be celebrated at the same time that they quietly helped the black students exist in the Westminster world. Black staff members such as Gladys, Lucile, Stanley, Ora, and Willie were pictured in the yearbook and lauded for their helpfulness.[55] Jannard had a close relationship with Willie Harris, the athletic trainer, who had been highlighted the year before in the school yearbook and newspaper. C. E. Lovelace,

Pressly's assistant, lived in Wanda Ward's neighborhood and volunteered to drive her and other black students to Westminster, a commute that felt incredibly long; it "was like to the other end of the world," according to Ward. But she recalled, "He was so proud of us that he often volunteered. He told my family if they would just drop me off at his house, I could ride to school. So there was a community pride, again, the significance of which I was not up on. So there was a lot—it meant a lot to the community, I guess, if you will, the communities from which we came."[56] The black staff helped to embrace the black students in ways that they needed, and the staff became an extension of the black students' home communities and priceless inheritances. The black staff members exhibited pride in having black students at Westminster, and the students channeled that pride as they navigated Westminster. These special relationships added to their overflowing backpacks of community support and the importance of education in the black community.

Some of the slight changes in the environment that students experienced the second year may also be linked to Westminster itself. Westminster students, like other independent school students across the country, began to become more actively engaged in community service in black neighborhoods. In Atlanta, Westminster students took a keen interest in Vine City. Fifteen Westminster students volunteered in the neighborhood during the summer. The student writer described how the "Vine City kids were a curious lot" to the Westminster students. In the school newspaper, one student wrote, "Their dialect was difficult to understand for one thing, and they fought all of the time—instant emotion, which was gone just as instantly. Their worst insult to each other was you 'nigger' which betrayed their serious identification problem."[57] The writer also noted that the Vine City students were behind academically and had limited experiences. As part of a collaboration between students and teachers, the service project showed Westminster students "that the society that they have inherited is one of great social disturbances between people, black and white, and rich and poor."[58] Over the course of the semester, students tutored after school, and on Saturday mornings, Westminster students took black children from Vine City to area locations such as Stone Mountain and the Zoo. Additionally, the Westminster volunteers gave a Christmas party.[59] The Girls National Honor Society also began a tutoring program in Clarendale, "a black, underprivileged pocket" that was located close to the Westminster girls' dorm.[60]

Although they had very good intentions, the Westminster students' actions and discourse reflected the deficit discourse of the era and the notion of noblesse oblige. The perspectives in the newspaper may also have been indicative of how some white students initially thought about the new black students. Clearly, some white students exhibited their disapproval through overt racial harassment. Most likely, however, there were other white students who thought that the black students could not achieve academically at Westminster. How Westminster's white students interacted with the first black students while also becoming more engaged in community service reflected national trends as community service increased among independent schools and as the number of blacks attending independent schools grew.

Pressly, who remained a national leader as an inaugural member of the NAIS minority affairs committee in 1967, began to address race and desegregation more forthrightly. In the 1968 report to the board, he made implicit references to race and desegregation as he wrote, "They will need to be able to live with their fellows, respecting differences, sympathizing with feelings."[61] These words suggested that the white students needed to understand their black peers. In February 1969, during a speech delivered at the Arlington School convocation, Pressly spoke out against segregationist academies, stating that to deny students on the basis of race is denying access to black students and an "adequate atmosphere" to white boys and girls; in his words, "it is a refusal on the basis of color, to recognize the worth of another human being." He then stated that the same admissions standards were applied to the twelve "Negro" girls and boys attending Westminster, asserted that current segregated schools needed time to desegregate, and concluded by discussing Christian love in accepting all students.[62] Pressly also referenced NAIS's October 1968 open enrollment statement which perhaps was NAIS's closest attempt at addressing the national climate following King's death and the increased focus on recruiting black students to independent schools.

Like Westminster, NAIS had not directly addressed King's assassination in the spring of 1968, although one might have thought that it would, considering the changes in the independent school world in the 1960s. Earlier in the decade, programs such as ABC and the Independent Schools Talent Search Program (ISTSP) had commenced. Other programs across the nation also supported the matriculation of black students. For example, independent schools helped to support and sponsor programs such as Upward Bound that were designed to compensate for the lack of educational access and opportunity historically experienced by black Americans. In 1967, the *Independent School Bulletin* (*ISB*) had included multiple articles on interactions with black students, having black students in independent schools, and independent schools' responsibility for promoting interracial relationships.[63] "The Story of an Integrated School" recounted the history of Georgetown Day School in Washington, D.C., that began in 1945 and included black students from the school's inception. "The Independent School and the Multiracial World" was formatted as a question and answer between Michael Lasser, chairman of the English department at The Harley School in Rochester, New York, and Dr. Elliot Shapiro, assistant superintendent of schools in New York City, who had spent the previous school year as director of the Center for Cooperative Action in Urban Education in Rochester, New York. During this interview, Shapiro suggested ways that independent schools could promote interracial interactions, and the positions that parents of children enrolled in independent schools could take on public education. These national changes most likely captured the attention of independent school leaders as the number of black students attending independent schools grew and as more southern schools desegregated.

The 1968 statement also reflected how NAIS remained middle-of-the-road on certain issues. Before publicly supporting open enrollment, the NAIS board of directors considered two points: "first, whether a voluntary membership organization should prescribe standards for its members, and second, whether a national organization which is recognized as a spokesman and standard-bearer for independent school education could fail to take a stand on an issue of such primary significance to all educational institutions and the American people." Based on recommendations by a special committee to study the issues, the board was persuaded to take a public stand because of the number of NAIS schools that "were either committed to, or making substantial strides toward, integration." But the statement did not exclude those schools that did not support integration because "the consensus was that the time had not yet arrived for an ultimatum from NAIS, and that the cause would be better served by a policy which would support rather than coerce those schools that were working hard to persuade their constituents that restrictive admissions practices were no longer tenable and should be changed."[64]

The 1968 policy included three points. The first stated that the "admission of students, as well as the employment of school personnel, should be open to all who are qualified regardless of race or color." Second, the NAIS board clarified its position on private schools intended to preserve segregation by including the following statement: "The Board . . . believes that such schools are contrary to the best interests of American society and, therefore, of the independent school, and it will not extend to such schools the services or privileges of the Association." The third point, therefore, urged all member schools to adopt nondiscriminatory policies and practices. The board then outlined several steps to be taken by NAIS, including surveys on black student enrollment, discussions about open enrollment at regional association meetings, and recruitment of black teachers.[65]

In its first six years, NAIS, having inherited the foci and challenges of previous national organizations, had developed during the civil rights movement. The position of NAIS reflected an embracing of the inclusion of more black students in independent schools, and independent school leaders across the nation had begun to take steps in earnest. Yet, NAIS leaders still technically allowed schools with discriminatory policies to be members of the organization. This might have occurred because NAIS was attempting to increase its number of member schools or because NAIS continued to discern how best to address the history of race and racism in independent schools and what it would mean to have more black students attending independent schools. NAIS leaders recognized how institutions of higher education responded to King's assassination and how some historically white elite institutions had begun to embrace racial diversity as an important factor for their schools. In the coming years, more black students would come to desegregate and attend independent schools, and NAIS would take an even more keen interest in their experiences. Westminster and other schools that had already desegregated were ahead of the curve and helped to bolster NAIS's position in 1968, but the realities of these schools indicated how much more would need to be done to support black students.

The students who had returned to Westminster for their second year had become even more involved in campus life, and they continued to hone their skills that had been nurtured prior to arriving at Westminster, allowing them to courageously navigate Westminster. And communities—whether of neighbors or of Westminster's black employees—were important to the black students' emotional stability. Both the school culture and the national changes remained paradoxical.

Making the New Pathways Even More Viable and Stronger

In the fall of 1969, four new black students joined the eleven black students who were continuing at Westminster; two boys enrolled in pre-first and third grades, and two girls enrolled in the fifth and seventh grades. During the third year of desegregation, interpersonal racism continued even as there seemed to be increased acknowledgment and integration of black culture and life. Old South vestiges remained, but individual white teachers and students were also of import as the black students continued to unpack their backpacks and utilized their skills and talents. Nationally, steps would be taken to more directly address minority affairs. The first black students, because of who they were, slow institutional change, and growing interpersonal support, continued to forge new pathways in their new school environment; they made those pathways more viable and stronger for others to follow.

One of the new students would be Joia Johnson. Similar to Malcolm Ryder, Joia Johnson, a new fifth-grade student, had experienced a majority white school prior to attending Westminster.[66] Joia, the only child of Aaron and Dr. Joyce Johnson, was raised primarily in Southwest Atlanta, but spent part of her early childhood outside of Atlanta. As Dr. Johnson completed her doctorate at Northwestern University in Evanston, Illinois, Aaron Johnson, a former teacher in Atlanta Public Schools (APS), worked in Rock Island, Illinois, and the family resided in Davenport, Iowa, near Rock Island. In Davenport, Joia attended St. Catherine's Catholic School, an all-white private school. Joia did not recall any racial issues at St. Catherine's nor did she recall any other black students attending St. Catherine's.

Upon returning to Atlanta, Johnson attended Oglethorpe, the same school that Ron and Michael McBay attended. At the time, her parents worked at Spelman College. Her father was the assistant to the president and her mother was a professor in the music department.[67] Johnson spent two years at Oglethorpe for second and fourth grades; she had been allowed to skip third grade. According to Johnson, one of her teachers recommended Westminster, and Aaron Johnson commented that he and his wife wanted Joia to be more academically challenged, despite the financial sacrifice of affording Westminster's tuition.[68]

Joia and the other black students would continue to experience racial harassment. For the younger students, this often meant their first encounters with racism. Joia vividly recalled,

> It was the first time I can remember name-calling about race and so that was just a big shock, and that was in the fifth grade and it was on the basketball court. You know it's the kind of thing you never forget. I was on the basketball court and there was another girl whose name I remember but I will leave out. . . . I think I stole the basketball from her or something and she didn't like that and she called me "a little

black sambo nigger." All of it in one. . . . We got into a fight and my mother had to come down to the school because you know it was my first year there.[69]

According to Johnson, both students were reprimanded. From this experience, Johnson came to understand "that there were people who would, you know, sort of denigrate you for your color."[70] Johnson did not recall other blatant racial incidents from her initial years at Westminster, but she spoke of a particular feeling that she would have: "It's just a feeling that you have when you're just an outsider."[71] Johnson experienced the effects of how white students used negative body language and racially charged humor around black students. This feeling of not belonging stood in stark contrast to Johnson's welcoming environment in the black community where she participated in her local Jack and Jill youth group, attended First Congregational Church, and enjoyed Spelman's campus.

Dawn and Ron, now both in the sixth grade, began to think about their experiences in different ways. Clark's feeling of being an outsider started to subside slightly. She recalled, "I had come to an appreciation of having the right to be there, and no one had the right to tell me anything else. But that was a process for me that took me a couple of years of being there and dealing with it every day . . . also by the time I was in sixth grade I realized what my parents were trying to do. First couple of years, I did not get it."[72] Dawn had endured racism as the first black girl to desegregate the younger grades, but as she settled into Westminster and more black girls joined her, she became more comfortable. Outside activities such as Girl Scouts with other black girls also helped, and she remained anchored by her parents, family, and larger black community.

Ron felt that he was living in two different worlds and acting differently in those worlds. He recalled that at school he "was a smart, skinny, 'nerd,' non-athlete." Back in his home neighborhood, he played sports and socialized. Some neighborhood children would denigrate other youth, including him, about how they spoke "proper" and did not "trash talk" on the basketball court. And although being smart did not always hold sway, on one particular night a young man older than Ron stopped giving him a hard time when he learned that Ron was a good student.[73] For Ron, "the upside of 'living in two worlds'" gave him "a very clear understanding from an early age of what things had to do with the particular environment and what things didn't." Navigating the world of home and school was an important part of Ron's early years as a student at Westminster. His experiences in both, or his double-consciousness, remained interconnected with how he understood himself in relation to others in terms of race, gender, and physical size. Often, he felt his physical size was a more significant factor in any harassment he experienced whether at school or in his home neighborhood. He faced challenges in both arenas, but seemingly found ways to cope with the challenges and to succeed.

In the upper grades, Malcolm, Wanda, Jannard, and Michael continued to grapple with race and racism, while finding even more ways to become a part of the Westminster community. The harassment Malcolm Ryder experienced as a freshman living in the dormitory negatively affected the fall semester of his sophomore year, but he would find an outlet that set him on a course for success during the spring of sophomore year. Having earlier retreated into a personal shell, he had sought solace in academics and thought that doing well academically would help him solidify an identity at Westminster.[74] Ryder came to realize that "getting good grades wasn't actually proving anything. . . . It didn't make anything else better. So I had played my ace and got nothing back in return, and just was lost . . . and I didn't want to go back [after Christmas break]."[75] But his mother insisted that he return to Westminster, and a white young woman living in the dormitory invited him to a chorale rehearsal. From that point forward, his experience changed dramatically. Ryder played the piano and was in the Westminster band, yet he had never thought of himself as a singer: "My mom and dad, both true artists, had sent me off in life with the predisposition to be an artist, but oddly I had just been going through the motions. I knew how to play piano because I was made to take piano lessons from day one, and all these things were just givens in the family. So I wasn't actually connected to it emotionally. [Frank] Boggs [director of the chorale] connected me to it emotionally, and then it just seemed like it was like somebody gave me the keys to the bank."[76]

Unlike the band—which Ryder described as a young orchestra, serious, and something he understood by training—he characterized the chorale by its energy and camaraderie. According to Ryder, "The chorale was a whole different thing. It was extremely social, and I think it was the most casual, yet developed group I'd ever been a member of." Boggs also infused the group with an infectious spirit:

He just had a belief in himself that no matter who you were if you didn't already know how to sing he could teach you to sing, and that singing was going to be the greatest thing that ever happened to you. That was the spirit that he had infused this whole outfit with so that whether you were in rehearsal, or at a concert, or just awake in the middle of the night, or standing in a bus stop or something, you had this feeling that he gave you that you could just sing and everything would be fine.[77]

Ryder adopted this spirit, and he found himself with new friends, new energy, and always busy with music. "Just this explosion of energy, all of it very upbeat. So it was a tremendous kind of breakaway and a chance to just reboot and start all over again at this place." Ryder became emotionally connected to music and even more so to his father's music because of Boggs's interest in it. According to Ryder, "So all these connections started happening, and he inspired me and challenged me at the same time."[78]

Other students would also speak of chorale in favorable ways. Having come from black communities and schools with deep ethics of care, black students responded to Boggs's leadership. Educational scholar Jacqueline Jordan Irvine, in discussing her more contemporary work with urban teachers, remarked that "students indicated that caring teachers laughed with them, trusted and respected them, and recognized them as individuals. . . . Students defined caring teachers as those who set limits, provided structure, had high expectations, and pushed them to achieve."[79] Boggs embodied these characteristics as he drew on a wide variety of music for the students to perform.

Other white teachers also drew on attributes of a care ethic as a way of supporting black student experiences. Jannard Wade fondly remembered Coach Sims, his soccer coach, and Sims's wife. Coach Sims, an early proponent of soccer, recruited football players who had never played soccer and taught them the game. According to Wade, Coach Sims was "just a great teacher and really took the time to teach us the skills so that we could become a decent soccer team."[80] Similarly, important to Wanda Ward's success on the basketball court was her coach, Sam Van Leer. She recalled, "He didn't pamper any of us but sort of recognized the talent. So if he recognized any talent, he would drive you, drive you, drive you."[81] Ward also has maintained contact with her chemistry teacher, Martha Thurmond, whom she described as "no nonsense" and chiefly concerned about her students getting the "'work right.'"[82] These particular white teachers and coaches helped Westminster to become an institution where black students could succeed, and by being supportive of all students, including their black students, they in part helped to shift the institutional culture because they were helping black students find ways to thrive.

Being a part of chorale launched a new persona for Ryder and a new start at Westminster. He came to recognize that many students were involved in many different facets of campus, and he would be no exception. Ryder stated, "I had my own routine, but it was very mixed. I was comfortable, but not because there was huge amount of repetition or simplification. It was kind of the opposite." Ryder became more outgoing, and Westminster "went from being kind of a terrible place . . . to being some place really wonderful." However, "Not every day was great. There was still plenty to complain about, but I just felt on top of it. Just on top of the school, the whole place . . . I felt like I had a lot of friends, so it was very supportive. The feedback was constant and generally pretty good. There was a lot of reward for being involved, involved with people and involved with different organizations."[83]

Sophomore year also brought changes for Jannard Wade and Wanda Ward. Wade, also a musician, developed into a standout all-around athlete on the varsity football, soccer, and baseball teams, and participated in the Fellowship of Christian Athletes.[84] Ward also excelled as a sophomore in academics, leadership, and sports, but the beginning of the year had brought new circumstances.[85] When Ward's family felt the financial toll of sending her to Westminster, her mother considered pulling her out, but Pressly and others offered Wanda a full scholarship to continue through high school. Just as importantly, Janice Kemp, the only other black girl in Wanda's grade, left following ninth grade. Kemp's departure profoundly affected Ward because for two years Janice and she could rely on one another in the girls' school, and after Janice left, Wanda's experience was "not peaches and cream." Ward believed that, in the eighth and ninth grades, Kemp and she both adjusted well to the academics at Westminster. The difference, in her estimation, was social integration. Ward, who earned her PhD in psychology, believed that she was "more integrated into the school socially," and that her being "an avid athlete and a leader in student government made the critical difference."[86]

The culture in the upper grades included certain teachers like Boggs, who supported and encouraged black students. The culture also included more inclusion of black life and culture in the academic curriculum. The experiences of African Americans were primarily addressed in English and history courses, both from the perspective of novels such as *Black Like Me* and *Cry, the Beloved Country* and from prowhite southern positions.[87] In 1969, a one-semester course, "The Negro in American History," was added to the girls' school curriculum. Taught by Ellen Fleming, the class sought to expand students' understanding of black history, contributions by black Americans, and the relevance and longevity of the freedom struggle. Fleming also wanted "to deepen student's understanding of the social sciences by pointing out the manifold nature of man, by fostering comprehension among people to overcome ethnocentrism, and to show American growth and limitations during various periods."[88]

While black students navigated their new school environments, white Westminster students continued their community service efforts, including tutoring, improving the Army Church in Vine City in collaboration with Morris Brown College students, and operating a wholesale grocery store with a student group from The Temple. In December 1969, the Vine City group invited to Westminster a group of students from Harper High School, a predominantly black public high school located in the Collier Heights neighborhood.[89] The stated purpose of the visit was "to better racial understanding among the youth in order to improve the problems between blacks and whites as they grow older."[90] Some Westminster students seemed genuinely interested in serving the community. For example, in January 1969, in a letter to the editor, the writer urged more students to volunteer in Vine City. Yet once more, the reasons for going to Vine City resonated with the era's white liberalism and stereotypes of black individuals. As one student wrote, "The answer to the 'why go down' question is easy. The ghetto child is born with a load to carry. This load, the one Vine City Project is interested in, is the one of poverty. Because of this poverty, they feel they are born to failure. . . . Their parents have other things on their minds than their children, but even without parental motivation, these kids are willing to work hard to learn. It is through learning that they will relieve and possibly get rid of the burden of poverty. They need all the help they can get."[91]

Despite these cross-cultural exchanges, the institutional culture remained one of progress and resistance. The slave auction continued through 1969, and in March 1970, as part of the Mardi Gras celebration, the freshman class float was described as "Dixie in the 1860s." Although the float came in fourth place, the class skit, "As Easy as Whistling Dixie," won first place.[92] Students harkening back to the antebellum and postantebellum eras of the United States showed their affinity for the Old South and how such culture remained embedded at Westminster as black students began to matriculate. Simultaneously, Westminster hosted black speakers, including William Borders and Vernon Jordan.[93] These events highlighted Westminster's culture and how the culture included space for events and activities that yielded to racist ideology and deficit discourse but that also presented opportunities to learn from and embrace the then leaders championing racial equality.

By the end of the 1969-70 school year, a total of sixteen black students had entered Westminster. Some of the first students had experienced racial harassment directly and indirectly; because of the small numbers, isolation was a factor. The slight increase in the number of black students during the first years of desegregation seemed to help, even if the black students were not close friends with one another. Westminster leadership did invite black speakers to campus, but the first black teacher was not hired until the early 1970s.

As the numbers of black students attending elite independent schools increased, NAIS began to grapple with questions of how best to support these students. In "The Black Student in the White Independent School," published in February 1969, Linda McLean, then associate director of the merged ABC and ISTSP programs, reported that "more than 1200 students have entered 110 ABC Schools, and 150 graduates have entered 102 colleges and universities."[94] Based on her observations and visits to ABC-ISTSP member schools, McLean addressed the effects of large and small numbers of black students on campus, areas of difficulties for girls at boarding schools, and the needs of black students on white campuses. McLean suggested that from students' perspectives that "when there are two or three black students in a school of a few hundred, the effects of their presence are minimal. They may be hardly noticed, as they 'fit in,' or they may be singled out for special treatment or attention." In contrast, McLean noted that psychological and behavioral options increase when the number of black students increased. McLean wrote, "Behaviorally, they are able to *contribute* something to schools as a significant group" as for example through programming related to "the black experience." McLean also believed that students will feel "more comfortable about 'being themselves.'"[95]

Accordingly, the psychological options were deemed more significant with increased numbers of black students because "primarily students are not then *psychologically intimidated*." McLean further wrote, "In a school where there are a few black students, they often feel pressure to spread themselves around. They sometimes are afraid to be seen in a group of two or three because they stand out and people accuse them of 'grouping together' or isolating themselves. More important, very often a school either *resents* this association of blacks or feels guilty if its black students are together. I am constantly presented with the statement: 'Since this black power thing, all the Negro students stay together.'" She encouraged schools "not only to reduce the psychological intimidation, but to enable black students to develop their personalities naturally and to establish and maintain their identities." She also suggested, "After all, most of the students will eventually be returning to an all-black world, and it would certainly be dysfunctional for schools to turn out products who cannot be accepted in the white world completely, and who are no longer functioning members of the black community."[96]

In addressing the needs of black young women, McLean pointed to three areas: academic adjustment, hair care, and dating. She observed that many girls had begun wearing Afros, both because of the era and the convenience and because often dorm mothers and fellow students did not understand about black hair care and processes. Problems with dating arose "1) because dating is usually assigned and 2) because students are not free to take off on weekends and find their own dates." With more black young men wanting to date black young women, the problem was apparently solved. Yet, McLean reminded readers, "It should be remembered that while academic pursuit is a student's first aim in attending school, if your social life is on the downswing, it is difficult to concentrate on academics." Finally, she recommended the importance of having black faculty at independent schools: "Most independent schools continue, almost in vain, to try to attract black faculty. However, the compensation and attractions available have been major stumbling blocks in making this a successful endeavor. Nevertheless, upon visiting our students, we have found that they desperately need the guidance, advice, attention, and presence of more qualified black faculty and residents. The students almost burst in animated excitement and pour out all of their feelings to any black person who comes to campus."[97]

These issues were not just isolated to participating schools in the ABC-ISTSP program. McLean's article provides insight for considering the experiences of students in a southern context. Although all the black students at Westminster were not necessarily close friends, the slightly enlarged number of black students attending Westminster may have helped to boost the spirits of students like Dawn and helped all students to excel inside and outside the classroom. Westminster had yet to hire a black teacher, but there were nods to black life, culture, and history through the additional course and guest speakers. There was not a space or club designated specifically for black students at Westminster, but the day students had both support at school and home which helped them to navigate the Westminster culture. More, however, needed to be done institutionally.

In the fall of 1969, NAIS took an additional step in offering support to black students by desegregating its office staff. President Cary Potter hired the first director of minority affairs, Dr. William Dandridge, an African American and, at that time, a twenty-nine-year-old teacher from Philadelphia. The son of an African Methodist Episcopal (AME) minister, Dandridge grew up in Pennsylvania in locations such as Monongahela, Pittsburgh, Lancaster, and Philadelphia. He attended high school in Philadelphia, completed his undergraduate work at Pennsylvania State University-University Park, and taught in Philadelphia. Dandridge recalled his first teaching experience, "In college, my first teaching assignment was in South Philadelphia and it overlapped with my father's parish so I worked with the kids both personally as well as professionally, and some of the children in the school were also members of my father's church. So they knew I wasn't going home at night because that was home."[98] When Dandridge met Cary Potter, then president of NAIS, he had decided to leave teaching, though his trajectory was pointing him in the direction of becoming a principal and eventually a superintendent. He remembered his chance meeting with Potter: "Cary's words were, 'Well, why don't you come with me just for three years? If you don't like it, you can come back and pick up with where you are now.' Somehow I didn't get back."[99] On November 1, 1969, Dandridge became the first African American NAIS staff member and the first director of minority affairs for NAIS, then headquartered in Boston.

Prior to working at NAIS, Dandridge was not familiar with independent schools, including the independent schools he often passed in Philadelphia. He stated, "I drove by Germantown Friends, Chestnut Hill Academy, all these schools, and never knew about them. . . . Then I go to NAIS, the chair of the minority affairs committee is Henry Scattergood, the head of Germantown Friends, and I'm saying 'Is that what this is all about? This is what these schools offer.' No one was talking to people of color about independent schools."[100] Dandridge became interested in working for NAIS because he was intrigued to work with Potter. He recollected,

His life history seemed a big puzzle to me, why he was so personally interested and committed to this issue of diversity. I could find nothing in his background that would give you a clue in terms of what led him to provide the leadership for this. . . . He was a quiet, dignified person, so he was not someone who was out beating the stump, and my sense of it was he felt that the Association needed to

lead by example if it was going to sort of make the case with its
membership. . . . The need to open their doors not only to children
of color, but to adults of color in all kinds of positions.[101]

As Dandridge settled into his new role, Reverend Canon John T. Walker,
then chaplain at St. Paul's School and later dean at the Washington National
Cathedral, became the first African American NAIS board member in 1970.
Black men had broken barriers at NAIS, and their presence and work would
begin to change the conversations in NAIS about race. NAIS still, however,
had not moved from its 1968 position to deny membership to schools with
discriminatory admissions policies, but continued challenges to federal
tax-exemption status would supersede NAIS's position.

IN THE MIDST OF these national, local, and institutional changes, the first
African American students used everything in their backpacks to navigate
Westminster. The first black students drew on their priceless inheritances,
their own schooling experiences, their intellect, their talents, and their
work ethic. Some black students did not stay at Westminster after enrolling
during the first years of desegregation. That they left does not mean that
they were not equipped to navigate Westminster's complex culture and to
succeed academically and in extracurricular activities. During the first years
of desegregation, the first black students did endure racism, yet they also
found some white students willing to connect with them and white teachers
and coaches who demonstrated great care.

In the coming years, Pressly's intriguing, changing position on race and
equality over nearly two decades ultimately earned him an opportunity to
speak to national policymakers. More black students enrolled at Westminster including the first black young women to live in the girls' dormitory.
The first black students would also graduate but not without speaking about
the racism and paradoxical culture at Westminster and about their experiences. How they succeeded and responded to their experiences grounded
their courageous navigation of a new school environment.

CHAPTER FIVE

Courageous Navigation

Nineteen more black students entered Westminster in the late 1960s and early 1970s, bringing the total number of African Americans who enrolled to thirty-five during the first years of school desegregation. As the number of black students grew and after the 1969 mayoral election, local politics shifted; in effect, the shift ended the once firm alliance between white businessmen on Atlanta's north side, including supporters of Westminster, and black businessmen and pragmatic civil rights leaders who pursued a gradual approach to desegregation. Atlantans elected Sam Massell, a prominent businessman, as mayor of Atlanta; he would be the first Jewish man to hold the position. The majority of local citizens also voted for Maynard Jackson; he became the city's first African American vice mayor. When Michael McBay, Malcolm Ryder, Jannard Wade, and Wanda Ward graduated from Westminster in 1972, Jackson was in the midst of what would be a successful mayoral campaign. By 1973, efforts at public school desegregation in the city basically ended. The majority of students attending Atlanta Public Schools (APS) were African American, and local National Association for the Advancement of Colored People (NAACP) members compromised by opting for more local control of the school district rather than using busing as a mechanism for desegregation since many whites had moved out of the city.

The students who entered Westminster and other independent schools during these years joined a group of black Americans who gained access to educational institutions that historically educated members of the white power structure and that reflected and reinforced the inequities of the larger society. By 1970, independent school leaders were confident enough in their progress to recruit black students to further argue what they believed to be their distinction from segregationist academies, especially when the Internal Revenue Service (IRS) required private institutions with tax-exemption status to have nondiscriminatory admissions policies. Pressly, president of Westminster and an appointee in 1969 to a newly established National Association of Independent Schools (NAIS) Committee on Governmental Relations, became a spokesperson on the differences between independent schools and segregationist academies. His presence in the national independent school community linked Westminster once more to national conversations about race, access, and equity.[1]

As black Americans and their lawyers sought legal remedies to enforce public school desegregation, black Americans also questioned the tax-exemption status of segregationist academies. By 1970, the Southern Regional Council estimated that 500,000 students attended segregationist academies, which was an increase of 100,000 just from the previous year.[2] In Mississippi, the Council School Foundation, "formed by the Citizens Council in response to the passage of the Civil Rights Act of 1964," operated segregationist academies.[3] Black Mississippians challenged the tax-exemption status of segregationist academies in *Green v. Kennedy* (1970), a case filed against David M. Kennedy, secretary of the treasury, and Randolph W. Thrower, commissioner of the IRS. The black plaintiffs questioned "whether or not the federal tax benefits normally conferred on private schools by sections 501 and 170 of the Internal Revenue Code of 1954 are valid when such schools are racially segregated."[4] Just the year prior, in *Coffey v. State Educational Finance Commission* (1969), "the court held unconstitutional state tuition grants, provided by the legislature of Mississippi by bills adopted in 1964 and amended in 1968, to Mississippi children attending private, segregated schools."[5] Drawing on the *Coffey* ruling, the court in *Green v. Kennedy* stated "that the tax benefits under the Internal Revenue Code mean a substantial and significant support by the Government to the segregated private school pattern" and "constitutes a derogation of constitutional rights."[6] With this decision, the court granted a temporary injunction and, in June 1970, a permanent injunction against the IRS from providing tax-exemption status to private institutions with discriminatory admissions policies.

That same summer, Pressly and Reese Cleghorn, director of the Leadership Project of the Southern Regional Council, testified before the Senate's Select Committee on Equal Educational Opportunity chaired by Senator Walter F. Mondale. Cleghorn argued that segregationist academies were "concentrated in certain areas and undermine the public schools." He also stated, "We cannot lightly dismiss any development which deprives large numbers of white children of good educations and frequently exposes them to anti-democratic nostrums and preachments; and which further postpones the South's coming to grips with the fact that it is a bi-racial society wherein both whites and blacks are deprived by the social and economic costs of separatism."[7] Cleghorn contended that how the South moved forward hinged on the quality of education afforded in a changing society.

The *Brown* decision implicated black children as the only ones negatively affected by segregation, but here Cleghorn seemed to suggest resistance to school desegregation harmed white children.

In his testimony, Pressly discussed that independent schools were part of a dual education system, which in his estimation, was a rationale for not supporting segregationist academies. Pressly stated, "Believing in both systems, then, we do not think that either ought to be segregated. Segregated independent schools, like segregated public schools, defy the ruling of the Supreme Court. Furthermore, such schools cannot prepare girls and boys for life in a country that wants to offer equal opportunity for all." Pressly's testimony clearly linked independent schools to the *Brown* decision, although the decision did not apply to independent schools. But he had evolved to see that segregation in any school setting hindered young people.

Pressly also spoke about the process of increasing open enrollment through admissions policies in independent schools. When NAIS declared the open enrollment policy in 1968, NAIS leaders did not necessarily drop schools with discriminatory practices from membership. Pressly now believed that the leadership was ready to reverse that policy. Pressly issued a strong challenge to segregationist academies by critiquing what he considered their low level of academic rigor, inadequate facilities, and underprepared teachers. He suggested that the low cost of tuition did not generate enough revenue to properly operate the schools.[8] Pressly also stated that proposals were being considered in Georgia "for the licensing of non-accredited independent schools." He concluded by suggesting the federal government needed to ensure integrated, adequate, and equal education in both public and private schools. The following year, in 1971, the IRS stipulated that private schools with racially discriminatory policies would not receive federal tax-exemption status.[9] The new tax-exemption policy firmly connected private schools with public policy, and NAIS could now rely on this tax-exemption status stipulation to enforce membership requirements.

Pressly, a southern *and* national independent school leader, now called for the equalization of schools on the brink of a new federal tax-exemption policy. When he became founding president of Westminster in 1951, he did not speak publicly against segregation. Nearly twenty years later, his position changed following the admission of black students at his own institution and as he continued to participate in national discussions about race in independent schools. Understanding Pressly's turnaround requires understanding the influence of context, the larger political and social changes, and the relationships school leaders had with stakeholders.

The constellation of factors that converged in the 1950s and 1960s created three incentives for independent school leaders. First the civil rights movement, the desire to be on the right side of history and not to be like segregationist academies, and the sense of noblesse oblige created a moral incentive for independent school leaders to respond to public matters. Second, maintaining the stature and growth of elite private schools and the threat of losing federal tax-exemption presented a financial incentive. Positioning their schools for success in a shifting U.S. society in which Jim Crow laws had been overturned offered a third incentive, as independent school leaders had long been concerned with public relations and their academic position in relationship to institutions of higher education, some of which desegregated or began to value racial diversification at the time.

Although independent school leaders acted on these incentives, institutional change at the school level was not immediate, and a push and pull between progress and regression continued. Nationally, there appeared to be progress. Though NAIS publications did little to address the experiences of black students who desegregated southern elite private schools, NAIS publications did offer more coverage of black students' experiences more generally. William Dandridge, the newly hired director of minority affairs, began to craft his network of black and white allies to advance a more equitable racial agenda within NAIS. Some independent schools outside of the South opened African American clubs and centers to accommodate the new students. For example, Choate and NAIS jointly sponsored the Choate Afro-American Resource Center; the center was also funded by a grant from the Henry Luce Foundation.[10] But, the culture of schools like Westminster remained thorny. Although white individual faculty and students were helpful to black students, black students continued to rely heavily on their backpacks, one another, black workers, and black communities to courageously navigate the space. In the coming years, they began to address more directly the troubling aspects of Westminster's culture and broke new barriers. Through their presence, involvement, and academic and extracurricular success, the first black students at Westminster countered old beliefs about the academic capabilities of black students and propelled institutional change.

Black Students Speak Back

As the 1970s began at Westminster, the black students continued to negotiate and to embody how students could be their own individuals. McBay,

Ryder, Wade, and Ward, now eleventh graders, were excelling as new students joined them. Among the five new black students who were set to enroll the following year was Corliss Blount, one of two of the first black female boarding students. Blount, like her other black peers, came from a two-parent working family. Her father, Louis Blount Jr., had worked as a police officer in Houston, Texas, for nearly twenty-one years after being a member of the first police academy class to include black men. Similar to other early black police officers, Louis Blount and the others faced restrictions such as being prohibited from arresting white individuals.[11] Louis and his wife, Lucille, were also entrepreneurs, who over time owned an Exxon gas station, a security business, a wrecker service, and a school bus transportation business.

As with other black students, what occurred in Corliss's community positively impacted her development. Corliss grew up in Houston's Third Ward close to both the University of Houston, a majority white institution, and Texas Southern University, a historically black university. She remembered her house as the location where everyone in the neighborhood liked to gather, in large part because her mother was a wonderful cook. Corliss enjoyed her experiences at neighborhood segregated black schools where she did well academically. Her teachers held her to high standards, and she was a student in the gifted and talented program. These experiences while growing up constituted her version of the priceless inheritance.

Because of her academic achievement—Corliss graduated from junior high as class valedictorian—and her involvement with Student Council, the dance club, the science club, and Girl Scouts, she was an ideal candidate for the Stouffer Foundation scholarship. John Ehle of the Stouffer Foundation recognized the importance of not allowing Corliss to desegregate the girls' dormitory by herself. By spring 1970, the Stouffer Foundation supported sixty-one students at eleven different schools throughout the South, and the Stouffer Foundation had received additional funding to support young women.[12] Upon receiving the Stouffer Foundation scholarship, the foundation leadership invited Corliss and other recipients to visit Westminster. Corliss was joined by Karen Meeks, another Stouffer Foundation scholarship recipient from Greenville, Mississippi, on a visit to Westminster. Prior to their visit, Ehle communicated with Don Westmoreland, principal of the girls' school at Westminster, and he addressed how the Stouffer Foundation did not want a black girl to desegregate the dorms by herself. He wrote, "Please like the girls as best you can and make your decision as you choose and let me know. If you do not like one of them or one doesn't like your school, we will try to help you find another one. We cannot, however, Don, as I mentioned last spring in our conversation, leave one Negro girl there to integrate the dormitory alone."[13] By this time, the Stouffer Foundation was most likely aware of how white students racially harassed black students, including some of their recipients, living in dormitories at historically white elite private schools in the South. This letter apparently was a precaution to avoid such future occurrences. The visit went well for Blount and Meeks, and they began at Westminster in the fall of 1970. Although Corliss's father was at first reluctant to let her leave home, Corliss welcomed the opportunity. Corliss ultimately understood that something bigger was at stake: "It was about the good that could come out of it."[14]

Occurrences at Westminster continued to reflect how Westminster leaders may not have known how to proceed through desegregation. When Blount began at Westminster, she "didn't feel like [she] had the weight of all black people on [her] shoulders." She was not angry or trying to make a statement. In her words, "I just think, overall, my parents had raised us to be well behaved and well mannered, and to take what life gives you and take advantage of it and do your best. I tried to do that." Yet her presence did make a statement. After moving into the dorm, Jan Reece, a white student from Duluth, Georgia, told Corliss about a meeting held the day before Karen and Corliss arrived at the dorm. According to Blount, "everybody else had been told to come the day before" we arrived. The white students were informed that two new girls were due the next day. They "were different" but students should not be "afraid."[15] Corliss said, "I'll never, ever forget that." That Westminster leaders thought it best to assuage white young women first rather than new black young women signaled the school's priorities, its culture of whiteness, and the lack of consciousness about how such actions might affect Corliss and Karen. Surely, administrators, faculty, and staff knew that students would talk about coming a day early and that Corliss and Karen would learn about the white students' early arrival.

Blount did not experience the same blatant racial harassment as Malcolm Ryder. She said, "There were a few that were curious. There were a few that were maybe a little wary. Then there were some that just genuinely didn't care." Blount suspected that the older dorm mother was uncomfortable. According to Corliss, "You could tell that probably, given a choice, she would not have embraced that. I don't think she had a choice. She knew there were a few more years before retirement." Corliss described a younger dorm mother who was "with the times and it was not an issue."[16]

Although Corliss Blount did not experience overt racial harassment, race certainly informed her experience. She and Jan became friends and roommates by the end of Corliss's first semester, despite the negative reaction of Jan's grandmother. Corliss recalled, "When her grandmother found out about it—in the expression of the day—she took to her bed, refusing food, and sent for Jan to come and see her. When Jan went to visit, she basically signed a blank check and told her that she could fill in any amount to move out of the room with me. Jan turned her down. I was like 'Why? We could have had. . . .' It was funny. It was very funny."[17] That the girls could laugh about Jan's grandmother disclosed the girls' close friendship. How white students dealt with parents and grandparents as they became friends with black students bared generational differences, although these differences did not necessarily absolve younger white students from holding negative notions about their black classmates and black America broadly.

As Corliss settled into life at Westminster, she and the other black students were active members of the student body. The 1971 yearbook listed black students on the honor roll and as members of the German club, Spanish club, and ecology club. They served on the Service Council Board and were members of the quest club. They played basketball, football, soccer, and baseball. Black students enjoyed singing in chorale, acting in the drama club, and performing in the band.[18] Of note, the American Friends Service selected Wanda Ward to travel abroad the summer of 1971 to Switzerland.[19]

The school newspaper reflected students engaged in the politics of the day. The paper covered Andrew Young's congressional race (the editorial board even offered their endorsement of Young) and the Vinings group continued as well.[20] On the other hand, the slave auction fundraiser was not mentioned in the Bi-Line or pictured in the Lynx. There was no discussion of the end of the slave auction fundraiser in the Bi-Line or the Lynx either, but the fundraiser being discontinued implied that individuals recognized that the event invoked the history of U.S. slavery and racism and that it needed to stop because black students now attended Westminster.

The era in which the black students found themselves, however, was still very clearly racially, politically, and socially charged. As high school students, Blount, Ryder, Wade, and Ward became more and more politically conscious. African American students desegregating previously all-white schools "faced enormous pressures," stated historian Gael Graham. She continued, "They had to get along with the white students, succeed academically, and serve as representatives of their race, all the while knowing that one misstep would have the white community shaking its collective head."[21]

Jannard Wade (seated), who was a stellar athlete, also enjoyed being a musician. In this candid shot, Malcolm Ryder, who enjoyed participating in chorale, and Jannard are having a jam session. Source: *Lynx* (Yearbook), 1971, 234, RG 21.03, Beck Archives-Westminster.

Graham argued that with the coming of Black Power, African American students in newly desegregated schools "became the arbiters of race and racism" and "white students lost the comparative advantage they had enjoyed in the early days of desegregation."[22] Unlike the other African American students, Michael McBay became one of those "arbiters of race and racism." As Malcolm Ryder stated, "Michael . . . was the radical . . . he did force us, I think, to be in touch, to get in touch if we weren't already."[23]

Researchers have noted that black high school students' social activism in the late 1960s and early 1970s took a variety of forms, including organizing school boycotts, starting underground newspapers, and participating in antiwar protests.[24] Michael McBay's writings and drawings in the school newspaper reflected the social activism of young people in the late 1960s and early 1970s. Throughout his junior year, McBay drew political cartoons to accompany news articles on important issues such as the teachers' dress code, grades in physical education, required attendance at school assemblies, and politics.[25] Michael McBay was very explicit in his protests. He was really disturbed by the culture of the school, including how white faculty and staff might not have been able to tell black students apart from each other; by the subtle racism that mired the campus; and by the fact that whites greeted black staff members differently than their white counterparts. He challenged white and black students to be aware of the climate in which they were attending school and of the world around them.

At the end of his junior year, McBay penned "McBay Voices Black Frustrations" in the *Bi-Line*. He asked, "How often do you see adults of your race, commanded like children cringe with an obedient 'Yes ma'am,' and then scurry to perform their assigned errands? . . . How often are you mistaken for Malcolm Ryder? Not often I should guess, unless you are a member of the minute black percentile of the Westminster student body." Through his political cartoon, McBay illustrated this point by presenting a common exchange between a black male student and a white female librarian. The exchange flowed as follows:

LIBRARIAN: Let's see now, Malcolm, our library list says you owe $2.35!
STUDENT: I'm not Malcolm!
LIBRARIAN: Oh well then, Isaac, you owe us 78 cents.
STUDENT: I'm not Isaac!
LIBRARIAN: Well then, Mike, you owe 4 cents.
STUDENT: I'm not Mike!
LIBRARIAN: Well, Jannard . . .
STUDENT: I'm not Jannard!
LIBRARIAN: Then who are you?
STUDENT: I'm Dante, Just Back from Hell!!

McBay also reminded African American students to be aware of the "subtle hostilities." He continued, "These are atrocities which should be abhorrent to your very natures, i.e. the witnessing of these affronts." McBay also questioned how the Westminster community addressed and treated black and white workers. White students, teachers, and administrators interacted regularly with African Americans, but not on the basis of equality. He asked, "Why is Mrs. Nixon [a white worker] "Mrs. Nix," while Betty [African American] is Betty"? Why is Gladys [African American], "Gladys," while Mrs. Nonie [white] is "Mrs. Nonie?" McBay questioned the language

Michael McBay, who withstood racial harassment on his very first day at Westminster in 1967, became one of the most outspoken students on campus in the early 1970s. As a writer and illustrator for the *Westminster Bi-Line*, Michael addressed the racial culture and racism apparent at Westminster and other school matters and broader societal issues, such as busing and Angela Davis's activism, and he reviewed albums of his favorite musical groups. Pictured here is Michael's depiction of a conversation between a school librarian and black male students at Westminster. Source: Michael McBay, "McBay Voices Black Frustrations," *Westminster Bi-Line*, June 5, 1971, RG 21.06, Beck Archives-Westminster.

used by Pressly when discussing workers at the school. "Dr. Pressly, why does our 'Physical Facilities Staff' become 'colored workers' when you address white peers, but quickly switches to 'black workers' when you address blacks?" With regard to the school's admissions policy, he asked, "Is it true that there is a maximum quota on the number of blacks accepted in our school?" McBay concluded his article, "[A]s I have stated before, these things are not wanton acts of oppression to be up in arms about, and the only way to meet them is to **outlast** them with resolve."[26]

Despite the subtle discriminatory behavior and overt hostility McBay observed and experienced, he had persevered. He had enough resolve to move forward after his eighth-grade year to excel academically and to find his niche in the campus community. He used the school newspaper as an avenue to raise questions about the culture of Westminster—the very culture that allowed his initial racial harassment. Like his counterparts across the country who agitated and advocated for better experiences on historically white campuses, McBay directly addressed the inequities that he believed characterized Westminster and thus the inequities that administrators, faculty, staff, and students absorbed as normal. His article pointed to what he believed needed to change. McBay's actions and words actually mirrored a growing realization among national independent school leaders as they made plans to increase their efforts to address the quality of the black student experience across independent schools. The leadership increasingly recognized that schools needed to move beyond admitting a few token students and to increase their focus on the recruitment of black teachers, administrators, and trustees.

During his initial years at NAIS, Dandridge began to recognize what needed to occur as he worked with the NAIS leadership team headed by President Cary Potter. When Dandridge entered NAIS, the executive staff was comprised of Cary Potter, president; John Chandler Jr., vice president; David Mallery, director of studies; John P. Downing, business manager; Frank R. Miller, director of administrative services; Adele Q. Ervin, staff associate; Esther E. Osgood, director of publications; Wellington Y. Grimes, director of academic services; Richard P. Thomsen, Washington representative; and Edward Yeomans, associate director for academic services. Wellington Grimes served as Dandridge's mentor by showing hospitality to the Dandridge family, partnering with Dandridge on travel trips for NAIS, encouraging him to move up the ranks in NAIS, and inviting him to attend the Teacher Services Committee.[27] Key board members during Dandridge's first year were Ben Snyder, then director of special and summer programs at the Cranbrook School in Detroit, Michigan, an independent school known for its Upward Bound program, and Howard L. Jones, then headmaster of the Northfield and Mount Hermon Schools in Massachusetts. When asked about the board's receptivity to him, Dandridge stated,

I think there were some board members who were more receptive than others and I think they were waiting to see how aggressive I was going to be. I'm not sure they knew what to expect, but a number of them, I think went out of their way to make sure that I felt comfortable and I felt welcomed in the group. They were wrestling with how to provide leadership without necessarily mandating and essentially they were moving toward a membership requirement that schools had to be on record as non-discriminatory in their admissions and trying to work through how do you support schools in making those transitions as opposed to mandating it and then perhaps losing members?[28]

While NAIS's goals and expectations were "broad and diffuse," it was clear to Dandridge that independent schools did not want to be seen as segregationist academies.[29] Dandridge believed that independent school leaders thought of their purpose and mission as more "legitimate" than the purpose and mission of segregationist academies. According to Dandridge, independent school leaders "saw themselves as providing a very nurturing and supportive educational development for the children they served. . . . So they saw themselves as being positive contributors to the education of American children and they saw the segregationist academies as being a cloud over all of them."[30] So a national priority became pushing member schools with closed admissions policies to change those policies; concurrently NAIS changed its membership requirement—all new schools now needed open admissions policies.

As Dandridge settled into his new role, he began asking the tough questions, because in his opinion, many in the independent school world had "no position on the question of diversity within their schools." He saw many stakeholders as being neutral. They were not necessarily "advocates for diversity, and they would only actively oppose it when it impacted their child directly."[31] Stakeholders also defined diversity primarily as "African American children and African American children from poor and disadvantaged neighborhoods." In response to this notion, Dandridge often asked those working in independent schools, "What makes you think that because you have provided an educational experience for children from very wealthy white families, you have the ability to do the same thing with an African American child from 120th Street in Harlem?"

Dandridge began questioning NAIS community members' assumptions about the African American community and African American students. Dandridge sought for "people to see the strengths that existed in those communities, that you could learn as much from the families and the people, and the agencies and the organizations. I tried to get them to understand that in your recruitment effort, if you want the support of black preachers and social workers and administrators—if you're talking about the community in which they live as though it is some kind of cesspool, that's not the way to build at all."[32] Because of these deeply embedded stereotypes and NAIS's need to focus on "the disadvantaged," NAIS leaders did not distinguish among African American children from different backgrounds. As

Dandridge stated, "when they were talking about minority students they were speaking more specifically about African American children, but African American children from poor communities and households." In Dandridge's estimation there was not enough dialogue or attention given to African Americans of all backgrounds, including those from different social classes.[33] Dandridge also inquired about the role of children as the propellers of change in independent schools. He recalled often asking: "How can you expect to serve children of color in isolation? Why are we expecting children of color to help lead the cultural change in the institution? Is this not the work that should be done by adults and adults of color? How were [white students to experience a diverse community] if they were never exposed to black adults in positions of authority and power?"[34] Dandridge, in essence, pushed those around him to realize that children should not be the only ones leading change. There needed to be more black administrators, board members, faculty, and staff in independent schools. Whites in independent schools needed to shed their biases, stereotypes, and misunderstandings of black America.

Dandridge's concerns and questions were reflected in *ISB*. In the fall of 1970, two articles followed up on an earlier piece, "Integrating the U.S. History Course: The Question of Balance," in which Ford Dixon called for the inclusion of more black history in the U.S. history curriculum. Agreeing with Ford, David G. Erdmann, chairman of the history department at Trinity-Pawling School in Pawling, New York, argued that including black history was important so that the "traditional myths concerning the Negro as held by whites and perpetuated in many textbooks" could be "closely examined if white America is ever to accept the black man as an equal."[35] He also contended about the importance of showing that African Americans were not passive prior to the twentieth century: "An objective account of the black man's chafing under slavery, a refutation of the myth that he was a docile slave in the hands of the master must be included in our history courses, if we are to achieve the proper balance." He further refuted the notion that African Americans made no contributions to U.S. society during and immediately after enslavement. Erdmann noted that white and black students needed to be instructed in how whites characterized African Americans as inferior because "only then shall we be able to break down the myths and eliminate the spirit of racism which still exists within in our society." Dandridge in "The Real Question of Balance" took up Dixon's concern. Dandridge suggested that black history and American history are inseparable and that the purpose of black history was the same as other history: "to retell the stories of the past, to glory in the nostalgia of one's heritage, and to create a positive image for ego building." Additionally, Dandridge argued that the inclusion of black history was important for an accurate understanding of history. He stated, "If minorities are to perceive their role in America and whites are to readjust their preconceived notion of minorities, the true story must be told."[36]

Reflections on the inclusion of black history indicated that NAIS leaders were contending with how whites had learned about African Americans through history textbooks and courses, and possibly how whites would interact with more black students in independent schools. Clearly, some southern white children had not thought very well of their first black classmates, and they acted accordingly. Even without overt racial harassment, black students still felt like outsiders. The NAIS leadership recognized this problem and turned its attention to both the quality of black students' experiences and the inclusion of more black individuals at all levels in the independent school world.

In a series of four articles, "Black Reflections of the Independent School," the black experience was considered from the perspective of Dandridge, black students, a black teacher, and a black trustee. An overriding theme in the series was that the black experience should not be tokenized and that black students wanted to belong and to be included but not to be expected to conform to white middle- and upper-class mores. As Dandridge stated, "Over the last few years, however, with a greater influx of blacks, there has been a major revolt, in which black students have rejected these prescribed roles and have begun to demonstrate their desire to create their own place in the school community." Similar to their counterparts in universities and colleges in the late 1960s and early 1970s, black students at independent schools were asserting themselves, and as Dandridge, just in his first year with NAIS, observed, "Many people are bewildered by the new attitude of black students and of the black community in general."[37] Dandridge challenged the notion that the admission of black students to independent schools was a reciprocal exchange between the students and the institution. With his utmost concern being that of the quality of the black student experience, he wrote, "At present, the institution is gaining substantially more from the presence of the black students than the black students are receiving in return from the institution."[38] Dandridge called for creative, open-minded thinking to address attitudes toward African Americans. He recognized the concern that black families and communities have in sending their children to independent schools, so he called for the inclusion of African Americans at all levels.

Four black students addressed not wanting to be seen as authorities on blackness, not always having similar interests as their white peers, needing time with other black students, and the mechanization of the academic curriculum. For the latter, Jean, one of the students, stated, "They teach us to relate to books. That's all they teach us. But they don't teach how to relate to people."[39] These four black students yearned for something more in their experiences at independent schools. In his reflection as a black alum of and teacher at Phillips Exeter Academy, E. L. Belton wrote from what he considered a unique perspective. He called on independent schools to ask themselves why they wanted a black teacher and shared the multiple issues that black teachers confront as they go about their work in the school.[40] In the final piece, the Reverend Canon John T. Walker, then a trustee of Milton Academy in Milton, Massachusetts, called for the importance of having black students, faculty, administrators, and board members, and he shared how a black board member or trustee can help the entire board understand matters of race. Yet he warned, "The Black Trustee is not a miracle man, and he may to some extent lose credibility by the very fact that he serves on the otherwise all-white Board of a school with token or near token black student representation."[41]

Together, these four articles illuminate how independent schools were dealing with race and the inclusion of more black students, and how black students and leaders responded. There was recognition that independent schools, like many of their public school counterparts, had participated in token desegregation practices. It was time to move on from such practices and to more robustly include more black students and more black adults in all aspects of the independent school community. The independent school culture had made black students feel the need to conform to the norms of historically white elite private schools. Dandridge and others realized that structural change needed to occur in schools. Though not explicitly stated, NAIS leaders more than likely believed that having more black teachers and administrators would provide a level of comfort for black students so that they could express themselves and be their own persons in such school environments. This national focus on race and the quality of experiences for black students was reflected in Westminster's complicated environment that Corliss Blount and Karen Meeks had experienced as new young black women living in the dormitory and that Michael McBay had illuminated through his contributions to the school newspaper. Black students had desegregated Westminster, and there were slight shifts in the institutional culture. Black workers also supported black students, but how Westminster leaders would address more directly the school culture, the need for black administrators and faculty, and the concerns posited by Dandridge and others, remained to be seen.

The Graduates

June 1972 would mark an important milestone—the graduation of Michael McBay, Malcolm Ryder, Jannard Wade, and Wanda Ward.[42] In their time at Westminster, they laid the groundwork for others to follow, and they achieved in a new school environment. A mixture of reasons kept them at Westminster during these initial years of desegregation, including their parents' commitment to schools with high academic standards, and they found ways, with the support of black and white individuals, to journey through a school culture not created with them in mind. They were part of a growing number of black students attending historically white elite private schools, albeit small in comparison to the number of black students enrolled in public schools. While the very role of independent schools in U.S. life may be questioned, black students and their families in the 1960s and 1970s continued to seek educational opportunities that might position them well in the larger society. Further, the state failed to implement public school desegregation in a way that significantly built upon the positive traits of segregated black schooling.

Michael, Malcolm, Jannard, and Wanda were four of the ten thousand black students attending independent schools according to the 1971-72 NAIS minority affairs survey. These ten thousand black students constituted the majority of the thirteen thousand reported minority students in 730 elementary and secondary schools that responded to the survey. Out of the total student population in independent schools, students of color were 5.5 percent of that population.[43] These figures suggest tremendous growth since the first survey during the 1966-67 school year. While Jannard, Malcolm, Michael, Wanda, and others had matriculated to Westminster, more black students were also attending independent schools. As noted about the differences in the surveys:

1. While total student enrollment in NAIS schools increased by approximately 12% since 1966-67, the growth rate for minority students since the last survey was 26% (1969-70) and 158% since 1966-67;
2. the Black student enrollment of 4.1% is comparable to the percentages for similar students enrolled in undergraduate colleges and universities, graduate schools, and professional schools;
3. independent schools spent 9.7 million dollars on financial aid for minority students in 1971-72; and
4. 92% of the reporting schools offered special courses and/or special units on ethnic studies.[44]

Under the leadership of Dandridge, NAIS continued to promote racial understanding. Videotapes of conversations between black students and their teachers about the independent school experience were to be featured at the 1972 NAIS annual conference, and black teacher recruitment efforts continued. Additionally, five local projects were "sponsored in cooperation with the area associations of independent schools: Boston (Independent Schools Association of Massachusetts), New York City (Independent Schools Opportunity Project), Philadelphia (Friends Council on Education), Baltimore (Association of Independent Schools), and Washington, D.C. (Association of Independent Schools of Greater Washington)."[45]

As the 1971-72 school year started, black students outside of Westminster continued to call for change. Cora Pressly, a black student who attended Milton Academy Girls' School in Milton, Massachusetts, voiced her opinion. She stated, "This world [the independent school world] has for the black student only academic attraction, coated with social and cultural repellents. The repellents make the school world sterile and lonely." Cora Pressly called for Milton to include more black literature in English courses and more communication "between parents of black day students and black boarders." She acknowledged that an important difference in her experience had been the addition of Mr. Milton Smith, a "black advisor, staff member, and defender." Cora Pressly offered the critiques and suggestions not because of "ingratitude"; it was precisely because the black students valued "the Milton experience" that they "criticize[d] and [sought] to improve it."[46] Cora's opinion echoed what Dandridge and others had believed to be true about the role of a black staff member who advised students academically and socially. Cora's piece also shed light once more on how black students felt in independent schools and the disconnect between their academic and social experiences.

As black students published pieces in *ISB*, Michael McBay wrote and drew for the *Bi-Line* at Westminster throughout the school year. He included a cartoon on busing as a remedy to school desegregation and his opposition to it. He depicted how adults thought young people did not have respect for the law, when it was in fact the adults who were opposed to the new busing decision.[47] He also reviewed Sly and the Family Stone's album *There's a Riot Goin' On* and penned an article on Angela Davis who was placed on trial after being falsely accused of participation in a Black Panther murder plot.[48] When Julian Bond visited the student body, Michael greeted him with a standing ovation.[49] Michael was now known as a student who made others aware about the world around them, and he showed his aptitude for understanding facets of life and culture through the varied topics he covered in the school newspaper.

During their time at Westminster, McBay, Ryder, Wade, and Ward contended with the realities of race and racism. Even on graduation day, as Westminster acknowledged all of her accomplishments, Wanda Ward dealt with a racial incident. As a senior, she was inducted into the National Honor Society, was one of twelve seniors to receive Senior Superlatives, served as president of the Service Council, and helped to lead the basketball team to the playoffs.[50] During Honors Day, the school leadership awarded her the Frances Isabelle Outler Award. Upon receiving the award, the following was read:

> Entering Westminster the first year that the school enrolled black students, she has accepted leadership positions in a most responsible and mature manner. She has maintained a diligent, thorough, and persevering record of academic performance. Her college acceptance brought her invitations to attend Princeton University, the University of Pennsylvania, Vassar College, and Colgate University. She will enroll in Princeton University as one of the first two girls we have sent to that distinguished institution. For her dignity, for her grace under the pressures of many difficult situations, for her unselfishness, stability, and strength of character, for the example she has left us in her role of pioneer in a changing world, we offer our gratitude and highest honor to Wanda Elaine Ward.[51]

Yet, when Wanda went to the podium to receive the award, the woman presenting the award did not readily greet her. Wanda "poignantly" recollected that the woman wore white gloves. When Wanda extended her hand to shake the woman's hand, Wanda remembered that "it became very apparent to me that she did not want to shake my hand. It was clear to me that it was a racial thing. But I extended my hand even further and she had to shake my hand. . . . It was noticed by everyone and it was clear to me that some of the administrators and some of the classmates were embarrassed. But that was life. I didn't care. I was graduating." Ward indicated that she "always had this sense of indifference. That was a defense mechanism, not deliberate, but it's like, hey just make it work."[52] Any number of factors contribute to student success, in particular to black student success, and Wanda, like the others, found coping mechanisms for being a student at Westminster. Wanda and the others discerned, even without fully realizing it, how to stay focused on the task at hand while drawing on all that they brought with them.

In the June 1972 edition of the *Westminster Bi-Line*, the four graduates offered their perspectives in Malcolm Ryder's article, "First Black Grads Voice Common Impressions, Ideas." They criticized "the lack of black students and black teachers." While they felt that they were able to maintain their identity as African Americans, having true friendships with white students was difficult due to "indifference, deceit, and tremendous competition on campus." Although in later interviews, African American graduates spoke of the importance of their home communities, Ryder, who would attend Princeton the following fall, wrote at the time that "they expressed feelings of resentment coming from the black community stemming from envy, misunderstanding, and a feeling that they did not belong 'up here' and should be with the rest of the black community—'with their own kind.' But they agreed that the gains outweighed the negative factors and resentment." Most importantly, they recommended that black students not matriculate to Westminster alone. As Michael McBay, who enrolled in Stanford, stated, "A black student should be able to depend on other blacks here."[53]

Wanda, Malcolm, Michael, and Jannard made the most of their years at Westminster and excelled inside and outside the classroom. What they brought in their backpacks, including their families, communities, talents, strength, and their experiences in segregated black schools, helped them. Jannard Wade, now a Morehouse College alumnus, maintained a balance between home and school that grounded him, allowing him to make the Westminster experience work for him. Reflecting on his childhood, Wade

Wanda Ward (front left), Michael McBay (back left), Jannard Wade (back right), and Malcolm Ryder (front right) graduated from Westminster in 1972, and they would attend Princeton University, Stanford University, Morehouse College, and Princeton University, respectively. They, along with Isaac Clark, who graduated a year earlier, were the first black graduates from Westminster. Each student courageously navigated Westminster's paradoxical school culture during the initial years of school desegregation. At graduation, Wanda received one of Westminster's highest honors—the Frances Isabelle Outler Award. In the June 1972 edition of the *Bi-Line*, Wanda, Michael, Jannard, and Malcolm shared their experiences and impressions of Westminster. Source: Malcolm Ryder, "First Black Grads," *Westminster Bi-Line*, June 1972, 3, RG 21.06, Beck Archives-Westminster.

commented, "My parents got me involved in going to a lot of those things so that I wouldn't lose my perspective on what was happening to our community." Throughout high school, Wade's social life centered on Southwest High School, a predominantly black middle-class public high school. He commented, "I was involved in the Scouts and that kind of thing, a lot in church [Flipper Temple AME Church]. I was really busy on the weekends in my community, kind of doing things. That really helped as far as giving me some normalcy as far as social life. All the girlfriends that I had were from public schools. So I was fortunate to have some really good friends, like I said, over at the other school."[54] Being an athlete also was a significant factor in Wade's Westminster experience. Wade noted that nearly the entire Westminster team and their parents attended his mother's funeral. Through sports, Wade believed, "You learn a lot of different things. You really get to know people. When you're in the trenches together and you have a common goal, the race thing kind of goes away because your goal is to win that championship."[55]

Similar to Wade, Wanda Ward, a Princeton alumna, attributed her initial experience and matriculation through Westminster to her family, her community, and her personal affect. Though her family was not actively involved in the civil rights movement, her church, Big Bethel, because of its location on Auburn Avenue and its membership, served not only as a foundation for "spiritual growth, but social activism."[56] Ward acknowledged that her path was different from most in her church. Yet, these differences were reconciled because, according to Ward, "it wasn't so exceptionally different because we were in that environment that valued the criticality of good education." Ward's own younger siblings attended public schools, thereby continuing to link her to the educational experiences of most black Atlantans. Additionally, Wanda remembered embracing the opportunity to attend Westminster with the sentiment, "Okay. Let's do it." Ward's mother, Elaine Jackson, was committed to the opportunity and very enthusiastic, especially because of Burch's outreach. When asked why Ward attended Westminster, Jackson responded, "Wanda was there for the academics, which she was quite capable of performing. I told her [an administrator at Westminster with whom she had a difference]: 'She's not here to make friends. She's here to take advantage of the academics that you provide.'"[57]

The black students' presence, involvement, and activism influenced and changed Westminster. David Mallery in *Negro Students in Independent Schools* indicated the belief that the presence of African American students would cause white students to confront their own stereotypes about black people. Anne Forsyth, who sponsored the Stouffer Foundation, also believed that African American students would impact racist beliefs and perceptions. For some white students at Westminster, this certainly occurred. Jane Haverty, along with her four siblings, attended Westminster, and, like many of her white classmates, black domestic workers helped to raise her. As president of Haverty Furniture Company (Havertys), her father, Rawson Haverty, was a member of the business elite in Atlanta. Jane, a 1972 alumna who dated McBay their senior year, maintained that African American students could not be ignored, because of their individual characteristics, academic abilities, and various talents, not just their physical appearance. Haverty came to "realize how smart they were, how capable they were, how talented they were, how much they suffered, how different their lives were, and how tall they stood in spite of all that, and you know, how accomplished they could be in spite of all that."[58]

In 1972, these first black graduates were not able to consider their impact on others because of the social and educational environment they navigated. Hill Martin, also a 1972 Westminster alumnus, acknowledged his part in harassing Michael McBay, Malcolm Ryder, and other African American students. He recalled growing up around adults who made disparaging comments about African Americans, and all the while, he was being looked after by a black housekeeper "as if [he] were her own" and worked alongside black workers in the Westminster kitchen. Hill, however, revealed "what [the African American students] cannot possibly know is that their example in my life changed the way I felt, thought, behaved, and believed about people ever since. I never knowingly, consciously made the mistake again of assuming something about someone strictly because of race."[59]

As indicated by white and black alumni, both groups were adjusting to different worlds and encountering one another in large part for the first time as peers; black workers had long been a part of the school and the lives of white students, who lived in all-white communities. With the desegregation of Westminster, white students' ideas about race were challenged first by the sheer presence of black students and second by their character and talents. Desegregating Westminster was not easy, for according to Ryder, Westminster was not a place that "went out of its way to do anything for me just because I was black. Once I got there it was just, 'Okay well now you're here and this is what the place is like.' It took me a while to kind of catch on to it, and when I did it worked out great."[60]

Shifting Institutional, Local, and National Terrains

By 1972, the school now attracted and enrolled black boys and girls in their day schools and boarding components. Westminster leaders had recruited black students from different backgrounds, although their families' educational attainment was similar. Included in this group now were children of well-known local black families such as Donata Russell, the oldest child and only daughter of Herman J. and Otelia Russell.

Donata grew up around kids of other black professionals, as her father was known for his work as a pioneering black businessman; he founded H. J. Russell Company in 1962 that remains one of the oldest and largest minority-owned businesses focused on construction and real estate development.

Donata was very well aware of the civil rights movement, in part, because her parents were friends with the Kings. Prior to attending Westminster, she had attended a Catholic school and a historically white public school, Margaret Mitchell on Atlanta's north side. Russell had known a couple of the students at Margaret Mitchell because of her father's business associations and friendships with some of the Jewish business owners, who also sent their children to Margaret Mitchell. According to Donata, her father's associates "suggested that he send us to this school."[61] Donata was fortunate that one of her teachers at Margaret Mitchell, Mrs. Johnson, was supportive. Mrs. Johnson, an African American, "was my favorite teacher of all my years in school. . . . And I think it was an easier transition for me because she watched out for me and she helped me."[62]

Donata did not want to attend Westminster because she wanted to attend school with her friends from her Collier Heights neighborhood. When Russell transferred to Westminster for eighth grade, other friends from Margaret Mitchell did also, and it helped to have Jewish friends at Westminster; they were also somewhat marginalized in Westminster's nearly all-white Christian school population. Donata enrolled in an eighth-grade class that included eight other black students. With the addition of more black students, they came to rely on each other; in comparison to those who had just graduated, the bonds among the younger black students were probably stronger. But those who entered in 1967 still found their way at Westminster, and they unconsciously paved the way for more black students to attend Westminster and to have deeper connections among one another. Although most boarding students had limited access to Atlanta, Corliss recalled going to the Omni Arena to an Atlanta Hawks basketball game with Donata, whose father at the time was partial owner of the Hawks. Corliss also remembered occasionally attending Wheat Street Baptist Church with Lisa Borders.

Like those who graduated before them, younger black students excelled academically, were active throughout the campus life of Westminster, and broke additional racial barriers at Westminster. During her senior year, Westminster students elected Corliss Blount, nicknamed "Peaches," Miss Mardi Gras in 1973, the first black student to hold the title. According to Blount, "I think the biggest thing—and I think that got probably more excitement than a lot of things when I was there . . . the girls pulling [the float] . . . were not of color. That was like a huge deal, and they—of course, it was the white swan, which years later people were like, 'Were you trying to make a statement?' At the time I don't think so."[63] Blount, who would graduate in 1973 and matriculate to Harvard University, had

Corliss Blount, also known as "Peaches," was one of two black young women to desegregate the girls' dormitory in 1970. Her peers selected Corliss as Miss Mardi Gras in the spring of 1973; she was the first black student to receive this honor. She is pictured here on top of the swan float during the festivities on campus. After graduating, Corliss matriculated to Harvard University. Source: *Lynx* (Yearbook), 1973, 183, RG 21.03, Beck Archives-Westminster.

demonstrated a comfortability in her new environment, whether through her friendship with Jan, being selected as Miss Mardi Gras, or because of whom she dated. At one point, Blount dated Perry Flynn, a white student who was also in chorale. She did not feel "any underlying [racial] tension" toward her interracial relationship. When her mother found out about them dating (Perry had written to her), Corliss said, "And then I did get the talk about not staying in my place, but just about rocking the boat, because she said, 'I know he is not black.' I said, 'How do you know?' She said, 'Because he would not be writing me and thanking me for having you.' It was so funny."[64]

As Pressly completed his tenure as founding president of Westminster, the independent school world had undergone significant change in a short of amount of time as was the case with other schools and institutions of higher learning across the country. *ISB* continued to include the voices of black students, but the students were mostly from outside the South. The black students' sentiments reflected similar concerns by black students as those in previous years, but their continued inclusion showed that NAIS was giving more attention to their experiences and was embracing more black students, teachers, administrators, and trustees. After Dandridge served three years as the inaugural director of minority affairs, Cary Potter changed his title to special assistant to the president. Dandridge became responsible for the association's administrative seminar, attended by all those preparing to be heads of independent schools, and chair of the Teacher Services Committee. This change in his title and responsibilities was a major help because the membership could no longer ignore him, "because I was the staff person for two or three key services that schools wanted."[65] Dandridge organized the seminar, met with interested attendees, selected participants (since there were typically more interested in attending than spaces available), and worked with the faculty involved with the seminar. As the staff person responsible for the Teacher Services Committee, Dandridge directed the association's annual meeting including organizing and selecting presenters. Additionally, the Teacher Services Committee was responsible for determining and organizing various summer workshops.

As special assistant, Dandridge's status in NAIS significantly changed: "It's one thing for you to be able to sit across from me as the head of school and we have conversations about your recruitment and staff of color, etc. It's when I leave the room, you can say, 'Well that was nice. We've done that, until maybe Bill will come back next year or something.'" Now "race would come up, but would come up in the normal course [of conversation] as opposed to saying, 'Oh here we go. We're going to have another conversation about race and deseg.'" Moreover, this position gave Dandridge an opportunity to build a network—"a network of many of the faculty and staff of color around the country where I could be a sounding board for them in helping them float through some issues they were wrestling with, and help people wrestling with similar problems to connect to each other to sort of build a conversation around how they could address those issues."[66]

Central to the network was Dandridge's friendship with Bill Walters, an African American educator in New York City independent schools. Dandridge described their chance meeting at an NAIS party in New York City:

NAIS had its annual meeting in New York City and the head of the school where Bill Walters worked at the time was on the board, and he gave a reception at his apartment. The NAIS board and NAIS staff were expected to attend. [The head of school's] administrative staff was expected to attend. Then we were walking across the room, looking across the room, there were three faces of color in the room: My wife, myself, and Bill Walters. . . . We just struck up a conversation there. It became a deep, deep, deep friendship that just went on, and on, and on.[67]

The friendship between the two Bills became central to the development of the network. Dandridge recollected, "He was my strategic partner and we developed a network of other people of color and my concern basically was as long as I was trying to work in isolation, I could get cut off, but if I built a network and a team of people, it would be harder for us to be ignored or cut off."[68] When Dandridge was in New York, Walters and he spent hours debriefing and strategizing. They thought through "how to find ways to use our heads rather than reacting from our hearts, thinking carefully about engaging in confrontations when it would not lead to positive outcomes. Being careful in heated situations not to over react with statements that conveyed personal attacks, and that could not be taken back."[69]

Though Dandridge and Walters found ways to navigate in meetings and in NAIS, they were not without reservations:

What do you say to the African American community when they see some of their brightest young people being pulled out of the community and sent off to these elite institutions? Are they going to be able to come back home again? How do you support the young people that you're sending off to Vermont? If they're there and there are only ten or twelve of them, what kind of experience are they really having? How do you look at a parent in the face and say to them, "It's all right for your kid to go to x school," when you might have reservations and thinking about how — so those are some of the questions that you raise with yourself. How do you sit in a meeting with a very diverse group of African American parents, those who are upset because their kids — they think their kids are being seen as those inner city kids who can't perform and they need full scholarships? On the other side of the room you have a parent who is doing the best he or she can to get their kid out of a difficult community situation, and they're willing to make the sacrifice. How do you help them find a connection?[70]

Dandridge captured many feelings with which black parents wrestled about educating their children and that continue to linger. Dandridge recognized that black parents were concerned about the academic, social, and emotional well-being of their children, and that determining which school could meet all of those needs was not easy. He also acknowledged the continued deficit perspective that permeated the educational conditions for black children and the interconnectedness of schooling and community for black Americans. Not all African Americans pursued school desegregation, and certainly the implementation of it and the continued battles in the 1970s concerning desegregation and equitable schooling conditions left some African Americans puzzled about next steps. In the midst of these dilemmas, Dandridge remained motivated to show the independent school world to parents, to help provide black children with new opportunities, and to highlight opportunities in which black students did not feel isolated.

Having a network of supportive individuals helped Dandridge's efforts. He encouraged those working in independent schools "to serve on different committees and [provided] them with off-the-record information about the committees and what they were doing in their histories and some of their personalities so they had some context for when they walked into meeting rooms or other things." Dandridge literally made an organizational chart, discerned the power bases, and worked to have individuals who were committed to minority issues involved with those power bases.[71] In addition to committees, Dandridge sought to have individuals attend regional meetings and partner with him on presentations, and he connected with other committed individuals on the regional level. In developing this network, Dandridge's goal "was to push the envelope so those schools could never go back to where they were to feeling that each area community or type of school had to find its own path. There was no one and only way. By counting on them to use their creative energies and resources, they'd figure it out." Dandridge did not want independent school communities to go back to their old ways "because I thought too many people had paid too high a price to get them to where they were."[72]

Comprising the network were Bill Walters, Bobette Reed Kahn, Bill Baeckler, Bobbie Swain, and Betty Ann Workman. Kahn, a black woman and an alumna of The MacDuffie School in Granby, Massachussetts, was on the admissions staff at Choate Rosemary Hall. Bill Baeckler, a white man, headed up Independent Educational Services, a teacher placement agency that Dandridge used as a model for the recruitment of black teachers to independent schools. Swain and Workman, African American women, taught at Brooklyn Friends in New York City and Germantown Friends in Philadelphia, respectively. In terms of NAIS committees, Kahn and Dandridge worked on the Admissions Committee; Walters and Workman served on the Teacher Services Committee; and Walters, Swain, and Kahn at times were on the Minority Affairs Committee. Dandridge's goal in having a network of individuals on a number of committees was to have other NAIS committees

NAIS Organizational Structure

NAIS Board of Directors (i.e. heads of schools)

|

Teacher Services Committee
(teachers; some heads of divisions)

Administrative Services Committee
(heads of schools in charge of administrative seminars)

Trustees Affairs Committee

|

Minority Affairs Committee; Publications Committee;
Admissions Committee

*Board of Directors met 4 times a year
*All other committees met 3 times a year
*Example of Ad Hoc Committee: Womens' Affairs Committee

Dr. William Dandridge, the first director of minority affairs for NAIS, strategically developed a network of individuals within the organization who were active throughout the NAIS organizational structure, depicted here. Dandridge and his network were committed to addressing long-held stereotypes about black students and all aspects of racial diversity within NAIS schools, including the need for black trustees, school leaders, and teachers. Since leaving NAIS in 1982, Dandridge has worked in the Boston Public Schools, served as dean of graduate programs in the College of Education and Human Development at the University of Massachusetts-Boston and as dean of the Graduate School of Education at Lesley University, and has been a program officer for the Woodrow Wilson National Fellowship Foundation. He also established two foundations to support teachers—the Boston Educational Development Foundation and the Massachusetts Foundation for Teaching and Learning. Source: The author recreated this chart based on her interviews with William Dandridge.

in addition to the Minority Affairs Committee take ownership of diversity issues. Dandridge wanted to "create the expectation that committees have to address board priorities around issues of diversity." Other individuals important to the network were Gerald Davis of Northfield Mount Hermon, Howard Johnson of the State University of New York at New Paltz, and Gardenia White of Equal Opportunity Programs.[73]

Like Dandridge and Walters, the group had "off-the-record" meetings as well. According to Dandridge, "At the annual meeting, we'd always find a way to have an off-the-record gathering or meeting to stay in touch. Whenever I did a program or a workshop, I always took one or two people with me. . . . I was trying to be as broad in outreach as possible. I had a feeling that the more people they saw and the more voices they heard, the better it would be than just one person."[74] Members of the network also thought it best to support one another in public. Dandridge recalled, "If someone was on a program presenting, everybody went to be part of the audience. . . . If we saw someone trying to field a tough question, someone on the floor would ask another question that was more a response to the tough question, but sort of shifting the focus . . . so we did our best to cover each other."[75] Those in the network supported one another as they prompted discussions about racial diversity in a number of NAIS settings.

NAIS leaders devoted more and more time to examining the experience of black students, and private schools, in particular in the South, increasingly became an educational option for white parents. The continued turn to the private signaled the resistance to public school desegregation in Atlanta, and the number of applications increased at Westminster. In the early 1970s, despite a ruling that declared Atlanta Public Schools unitary, segregation continued. By 1973 when Maynard Jackson was mayor, "the percentage of black students in the Atlanta system had reached almost eighty percent, with only slightly more than twenty percent of whites remaining."[76] White students leaving APS fled either to suburban schools or private schools. In citing Research Atlanta's survey of 1973, Gong noted, "The city's private school enrollment for the school year of 1972-1973 was 20,146, an increase of about 2,000 students over the 1971-1972 total and an increase of 5,000 from the total enrollment for 1970-1971."[77] Private schools had also increasingly become an option for black parents. Included among those students attending private schools were black students who "accounted for 13 percent of the private school enrollment in metro Atlanta."[78] For the majority of black students in public schools, however, the struggles over public school desegregation continued.

The NAACP and school board, under court order, submitted new desegregation plans in January 1973 which included busing options, but local NAACP and other black leaders, joined by a group of white business and professional leaders, agreed to abandon such plans, leading to the compromise of 1973. The compromise consisted of four main sections: (1) student assignment plan, (2) plan for staff desegregation, (3) majority to minority transfer plan, and (4) plan for desegregation of administration. The plan called for every school to have a minimum black student enrollment of

30 percent, which in turn, left many schools all black, and African Americans became more integral in the administrative control of the largely black school system including the appointment of a black superintendent and 50 percent of all administrative posts.[79]

As the compromise ushered in new black leadership for APS, Pressly's tenure ended at Westminster with much appreciation and fanfare. The main administration building was named in his honor and the 1973 Westminster *Lynx* yearbook was dedicated to him. In his twenty-two years as founding president of Westminster, the school had grown tremendously in the size of its student body, physical location, fundraising, and stature, and he had led the school through its first years of desegregation, culminating in the first black graduates in the early 1970s. Institutional and interpersonal racism were real. The school culture was a mixture of contradictions from its early heralding of the Old South to later reflecting the changing political and social climate of the era.

Three years after Pressly's retirement, Dawn Clark and Ron McBay graduated. Dawn, the first and youngest black girl to enroll at Westminster, felt isolated as the only black girl in the lower grades. Clark experienced racial discrimination in her initial years at Westminster, but her experience became more balanced as she developed interest in the subject of religion, participated in extracurricular activities, and enjoyed familial relationships with other black students. Dawn candidly reflected on her own sensitivity, which she openly discussed, yet if teachers in those early years honored the Westminster handbook's expectation that they should be attuned to students' individual needs, perhaps Clark would not have felt as isolated as she did.[80] Moreover, school leaders could have taken a more proactive stance in communicating expectations to *all* students concerning race. Ron McBay "felt accepted, special in a good way but not so terribly different," and race, at least implicitly, informed some of his daily interactions. For example, it was not a surprise that he played "Rudolph" in the class Christmas skit, "Rudolph: The Red-Nosed Reindeer," and he enjoyed being the star of the Christmas play. McBay recalled how a few students gave him the nickname "Fuzzy." In his words, "It was just as new for them to be around someone black as it was for me to be around white people. They would rub my hair and think it was cool and different. It probably sounds bad, but it was innocent and sweet."[81] Ron communicated a nuanced understanding about his years at Westminster that was connected to how he felt about himself physically and how he experienced a certain double consciousness or twoness between his school and home communities. That Ron reflected on his

After beginning at Westminster during the early years of desegregation, Dawn Clark (top left) and Ron McBay (top right) graduated in 1976, and Joia Johnson (bottom left) and Donata Russell (bottom right) graduated in 1977. Like the earlier graduates, they excelled and helped to pave the way for future black students at Westminster. Upon graduation, Dawn attended St. Andrews Presbyterian College, Ron began at Princeton University, Joia attended Duke University, and Donata matriculated to the University of Pennsylvania. Sources: Dawn Clark and Ron McBay, *Lynx* (Yearbook), 1976, 34, 51, RG 21.03, Beck Archives-Westminster; Joia Johnson and Donata Russell, *Lynx* (Yearbook), 1977, 143, 153, RG 21.03, Beck Archives-Westminster.

experiences with such nuance also shows the complexity of his experience and, most likely, that of many other black students.

AGAIN, THERE WAS no full template for schools like Westminster or students like Corliss Blount, Dawn Clark, Joia Johnson, Ron McBay, Michael McBay, Malcolm Ryder, Donata Russell, Jannard Wade, and Wanda Ward to follow. A constellation of factors in the 1950s and 1960s coalesced to push schools like Westminster to desegregate when they were not legally obligated to do so. The moral consciousness of independent school leaders, the desire not to be like segregationist academies, the civil rights movement, and the influence of the federal government in public *and* private education led independent school leaders to act in public and private ways, to recruit and retain black students, and to desegregate their schools in some cases. Most of the first black students to desegregate and graduate from schools like Westminster came from working- and middle-class homes. Their parents, educated in the Jim Crow South, were professionals, including educators. Such students were not readily represented in the national discussion of the recruitment and retention of black students to independent schools in the late 1960s and 1970s.

The first black students at Westminster brought with them an inheritance rooted in the public and private black schools of the Jim Crow South. They also relied on a host of experiences in segregated black schools and in their families and communities and on their own gifts and talents. For those who stayed at Westminster through graduation, a mixture of factors affected their achievement. Although individual white administrators, teachers, coaches, and students were incredibly supportive of these first black students, substantial institutional change was not one of those factors. That Westminster and other elite schools became accessible to more and more African American youth in the 1960s and 1970s signaled a shift in student demographics and illuminated the abilities and talents of black youth across the South and the nation. The work to change the institutional culture had just begun.

Epilogue

Grappling with the multifaceted history of black educational experiences in the United States deepens and expands our knowledge about the role of formal schooling in the African American freedom struggle. For many have sought and seek formal schooling as a means of liberation and collective and individual mobility. Historically white institutions, whether public or private, K–12 or higher education, were not exempted from larger historical, political, and social changes during the mid-twentieth century, and black students courageously navigated these institutions. These complex lessons from the past help inform questions that a) contemplate contemporary challenges in meeting the needs of African American students, b) deeply examine the school cultures in which they find themselves, and c) consider the intricate relationships among schools and local, regional, national, and international contexts. One might ask: what are the responsibilities of students to change institutional culture? What are the benefits and costs to the students for shouldering this responsibility? What are the responsibilities of all educational institutions to address the roles of race and racism in their school cultures and in their students' everyday lives? And what must we consider about all facets of past school desegregation and the current racial demographics of schools in the United States?

The first black alumni succeeded at Westminster during the era in which policymakers adhered to the Coleman Report. Coleman, in essence, argued that family life had a greater effect on children than that of the school. Although Coleman was focused on public schools in the late 1960s, one might contend that the success of the first Westminster students follows a similar line of thinking—that their familial backgrounds which nurtured their personal attributes predetermined their excellence in schooling. Doing so misses a significant point. The first black students to desegregate Westminster succeeded in large part because of their backgrounds and personal attributes, but they entered a school culture that had been created without them in mind, which was an effect in and of itself. That they succeeded did not absolve Westminster of advancing institutional change. These black students and others across the South helped to spur institutional change in schools intended to position graduates for greater social mobility.

Today these first black alumni lead diverse professional and personal lives that are worthy of recognition, but historical scholars have not robustly studied their experiences and the experiences of others like them at academic institutions across the country. As we contend with the intersection of school desegregation and African American education during the mid-twentieth century, it is critical to do so.[1] From personal observation, Westminster currently appears to have a deep commitment to diversity and inclusion, although the school community continues to work on reconciling with parts of its past. Further, independent schools more broadly continue to address what it means to be open in an unequal society. Independent schools pivoted toward racial inclusion at the same time that other schools retreated from it in the mid-twentieth century. This work is continuous, and those in control at present have much to learn from the processes of their predecessors.

Currently, there are over 47,000 African American students attending independent schools, more than six times the number than those attending such schools in the early 1970s. At Westminster, students of color make up more than 30 percent of the student body population. The first students to attend and desegregate Westminster, along with their counterparts in other independent schools throughout the nation, helped to increase these numbers. The schools themselves, especially those schools located in major cities like Atlanta, reflected and continue to reflect not only the tenor of national independent schools but state and local politics. Because of these intersecting contexts, historically white elite private schools are highly politicized spaces. Over time, as independent schools have taken up the banner of diversity and inclusion, independent school leaders positioned themselves to be different, both among some private schools and among many public schools that remain relatively homogenous. Even so, independent schools are subject to analyses. Independent schools are part of an interplay between public and private schools, as private school leaders also contend with public matters. Independent schools' policies and practices affect schooling opportunities for marginalized groups, and the policies and practices inform how students of color and their families navigate this tenuous terrain to secure educational access to both academics and the larger political economy.

My arguments about how independent school leaders blurred public and private lines in relationship to their decision making in the mid-twentieth century—and how black students courageously navigated a difficult school climate—rely on multiple story lines related to the history of school desegregation, historically white elite private schools, and Atlanta during the civil rights movement and the Black Power movement. In this contemporary era of social protest and tension between diverse populations and institutions, the historical implications for considering the desegregation of Westminster as I have in this work resonate deeply. Looking to these histories illuminates how schools can perpetuate and disrupt racist narratives, the continued need for understanding institutional and interpersonal change, and issues of contemporary school choice. Indeed, recent history certainly calls for this and more.

I undertook this project during Barack Obama's presidency of the United States; he is a graduate of the Punahou School, a historically white elite private school in Hawaii. Barack and Michelle Obama's daughters, Malia and Sasha Obama, have also been educated in elite independent schools, including Sidwell Friends in Washington, D.C. The historical significance of the first family reminded us every day of what was possible but also what was enduring about institutional and interpersonal racism in the United States. Michelle Obama, former first lady, prompted us to consider how the first family's story was connected with the past: "the story of generations of people who felt the lash of bondage, the shame of servitude, the sting of segregation, but who kept on striving and doing what needed to be done so that today I wake up every morning in a house that was built by slaves."[2] Many appreciated the promise of progress that the Obamas represent, but this history recounted by Michelle Obama haunted us during the Obama presidency, as activists launched #blacklivesmatter because of the killings of unarmed black citizens, in particular, black young men, at the hands of security guards and police. Protests, in new but familiar ways, erupted around the United States and the world. Many of them began on college campuses. From Yale and Georgetown to the University of Missouri, black students and their racially diverse allies courageously asked us to consider how the legacies of racism that permeate these institutions have impacted, and in many cases defined, their experiences. For those of us concerned about the past, present, and future experiences of students with marginalized identities, they awakened (or "woke") us to the urgency of the work that continues for equity and true inclusivity in all schools and institutions of higher learning, including historically white elite private schools.

Independent schools, like other historically white institutions, are called to reconcile their past and present and to understand and embrace their position in a U.S. society that remains very unequal. It was in the interest of white independent school leaders to side with the civil rights movement and the changing racial tenor of the United States. The decision to desegregate Westminster, which included the preservation of its image, may be what critical race theorists deem a moment of "interest convergence." As Derrick Bell argued, "the interest of blacks in achieving racial equality will be accommodated only when it converges with the interest of whites in policy-making decisions."[3] A relatively small group of African Americans gained access to an elite institution. In spite of experiencing racial harassment and feeling like outsiders, they succeeded and matriculated to historically white and black elite higher education institutions. Concurrently, Westminster gained further stature in the independent school world and distinguished itself from post-*Brown* segregationist academies, and its white students were changed by their interactions with black peers. How institutional leaders make decisions is influenced by any number of factors, including larger forces related to race, because institutions do not exist in a vacuum. Part of this process of understanding the past is in the work of understanding why decisions were made and acknowledging the paradoxical culture that exists in many educational institutions, because U.S. society is not, as many argue, "post-racial."

We need not only understand the history of complex and contradictory school cultures, but how such cultures are sustained so that they might be disrupted, directly addressed, and remedied. Bridging the history and contemporary realities of school cultures is important for engaging this work. Scholars of the contemporary era such as Prudence Carter, Leigh Patel, and Shamus Khan show that culture is an essential factor in students' school experiences, due to its impact on learning outcomes, personal development, and students' understanding of the larger society. Prudence Carter, who "differentiate[s] between the school's mobility and sociocultural contexts," examined four contemporary public high schools and contended that the "underlying premise . . . that student success, engagement, or well-being is not simply indicated by tests." She continued by arguing, "Several other outcomes that pertain to schooling, including their sense of 'engagement' and 'incorporation' within their school, are probably related either directly or indirectly, to students' attainment and achievement."[4] In her study of undocumented high school students, Leigh Patel eloquently captured Franklin High School, the public school attended by the youth illuminated in her text. Patel's study revealed "a complicated set of relationships between oft-invoked discourses about multiculturalism, diversity, and the lived realities of racism and discrimination."[5] According to Khan's *Privilege*, in which he focuses on the new forms of elitism in historically white elite private

schools, students cross and mix cultural boundaries within their school setting as they wax and wane with understanding and perpetuating their new
form of elitism. As Khan wrote, "Students learned not to value elite knowledge or savor (or hide behind) the things that distinguished them. They
learned to absorb it all and to *want* to absorb it all."[6] How students experience, interact with, and make school culture is multidimensional, and this
culture affects their academic achievement and their social, cultural, and
psychological development. *Transforming the Elite* can help us uncover and
investigate more deeply the daily conditions, lived realities, and contexts
that influenced how African American students experienced schools historically. Engaging in these processes inevitably raises questions about the
contemporary.

Parents (and sometimes students) choosing independent schools reflect
an array of hopes and beliefs about what such schools can provide in terms
of academics, extracurricular activities, and social life. For African American parents, however, choosing the best schools for their children includes
an additional consideration: positioning them for success in a society undergirded by racist policies, practices, and ideologies.[7] Thus, contemporary
school choice can often be a gray matter for black parents.[8] As noted in *Both
Sides Now*, Amy Stuart Wells and a team of researchers interviewed over 280
high school graduates from the class of 1980 who attended racially mixed
public high schools. Part of what Wells and her researchers considered is
how those graduates make decisions for their children today. Wells et al.
observed:

> Graduates of color talked about the difficulties they faced in finding
> schools for their children that were both academically rigorous and
> diverse in the sense that their children would not be the only minori-
> ties in their classrooms. They knew that schools enrolling larger
> numbers of white students were more likely to have more resources,
> the most qualified teachers, and a challenging curriculum—the white
> powerful parents would ensure this. At the same time, they did not
> want their children to be "tokens" in schools that catered to the
> demands of white families.[9]

African Americans are not exempt from conversations about the privatization of public schooling, but the contemporary debates on the privatization
of public schools and the implications for African Americans are not di-
vested from the historical role of private schools in the education of African Americans. Also, these debates cannot ignore considering how African

Americans' school choices are part of their way for establishing full participation in the larger U.S. political economy. African American families are choosing among traditional public schools inside and outside their neighborhoods, magnet schools, charter schools, parochial schools, private schools, and home schooling—but as noted by DeCuir and Dixson and a host of other scholars, racism transcends school type.[10]

Scholars and educators continue to address the "educational debt" in the United States, a concept that considers the accumulation of historical, moral, sociopolitical, and economic debts owed to students of color as a framework for understanding the achievement gap or the disparities in test scores between students of color, in particular African American and Latina/o students, and white students.[11] Rather than viewing the achievement gap as a contemporary phenomenon, Gloria Ladson-Billings' notion of the educational debt calls for a longer consideration of why these differences exist. Critical literacy scholars such as Django Paris also call for us to recognize the literacy gifts that African American students bring to the classroom and how to substantiate and connect with those practices and, in turn, those students as we "ask ourselves that age-old question: What is the purpose of schooling in a pluralistic society?"[12] To engage in debate about why the educational debt persists begs investigating why we cannot seem to answer that age-old question. We must consider the many factors that influence student achievement, especially the challenges that function as barriers to the achievement of students who are marginalized by race and other social identity markers. We learn from history how black institutions met these challenges and how black students, whether in black schools or historically white schools, fared. We also learn how and why institutions begin to change and the culture that students inherit, create, affect, and navigate. Many African American children have not fared well in U.S. schools; too often our policies, practices, and ideologies hinge on the perceived beliefs about individual deficiencies without holding the state accountable for its debts.[13] And despite the legacy of state debt, some have fared well. Those of us concerned about the history of race, culture, and the struggle for equity in education are called on to be cognizant of the nuanced ecology of the black academic experience so that we might find an answer to that persistent question and the many other questions that encircle our pursuits for justice and equity. With such a nuanced understanding, our efforts can create educational opportunities in which all children, in particular, those born into the "educational debt," are more likely to reach their highest potential.

Acknowledgments

The late James E. McLeod often stated, "An education is an extraordinarily valuable process. It's transformative. It makes you a different person." Researching and writing this book has been a transformative educational experience for me because of what I have learned through the process. This process was both an individual and a collective effort because of the many who supported me in this endeavor, in small and large ways, to offer the history presented in the following pages. I say thank you to each person, named and unnamed, who has offered words of encouragement, advice, and support.

Having my first book published by the University of North Carolina (UNC) Press has fulfilled one of my long-held professional goals. I first met Brandon Proia, my editor at UNC Press, in the spring of 2013. Since then, he has patiently nurtured and championed this book. His comments on my drafts, flexibility with my schedule, and prompt responsiveness to my queries have been invaluable. I feel fortunate to call Brandon my editor, and I deeply value his work on my behalf. I am also grateful to Catherine "Cate" Hodorowicz, editorial assistant at UNC Press, for her efforts to carefully prepare my manuscript for publication and for answering all of my questions; to David Perry, former editor-in-chief at UNC Press, for his feedback on my initial book proposal; to Dino Battista and the UNC Press Marketing Department for their assistance; to Kim Bryant and the UNC Press Design and Production Department for their work on the book cover design and interior images; to Erin Davis and the Westchester Publishing Services staff for their diligent work on copyediting and typesetting the manuscript; to Margaretta Yarborough for proofreading and Mike Taber for indexing the book; and to Patrick Taylor at St. Andrew's Episcopal School for his photography. I also sincerely appreciate my external readers for their detailed constructive criticism that helped to push my thinking, further develop and refine my arguments, and strengthen my historical analysis.

This book is based on both archival research and oral history interviews. Each complements the other, allowing me to develop a historical account that is richly informed by national organizations, institutional history, and the student experience.

To everyone I interviewed, I thank you for responding, for communicating with me whether in person, on the phone, or by email, and for your steadfast support. Dawn Clark, Corliss Blount Denman, Joia Johnson, Michael McBay, Ron McBay, Donata Russell Ross, Malcolm Ryder, Jannard Wade, and Wanda Ward went back in time as I researched the first black students to desegregate a historically white elite private school in the South. Talking about their experiences was not always easy, but I am grateful that they entrusted me with their life histories. William Dandridge, whom I now consider a mentor, helped to connect the dots between local and national contexts through our various discussions about his role as the first director of minority affairs for the National Association of Independent Schools (NAIS). Aaron Johnson, Johnnie Clark, and Elaine Jackson provided black parental perspectives that I could not have gained otherwise. Hill Martin, Jane Haverty, Jere Wells, Nan Pendergrast, and the late John Ehle spoke with candor about their experiences as white alumni of Westminster, as a white parent of Westminster alumni, and as a white leader of the Stouffer Foundation. I also thank Linda Churchwell for introducing Ron McBay to me and Leslie Sargent, David Roseman, and Patricia Thomas for their hospitality on my research trips.

I am indebted to those in archives and libraries who assisted me. In particular, I thank Cathy Kelly, the former archivist at the Lewis H. Beck Archives at The Westminster Schools in Atlanta, Georgia, and Pamela Nye, current archivist at the Beck Archives-Westminster, for allowing me full access to archival materials, for taking a deep interest in my work, and for assisting me in acquiring the photos for this book. I extend gratitude to Marie Hansen, interlibrary loan coordinator for the Robert W. Woodruff Library at Emory University, Matthew Turi, manuscripts research and instruction librarian in the Southern Historical Collection at the University of North Carolina-Chapel Hill, and Kathy Shoemaker, reference coordinator at the Stuart A. Rose Manuscript, Archives, and Rare Book Library at Emory University, for their willingness to help me identify sources and to secure materials from individuals and multiple libraries across the nation. I also am appreciative of the librarians and staff of the John M. Olin Library at Washington University in St. Louis for their support in acquiring a number of sources.

The financial support of Emory University, Michigan State University, Washington University in St. Louis, and the Spencer Foundation benefited this book. Thank you for trusting me as a researcher and for providing opportunities to focus on this project and to interact with other scholars.

I owe a debt of gratitude to a number of scholars, mentors, and administrators who have facilitated my intellectual pursuits in education, history, and African American studies. I harken to many lessons learned from these individuals as I research, write, teach, and offer service as an assistant professor. For their mentorship of this project, I thank Vanessa Siddle Walker and Mary Ann Dzuback. Vanessa first shepherded this project. She modeled for me a balance of nuanced historical inquiry into the black educational experience, detailed and stimulating writing, a conscientious approach to reviewing archival materials and conducting interviews, and inventing revision of one's writing. Vanessa also encouraged me to pursue UNC Press as a potential outlet for my work and took the time to have key conversations related to this project over the last several years. From Mary Ann, my first mentor in the history of education, I garnered early lessons on how one critically reads and absorbs historiography, analyzes archival documents, and writes meticulously. Mary Ann, now my colleague, carefully and critically read drafts of the manuscript at different stages during the revision process and provided thorough feedback that strengthened this publication. In addition to their intellectual support, I also thank Vanessa and Mary Ann for supporting me personally when I needed it most.

I am appreciative of mentors, trusted colleagues, and dear friends for their helpfulness on this phase of my academic journey. I am especially grateful to Vera Stenhouse, Kevin Zayed, and Keona Ervin, dynamic scholars of education and history, for their belief in this project, for their careful attention to my work, and for their unwavering encouragement and friendship as I completed this book; to Summer McDonald for her editorial suggestions and for asking the necessary questions when I thought I had nearly answered them all; and to Sarah Murphy for her editorial and research assistance, especially as I completed final revisions.

It is a gift to have one's work read by scholars whose work you admire and to have them offer thoughtful and helpful comments. For this I thank James Anderson, Nancy Beadie, Martha Biondi, Kristen Buras, Joe Crespino, Dionne Danns, Leroy Davis, Ansley Erickson, V. P. Franklin, Brett Gadsden, Karen Graves, Carole Hahn, Jon Hale, Michael Hevel, Hilary Moss, Jonna Perrillo, Christopher Span, Joy Ann Williamson-Lott, and Vincent Willis. Their work as educational researchers and as historians has deepened my knowledge of African American educational history, U.S. educational history, southern history, school desegregation, private schools, and issues of race, culture, and equity. I value the time and energy that they have extended to my scholarly development.

I am also indebted to those who affirmed my pursuit of this project from the beginning, offered important intellectual inspiration and guidance, and held me accountable along the way. I especially thank the late Leslie Brown, Jade Caines, Bernadette Castillo, Brittney Cooper, Sheryl Croft, Erica Dotson, Alyssa Dunn, Terry Flennaugh, Jillian Ford, Theda Gibbs, Keisha Green, Joy Hannibal, Jacqueline Jordan Irvine, Alisha Johnson, Kathy Knight, Mark Knight, Dali Martinez, Margo McClinton, David Morris, Django Paris, Rae Paris, Solana Rice, Nicole Russell, Crystal Sanders, Elizabeth Todd-Breland, Natasha Trethewey, Jyotsna Vanapalli, Maisha Winn, and Ashley Woodson.

I appreciate the support of many in Washington University's Department of Education, Interdisciplinary Program in Urban Studies, Center on Urban Research and Public Policy, Department of African and African-American Studies, and Program in American Culture Studies; Michigan State University's Department of Teacher Education; and Emory University's Division of Educational Studies, including those who worked in the basement and were members of the Graduate Student Research Roundtable (GSRR). For their administrative support, collegiality, and advice as I have undertaken this project, I thank William Tate, Cindy Brantmeier, Kit Wellman, Carol Camp Yeakey, Rowhea Elmesky, Garrett Duncan, Odis Johnson, Andy Butler, Ebony Duncan-Shippy, Marilyn Broughton, Natalia Kolk, Roshonda Ludy, Michele Augustin, Ron Banfield, William Clark, Mark Hogrebe, Cheryl Holland, Habiba Ibrahim, Judy Joerding, Judy Lamb, Brenda Pierce, Madonna Riesenmy, Adrienne Davis, Wayne Fields, Gerald Early, Tim Parsons, Rafia Zafar, Sowandé Mustakeem, Monique Bedasse, Lerone Martin, Jonathan Fenderson, Douglas Flowe, Jean Allman, John Baugh, Iver Bernstein, Bill Maxwell, Jeffrey McCune, Shanti Parikh, Rebecca Wanzo, Rudolph Clay, Samba Diallo, Ron Himes, Mungai Mutonya, Janary Stanton, Suzanne Wilson, Avner Segall, Dorinda Carter Andrews, Sandra Crespo, Peter Youngs, Anne-Lise Halvorsen, and Jeff Bale. I recognize Carleen Carey and Jon Wargo for their research assistance, and I deeply appreciate all of my colleagues and students for their questions and insights that have caused me to think more deeply about my research, writing, pedagogy, and mentorship.

Likewise, I have been supported in tangible and intangible ways by many others who have contributed to my professional and personal development. For my entire life, the pastors, vicars, and members of Epiphany Lutheran Church (formerly St. Philip Lutheran Church) in Jackson, Mississippi, have supported my endeavors, kept me in their prayers, and provided many good wishes for my success. I am also indebted to the administrators, faculty, staff, and students at Jackson State University where my parents were employed, and those from the greater Jackson community who have taught, guided, and encouraged me. As a student, administrator, or assistant professor at St. Andrew's Episcopal School, Washington University in St. Louis, Emory University, and Michigan State University and as an active member of my professional associations, I have developed a large and wonderful compilation of mentors, colleagues, friends, sorors, associates, and students. I thank those in this dynamic group who share my commitments to social justice, educational equity, humanizing research, and lifelong learning. I also acknowledge those who help me to cope with life's challenges, are my sounding boards about important matters, and offer affirmations at exactly the right time. Further, I signal those who provide a little levity whether through our love of sports, or our affinity for good music and dancing, or our discussions about faith, politics, and pop culture. Of note, I am especially thankful to the late James E. McLeod, Clara McLeod, Dorothy Elliott, the late Adrienne Glore, Robyn Hadley, Laura Stephenson, Wilmetta Toliver-Diallo, Fernando Cutz, Keri McWilliams, Sharon McWilliams, Angela Roberts, Lynnell Thomas, Marie Winfield, and the entire John B. Ervin Scholar family; E2K1 (i.e. Shola Cole, Nate Dewart, Joe Donlin, Natalie Donlin-Zappella, Amit Goyal, Harpreet Khera, Pranav Kothari, Vinita Kumar, Solana Rice, Maritza Roberto, and Joel Schroeder) and their families; Beta Delta sorors, in particular Stephanie Baker, Alicia Bond-Lewis, and Kia Davis; and to many others with whom I have connected at Washington University including Christyn Abaray, Melanie Adams, Danielle Anderson, Gail Boker, Jill Carnaghi, Zelon Crawford, Patti Curtis, Phyllis Jackson, Tamara King, Mary Laurita, Delise LePool, Steve Malter, Leah Merrifield, Kimberly Norwood, Sean Phillips, Barbara Rea, Julie Shimabukuro, Jonathan Smith, Kirsten Smith, Rochelle Smith, Sharon Stahl, Jill Stratton, Sue Taylor, Karen Tokarz, Lori White, and Rob Wild.

I am also indebted to the Allen and Purdy families, with roots in Mississippi and Arkansas. I recognize and embrace the legacy of those who have come before me, including my late maternal grandfather, James Allen Sr., and my late paternal grandfather, Jessie Purdy. They were hard workers and devoted family men and community members. I wish I could have met and spent time with them before they passed away. I celebrate the dedication of the educators in my family, including my late paternal grandmother, Mollie B. Purdy, whom I knew as a child, and my late maternal grandmother, Pearl M. Allen, fondly known as MaDear, whom I knew for a little over thirty years as she lived to be one hundred years of age. I am grateful for MaDear's belief in me and the example that she set for me to follow. I also am thankful for the support of the late James Allen Jr., Cecelia Dorsey, Polly Brown, Carolyn Jean Crawford, Gloria Evans, and their families as I have undertaken this project.

This book is dedicated to my first teachers—my parents and my brother. They afforded me opportunities to explore my varied interests and have supported my educational endeavors. I am grateful for their love, patience, understanding, assistance, and so much more. My brother, Paul W. Purdy Jr., who is six and half years older than I am, first asked about attending St. Andrew's Episcopal School in Jackson, and I thank him for helping to pave the way there. I honor my late father, Paul W. Purdy Sr., for showing me how one perseveres and for instilling in me a deep interest in politics and history. And I salute my mother, Mitchell Pearl A. Purdy. I am forever grateful for her attention to details, devotion to family, prayers, gentle pushing, and words of encouragement.

My parents provided me unique educational opportunities as I grew up, including the opportunity to meet some of their educators such as the late Margaret Walker Alexander. As I have combined my interests in education, history, and African American studies since my undergraduate days, I often reflect on Alexander's poem "For My People"—especially these lines:

> For the cramped bewildered years we went to school to learn
> to know the reasons why and the answers to and the
> people who and the places where and the days when, in
> memory of the bitter hours when we discovered we
> were black and poor and small and different and nobody
> cared and nobody wondered and nobody understood.

This passage makes me think about the African American educational experience, past and present. African Americans have long valued education even when no one else thought it mattered for them or when it was a threat to the social order. As a child I often played school, and I am grateful now to have the opportunity to contribute to what we know about the history of education in the United States including the intersection of historically white elite private schools, school desegregation, and African American educational experiences. I hope that children of all backgrounds will know that someone cares, that somebody wonders about them, and that someone understands them.

The Fearless Firsts since Graduating from Westminster

Dawn Clark, M.B.A, following her graduation from Westminster in 1976, attended St. Andrews Presbyterian College (now St. Andrews University) in Laurinburg, North Carolina, and graduated in 1980 with a degree in theater. After college, Dawn returned to Atlanta and worked for Citizens and Southern National Bank (now a part of Bank of America), the National Processing Center, and Mellon Bank (now the Bank of New York Mellon), primarily in the lockbox departments. In addition, she operated her own business, "It's Cookie Time." In 1992, Dawn earned her master's of business administration from the University of Tennessee. Between 1998 and 2001, Dawn served as head of the business department and as a professor at Knoxville College. Though unable to work full time due to multiple sclerosis, she continues to consult on an occasional basis.

Corliss Blount Denman, M.S., is the executive director in the Office of the Deputy President and Chief Operating Officer at M. D. Anderson Cancer Center in Houston, Texas. Following her graduation from Westminster in 1973, Corliss matriculated to Harvard University and graduated with majors in psychology and social relations. After a couple of years as a social worker, Corliss worked with AT&T for ten and a half years, through 1990, during which time she moved to Washington, D.C., and then returned to Houston. After spending two years at home with her children, Corliss resumed working at Methodist Hospital until 2001. At Methodist, she led the transplant program, and concurrently earned a master's of science in healthcare administration from Texas Woman's University (TWU). Since 2001, she has been with M. D. Anderson, working in the blood and marrow transplant department. Additionally, she has remained committed to helping students think widely about their future possibilities through programs such as Junior Achievement and by serving on the healthcare administration advisory council at TWU.

Joia Johnson, M.B.A. and J.D., is chief administrative officer, general counsel, and corporate secretary for Hanesbrands, Inc. Following graduation from Westminster in 1977, Joia attended Duke University and graduated with majors in public policy and economics. She then earned a master's of business administration from the Wharton School at the University of Pennsylvania and a Juris Doctor from the University of Pennsylvania Law School. Joia returned to Atlanta and began her legal career at Long & Aldridge (now McKenna Long & Aldridge). In 1989, she became the first general counsel for H. J. Russell and Company and remained there until 1999. She then became the first general counsel for Rare Hospitality International, Inc., a restaurant company. After approximately eight years, Joia joined Hanesbrands as executive vice president, general counsel, and corporate secretary.

Michael McBay, M.D., periodically alternates between the professions of medicine and music in Los Angeles, California. Following graduation from Westminster in 1972, Michael matriculated to Stanford University with the assistance of a partial scholarship from the National Science Foundation. While performing commercial rock music semiprofessionally and continuing his passion for competitive martial arts, Michael earned his medical degree from the University of California-Los Angeles and trained in emergency medicine at King/Drew Medical Center, also in Los Angeles. Michael is also the coauthor of *Spiritual High: Alternatives to Drugs and Substance Abuse*, published in 2005 with his spiritual teacher of thirty years, John-Roger.

Ron McBay, M.B.A., is an independent computer consultant in Atlanta, Georgia. Following graduation from Westminster in 1976, Ron matriculated to Princeton University and graduated with a bachelor's degree in mathematics. He also earned a master's of business administration from Stanford University. Following Stanford, Ron worked briefly as an account manager for AT&T. Additionally he has been a computer programmer in the private sector and at the Atlanta University Center.

Donata Russell Ross is CEO of Concessions International, LLC, and president of the Herman J. Russell Foundation, her family foundation in Atlanta, Georgia. Donata's father, the late Herman J. Russell, founded H. J. Russell Company in 1962 and Concessions International, LLC, in 1979. Both companies are currently led by the second generation, Donata and her two younger brothers, Jerome and Michael. H. J. Russell Company is the country's oldest and one of the largest minority-owned enterprise real estate firms specializing in construction and real estate development. After graduating from Westminster in 1977, Donata attended and graduated from the University of Pennsylvania with a bachelor's of economics in management and marketing. Immediately following college, she worked for IBM in Philadelphia. She soon realized that returning home to work with the family business would provide her more exposure and experience. After working within the property management division of H. J. Russell and Company for a year and a half, Donata transitioned to Concessions International, which currently operates over forty food and beverage concessions in eight airports. The company's portfolio includes franchised, licensed, and proprietary concessions, including casual dining, quick service, snack, deli, and bar and grill. The company is a franchisee of major national brands including Chick-fil-A, Fresh To Order, and Einstein Bros. Bagels.

Malcolm Ryder is a strategist and product architect at TechSoup Global. Prior to joining TechSoup in 2016, Malcolm operated his own consulting firm in IT strategy and management, including various tours of staff duty or business partnerships with clients including startups, Fortune 500 enterprises, and nonprofits. Malcolm received his bachelor of arts from Princeton. He was an independent major in visual arts and was one of the first photography graduates from Princeton outside of the art history program. Upon completing college, he worked as professional photographer, which led to him work with the National Endowment for the Arts. Following his time at the National Endowment for the Arts, Malcolm created the IT programming for the arts funding departments' business operations at the New York Foundation for the Arts and the NY State Council on the Arts, and he was a member of the advisory council for the National Association for Arts Information Exchange. After moving to Oakland, California, with his family, he began working for a small consulting firm in San Francisco's financial district and continued in IT as an executive or strategy consultant until his present position with TechSoup.

Jannard Wade graduated from Morehouse College in 1976 with a bachelor of arts in music and has since worked in financial services in Atlanta, Georgia. Immediately following college, Jannard began working for New York Life in sales and sales management. In 1999, he was voted president of the Atlanta Association of Life Underwriters, an organization that encompasses all life insurance agents in Atlanta. After twenty years with New York Life, Jannard was recruited by New England Financial in 2001, for which he worked as a sales manager. Since the end of 2008, Jannard has been an independent insurance broker.

Wanda Ward, *Ph.D.*, is senior adviser to the director at the National Science Foundation (NSF). Previously she served as the National Science Foundation's head of the Office of Integrative and International Activities and deputy assistant director of the Directorates for Education and Human Resources and Social, Behavioral, and Economic Sciences. From June 2015 to March 2017, she served as assistant director for broadening participation at the Office of Science and Technology Policy, White House Executive Office of the President, on detail from the NSF. Wanda earned her bachelor of arts in psychology and the Afro-American studies certificate from Princeton University in 1976 and her doctorate in psychology from Stanford University in 1981. Before joining the National Science Foundation in 1992, Wanda was an associate professor of psychology and founding director of the Center for Research on Multi-Ethnic Education at the University of Oklahoma, Norman. She has received numerous awards, including a Ford Foundation Fellowship; the American Psychological Association (APA) Presidential Citation (2005); the Federation of Behavioral, Psychological, and Cognitive Sciences' Richard T. Louttit Award (2006); and the U.S. Presidential Rank Award of Distinguished Executive (2006).

Notes

Abbreviations in Endnotes

Beck Archives-Westminster
    Lewis H. Beck Archives-The Westminster Schools
ISB   *Independent School Bulletin*
NAIS   National Association of Independent Schools
NAISR   *National Association of Independent Schools Report*
NCIS   National Council of Independent Schools
NCISR   *National Council of Independent Schools Report*
RG   Record Group
Rose Library   Stuart A. Rose Manuscript, Archives, and Rare Book Library, Emory University
SHCUNC   Southern Historical Collection, Louis Round Wilson Special Collections Library, University of North Carolina at Chapel Hill

Introduction

1. Jere Wells, personal communication with author, October 21, 2016, Atlanta, Ga.

2. Jannard Wade, interview with author, June 30, 2009, Atlanta, Ga.

3. The school name, The Westminster Schools, represents the once separate boys' and girls' schools for grades seven to twelve that existed until 1986. Currently all grades are coeducational. See The Westminster Schools, "About Us: History" (website).

4. Fabrikant, "At Elite Prep Schools"; "The Westminster Schools: Tuition and Financial Aid."

5. The Westminster Schools, "2015-2016 School Profile" (brochure); Dilonardo, "One Size Doesn't Fit All."

6. The Westminster Schools, "2015-2016 School Profile."

7. National Center for Education Statistics, "SAT Scores" (website).

8. The Westminster Schools, "2015-2016 School Profile."

9. Orsini, "A Context for Understanding Faculty Diversity," 43; Speede-Franklin, "Ethnic Diversity," 23.

10. Hardiman, Jackson, and Griffin, "Conceptual Foundations," 27-28.

11. For the full text of the decisions, see *Brown v. Board of Education of Topeka I*, 347 U.S. 483 (1954); *Brown v. Board of Education of Topeka II*, 349 U.S. 294 (1955).

12. Hall and Stevenson, "Double Jeopardy," 1-2. For definitions of elite schools, see Baird, *Elite Schools*; Chamberlain, *Our Independent Schools*; Gaztambide-Fernandez, "What Is an Elite Boarding School?"; Kraushaar, *American Nonpublic Schools*. Please also note that some parochial schools, however, are members of the National Association of Independent Schools.

13. The term *desegregation* will be used to describe Westminster's process for changing its admissions policies to consider children from all backgrounds. At times, *integration* will be used within text rather than desegregation, as dictated by the material under discussion. Based on a review of legal and social science literature, desegregation is not synonymous with integration, though they are often used as such. Integration or racial integration refers to a transformed society, and desegregation is one step toward fulfilling that transformation. For definitions of desegregation and integration, see Adair, *Desegregation*, 181 and 183; powell and Spencer, "Response: *Brown* Is Not *Brown*."

14. National Association of Independent Schools, "NAIS Independent School Facts at a Glance" (website); for public and private school statistics, see the Center for Education Reform, "K-12 Facts" (website); National Center for Education Statistics, "Digest of Education Statistics" (website).

15. National Association of Independent Schools, "What Is the Difference?" (website); Rickford, *We Are an African People*.

16. Hall and Stevenson, "Double Jeopardy," 2; Bourdieu, "Forms of Capital." Note that some historically black K-12 private schools are also independent schools. Nineteenth-century white academies, having supplanted the Latin grammar schools that had existed as feeder schools to colleges, proliferated between the American Revolution and the Civil War. These schools included college preparatory schools, female academies, college preparatory departments, military academies, and Roman Catholic academies. For historical accounts on the origins of independent schools and private education, see the following examples: Kraushaar, "Independent Schools and Their Antecedents," in *American Nonpublic Schools*, 54-88; Reese, "Changing Conceptions of 'Public' and 'Private'"; Sizer, "Academies: An Interpretation"; Tolley and Beadie, "School for Every Purpose."

17. Chamberlain, *Our Independent Schools*, 7; Arthur Powell, *Lessons from Privilege*, 62. Various kinds of independent schools exist: "The schools differ also as to their educational philosophy and goals. There are college preparatory schools, military schools, tutoring schools, laboratory and demonstration schools, conventional schools, and progressive experimental schools, schools specializing in foreign languages, in world mindedness, in community involvement, in music or fine arts, in choir singing, in athletics, in character building, in work-study programs, in no-nonsense discipline or in an informal, permissive, first-name atmosphere." See Kraushaar, *American Nonpublic Schools*, 54.

18. National Association of Independent Schools, "What Is the Difference?" (website).

19. Denominational schools are often categorized as Catholic, Protestant, or Jewish schools. Further, among Catholic schools, there are those considered parochial schools, diocesan schools, and "private" schools and academies. See Kraushaar, *American Nonpublic Schools*, 27-28, 54.

20. Chamberlain, *Our Independent Schools*, 114-18.

21. Wilson and Frank, *They Took Their Stand*, 9.

22. Arthur Powell, *Lessons from Privilege*; Wilson and Frank, *They Took Their Stand*.

23. For example, see Kraushaar, *American Nonpublic Schools*.

24. Cary, *Black Ice*; Judith Berry Griffin, "Human Diversity and Academic Excellence"; Arthur Powell, *Lessons from Privilege*; Slaughter and Johnson, *Visible Now*; Zweigenhaft and Domhoff, *Blacks in the White Elite*.

25. William Dandridge, interview by author, October 22, 2009, Philadelphia, Pa.

26. Kaestle, *Pillars of the Republic*; Fraser, *School in the United States*.

27. The vast historiography of school desegregation includes Liva Baker, *Second Battle of New Orleans*; R. Scott Baker, *Paradoxes of Desegregation*; Bolton, *Hardest Deal of All*; Douglass, *Reading, Writing, and Race*; Hoppe and Speck, *Maxine Smith's Unwilling Pupils*; and Pratt, *Color of Their Skin*. Scholars have also provided accounts of *Brown*'s role in the Civil Rights Movement, and its influence on public education since the 1950s. Examples include V. P. Franklin, "Introduction: *Brown v. Board of Education*"; Klarman, "How *Brown* Changed Race Relations"; Ladson-Billings, "Landing on the Wrong Note"; Orfield and Eaton, *Dismantling Desegregation*.

28. Erickson, *Making the Unequal Metropolis*; Gadsden, *Between North and South*; K'Meyer, *From* Brown *to* Meredith.

29. Danns, *Desegregating Chicago's Public Schools*; Delmont, *Why Busing Failed*.

30. Delmont, *Why Busing Failed*, 3-4.

31. Lassiter and Crespino, *Myth of Southern Exceptionalism*.

32. The historiography on Southern black education in public and private schools following the Civil War is a robust field of study; this note and others below provide a limited number of examples. On public and private segregated black schooling, see James Anderson, *Education of Blacks in the South*. For histories of black private institutions, see Thomas Jesse Jones, *Negro Education*; Grant and Grant, *Way It Was in the South*; Cooper, *Between Struggle and Hope*; Wadelington and Knapp, *Charlotte Hawkins Brown & Palmer Memorial Institute*.

33. Discussion of this ideological tension has been well documented. Some examples include James Anderson, "Education and the Race Problem in the New South: The Struggle for Ideological Hegemony," in James Anderson, *Education of Blacks in the South*, 7-109; Du Bois, "Of Booker T. Washington and Others"; Washington, *Up from Slavery*; and Alridge, *Educational Thought of W. E. B. Du Bois*.

34. On excellent segregated black schooling, see Faustine Childress Jones, *Traditional Model of Educational Excellence*; Pierson, *Laboratory of Learning*; Stewart, *First Class*; and Walker, *Their Highest Potential*. On teachers and principals, examples include Fultz, "African American Teachers in the South, 1890-1940"; Walker, "Black Educators as Educational Advocates"; and Walker, *Hello Professor*. On fights for equalization, see Thuesen, *Greater Than Equal*. On cultural capital, see Franklin and Savage, *Cultural Capital and Black Education*.

35. On the history of African Americans in parochial schools see Franklin and Mc-Donald, "Blacks in Urban Catholic Schools in the United States"; Katrina Sanders, "Forgotten or Simply Ignored"; Hayes, "The Rise and Fall of a Black Private School"; Irvine and Foster, *Growing Up African American in Catholic Schools*.

36. Examples include Patillo-Beals, *Warriors Don't Cry*; Bates, "The Long Shadow of Little Rock"; Hampton and Fayer, *Voices of Freedom*; Wells et al., *Both Sides Now*.

37. For desegregation effects on black schooling, see Cecelski, *Along Freedom Road*; Fairclough, "Costs of *Brown*"; Fultz, "Displacement of Black Educators Post-*Brown*"; Ladson-Billings, "Landing on the Wrong Note."

38. Jon Hale, *Freedom Schools*; Crystal Sanders, *Chance for Change*.

39. Dougherty, *More Than One Struggle*; Perrillo, *Uncivil Rights*; Podair, *Strike That Changed New York*; Todd-Breland, "Control and Independence."

40. Biondi, *Black Revolution on Campus*; Cecelski, *Along Freedom Road*; Danns, "Chicago High School Students' Movement"; De Schweinitz, *If We Could Change the World*; Rogers, *Black Campus Movement*; Williamson, *Black Power on Campus*; Willis, "'Let Me In.'"

41. Brown, "'Opening the Gates'"; Gannon, "From White Flight to Open Admissions"; Kruse, *White Flight*; Morris, "Forcing Progress."

42. For a discussion of how the southern economy changed during the twentieth century, see Schulman, *From Cotton Belt to Sunbelt*.

43. Bayor, *Race and the Shaping of Twentieth-Century Atlanta*; Brown-Nagin, *Courage to Dissent*; Grady-Willis, *Challenging U.S. Apartheid*; Walker, "Black Educators as Educational Advocates"; Walker, *Lost Education of Horace Tate*.

44. Roche, *Restructured Resistance*; O'Brien, *Politics of Race and Schooling*.

45. Kean, *Desegregating Private Higher Education in the South*, 1.

46. Gannon, "From White Flight to Open Admissions." For a discussion of elite private schools with religious affiliations, see Kruse, *White Flight*, 171–79.

47. Hein, "Image of 'A City Too Busy to Hate'"; Harold H. Martin, *William Berry Hartsfield*; Jackson, "Desegregation: Atlanta Style"; Plank and Turner, "Changing Patterns in Black School Politics"; Hornsby Jr., "Black Public Education in Atlanta, Georgia, 1954–1973"; McGrath, "From Tokenism to Community Control."

48. Lassiter, *Silent Majority*.

49. Champagne, "Segregation Academy and the Law," 58. Other documentation of the 1970 decision may be found in Kraushaar, *American Nonpublic Schools*, 257.

50. Speede-Franklin, "Ethnic Diversity," 23.

51. Keith Evans, personal communication with author, October 21, 2016, Atlanta, Ga.; Keith Evans, email communication with author, April 23, 2017.

52. Kevin Kruse, "Beyond the Southern Cross."

53. Borstelmann, *The 1970s*; Freund, "Marketing the Free Market."

54. Borstelmann, *The 1970s*; Schulman and Zelizer, *Rightward Bound*.

55. Friedman, "Role of Government in Education"; Chubb and Moe, *Politics, Markets, and America's Schools*.

56. Stevens, *Creating a Class*, 146.

57. Stevens, 154.

58. Stevens, 144–55.

59. Gaztambide-Fernandez, "What Is an Elite Boarding School?," 1109; Hall and Stevenson, "Double Jeopardy," 2.

60. Khan, *Privilege*, 13.

61. Khan, 5.

62. Khan, 17, 197.

63. Orfield and Frankenberg, with Ee and Kuscera, *Brown at 60*.

64. *Parents Involved in Community Schools v. Seattle School District No. 1*, 551 U.S. 701 (2007).

65. Merriam, *Qualitative Research*, 35.

66. Lepore, "Historians Who Love Too Much," 133.

67. Dougherty, "From Anecdote to Analysis"; Noblit and Dempsey, *Social Construction of Virtue*; Portelli, "Peculiarities of Oral History"; Walker, *Their Highest Potential*, 221-26; Yow, *Recording Oral History*.

68. DeCuir and Dixson, "'So When It Comes Out, They Aren't That Surprised That It Is There.'"

Chapter One

1. Mira B. Wilson, "Colored Students Are an Asset," *ISB* Series '48-'49, no. 3 (February 1949): 12.

2. Wilson, "Colored Students Are an Asset," 13.

3. "The School Atlanta Needs," RG 13.07, box 1, folder: 1952 Promotional Materials (3 of 3). Office of Institutional Advancement, Campaigns and Promotional Materials, Beck Archives-Westminster.

4. "The School Atlanta Needs."

5. Litwack, *Trouble in Mind*, xv-xvi.

6. Kruse, *White Flight*, 12.

7. Brown-Nagin, *Courage to Dissent*, 211.

8. Kruse, *White Flight*, 23.

9. Plank and Turner, "Changing Patterns in Black School Politics," 589.

10. Gannon, "From White Flight to Open Admissions," 19.

11. Kruse, *White Flight*, 36.

12. Bayor, *Race and the Shaping of Twentieth-Century Atlanta*, 26.

13. Bayor, 27.

14. For studies on the NAACP Legal and Educational Defense Fund, Inc., and the legal development of *Brown v. Board of Education*, see Kluger, *Simple Justice*; Waldo E. Martin, Brown v. Board of Education; McNeil, *Groundwork*; Tushnet, *NAACP's Legal Strategy*.

15. O'Brien, "Georgia's Response to *Brown v. Board of Education*," 93.

16. NCIS, "Independent School Associations—Membership Standards," *NCISR*, no. 15 (June 1950): 7.

17. NCIS, "Southern Association of Colleges and Schools," *NCISR*, no. 17 (December 1950): 5.

18. NCIS, *NCISR*, no. 18 (March 1951): 3.

19. NCIS, "Georgia: Minimum Salaries," *NCISR*, no. 19 (June 1951): 2.

20. NCIS, "Georgia: Minimum Salaries," *NCISR*, no. 20 (September 1951): 5.

21. NCIS, "Legislation, Accreditation, Etc.: Southern Association of Independent Schools," *NCISR*, no. 22 (March 1952): 9.

22. Gannon, "From White Flight to Open Admissions," 49.

23. Gannon, 49.

24. Pressly, *Formative Years*, v-ix, 1-9.

25. Stuart R. Oglesby, "Presbyterian News Notes," ca. 1951, RG 5.01, box 2, folder: Clippings, Office of the President [Restricted], Pressly, Dr. William L., Beck Archives-Westminster.

26. Oglesby, "Presbyterian News Notes."

27. Pressly, *Formative Years*, 8-9.

28. Pressly, 8.

29. William L. Pressly to Dr. Vernon Broyles and Westminster Board, May 17, 1951, RG 5.01, box 7, folder 2: Correspondence, Dr. V. Broyles from Dr. Pressly, Office of the President [Restricted], Pressly, Dr. William L., Beck Archives-Westminster.

30. "The Physical Development of the School," RG 5.01, box 1, folder: Administrative Records 1956-1961, Office of the President [Restricted], Pressly, Dr. William L., Beck Archives-Westminster.

31. Minutes, June 23, 1953, RG 4.03, box 1, folder: Minutes—August 1952–June 1954. Board of Trustees [Restricted], Minutes, Beck Archives-Westminster.

32. Minutes, November 24, 1952, RG 4.03, box 1, folder: Minutes—August 1952–June 1954. Board of Trustees [Restricted], Minutes, Beck Archives-Westminster; Pressly, *Formative Years*, 33, 35.

33. Fund for the Advancement of Education, letter to Pressly, December 16, 1953, RG 4.05, box 1a, folder: Fund for the Advancement of Education, 1953-1956, Board of Trustees [Restricted], Correspondence, Beck Archives-Westminster.

34. "The Westminster Schools," advertisement, *Rush*, November 5, 1953, RG 5.01, box 2, folder: Clippings, Office of the President [Restricted], Pressly, Dr. William L., Beck Archives-Westminster; "Expenses," RG 5.01, box 1, folder: Administrative Records, 1953-1954, Office of the President [Restricted], Pressly, Dr. William L., Beck Archives-Westminster; "The Physical Development of the School," RG 5.01, box 1, folder: Administrative Records, 1956-1961, Office of the President [Restricted], Pressly, Dr. William L., Beck Archives-Westminster.

35. Celestine Sibley, "A Quiet Man with Ideas," *Atlanta Constitution*, July 2, 1953, RG 5.01, box 2, folder: Clippings, Office of the President [Restricted], Pressly, Dr. William L., Beck Archives-Westminster.

36. Kruse, *White Flight*, 39-40.

37. "A Great City, A Great School," RG 13.07, box 1, folder: 1954 Campaign, Office of Institutional Advancement, Campaigns and Promotional Materials, Beck Archives-Westminster.

38. "Great City, A Great School"; Gannon, "From White Flight to Open Admissions," 55.

39. Pressly, *Formative Years*, 52.

40. Kluger, *Simple Justice*, 713.

41. O'Brien, "Georgia's Response to *Brown v. Board of Education*," 131.

42. Prior to 1971, the Georgia Education Association served white teachers, whereas black teachers belonged to the Georgia Teachers and Education Association. In 1971, the two organizations merged and became the Georgia Association of Educators.

43. O'Brien, "Georgia's Response to *Brown v. Board of Education*," 137.

44. McGrath, "Great Expectations," 62.

45. Adamson, "Few Black Voices Heard," 340-41.

46. Adamson, 342.

47. Regina Turner, a black student who remained at Clinton for two more years after the fall of 1956 but graduated from an all-black high school in Tallahassee, Florida, and Jo Ann Allen, another student who also moved from Clinton with her family, aptly describe their experiences. See Adamson, "Few Black Voices Heard," 344, 347. For examples, especially during this stage of desegregation, see Bates, "Long Shadow of Little Rock"; Hampton and Fayer, *Voices of Freedom*.

48. O'Brien, "Georgia's Response to *Brown v. Board of Education*," 149-67.

49. O'Brien, 171.

50. The students now known as the Little Rock Nine were Carlotta Walls, Jefferson Thomas, Elizabeth Eckford, Thelma Mothershed, Melba Pattillo, Ernest Green, Terrance Roberts, Gloria Ray, and Minnijean Brown. Prior to their desegregation of Central High, Faubus had declared that "'blood will run in the streets' if Negro pupils should attempt to enter Central High School." See Bates, "Long Shadow of Little Rock," 98.

51. Hampton and Fayer, *Voices of Freedom*, 47.

52. United States Census, "Statistics of Population," 1900 Census (website); United States Census, "Number of Inhabitants, United States Summary," 1950 Census (website).

53. Steffes, *School, Society, and State*, 2, 5.

54. Adams, *Education for Extinction*; Mirel, *Patriotic Pluralism*; Sanchez, *Becoming Mexican American*; Tamura, *Americanization, Acculturation, and Ethnic Identity*.

55. Steffes, *School, Society, and State*, 173.

56. Steffes, 174-75.

57. Reese, "Changing Conceptions of 'Public' and 'Private,'" 104.

58. Steffes, *School, Society, and State*, 4.

59. Arthur Powell, *Lessons from Privilege*, 62-63.

60. Cary Potter, "NAIS 25 or 62?," *Independent School* 47, no. 1 (Fall 1987): 57.

61. Potter, 58.

62. Kraushaar, *American Nonpublic Schools*, 54; Reese, "Changing Conceptions of 'Public' and 'Private,'" 100.

63. Chamberlain, *Our Independent Schools*, 7; Arthur Powell, *Lessons from Privilege*, 62.

64. Powell, *Lessons from Privilege*, 62.

65. Powell, 62.

66. Potter, "NAIS 25 or 62?," 59.

67. Potter, 59.

68. NCIS, *National Council Report*, no. 2 (December 1946): 4.

69. Potter, "NAIS 25 or 62?," 60.

70. Potter, 60-61.

71. Powell, *Lessons from Privilege*, 85; Zweigenhaft and Domhoff, *Blacks in the White Elite*, 27.

72. Mallery, *Negro Students in Independent Schools*, 59.

73. "What the Schools Are Doing," *ISB* Series '49-'50, no. 2 (January 1949): 43.

74. Perkins, "First Black Talent Identification Program," 174.

75. Mallery, *Negro Students in Independent Schools*, 11.

76. "What the Schools Are Doing," *ISB* Series '55-'56, no. 4 (May 1956): 25.

77. Zweigenhaft and Domhoff, *Blacks in the White Elite*, 27.

78. Zweigenhaft and Domhoff, 27-28.

79. NCIS, "Independent Schools and the 'Crisis': Policy Statement," *NCISR*, no. 46 (December 1957): 11.

80. Miller, *Racial Discrimination and Private Education*, 19.

81. James V. Moffat, "The Admissions Officer in Public Relations," *ISB* Series '55-'56, no. 2 (January, 1956): 17.

82. Miller, *Racial Discrimination and Private Education*, 22.

83. Miller, 29.

84. "May Day Pageant Held Friday, May 30," *Westminster Tattler*, June 3, 1952, 1, RG 21.03, Beck Archives-Westminster.

85. Grace Elizabeth Hale, *Making Whiteness*, 52-53.

86. Hale, 52-53.

87. "The Pickaninny," advertisement, *Westminster Tattler*, April 1954, 3, RG 21.03, Beck Archives-Westminster.

88. Pilgrim, "The Pickaninny Caricature" (website).

89. "The Parade of the Floats," *Westminster Chimes*, March 1956, 3, RG 21.04, Beck Archives-Westminster.

90. "Slave Market Provides Rat's Revenge on Seniors," *Mark Sheet*, January 13, 1962, 2, RG 21.05, Beck Archives-Westminster.

91. Woodson, *Education of the Negro Prior to 1861*, 5.

92. Williams, *Self-Taught*, 203-13.

93. Williams, 7.

94. Hager, *Word by Word*.

95. Hager, 181.

96. Jacqueline Jones, *Soldiers of Light and Love*, 9.

97. James Anderson, *Education of Blacks in the South*, 19.

98. Anderson, 27, 31.

99. Bond, *Education of the Negro in the American Social Order*, 98; Bullock, *History of Negro Education in the South*, 74.

100. Du Bois, *The Souls of Black Folk*, 44.

101. Alridge, *Educational Thought of W. E. B. Du Bois*, 55.

102. In addition to James Anderson, *Education of Blacks in the South*, other scholars have examined how white philanthropy and black education were intertwined throughout the first half of the twentieth century, and how white southern policy-makers have been part and parcel of segregated black education and black educational opportunities throughout the twentieth century. See Anderson and Moss, *Dangerous Donations*; Watkins, *White Architects of Black Education*.

103. James Anderson, *Education of Blacks in the South*, 92, 94.

104. Anderson, 184-85.

105. Plank and Turner, "Changing Patterns in Black School Politics," 593.

106. Litwack, *Trouble in Mind*, 63.

107. Plank and Turner, "Changing Patterns in Black School Politics," 594. Also see Bayor, *Race and the Shaping of Twentieth-Century Atlanta*, 197-207.

108. Sowell, "Patterns of Black Excellence," 31.

109. James Anderson, *Education of Blacks in the South*, 181.

110. Anderson, 188, 197.

111. Anderson, 197. Orr, *History of Education in Georgia*, 295-96. See also Thomas Jesse Jones, *Negro Education*.

112. Cooper, *Between Struggle and Hope*, 14.

113. Reynolds, "Charlotte Hawkins Brown and the Palmer Institute," 12.

114. Wadelington and Knapp, *Charlotte Hawkins Brown & Palmer Memorial Institute*, 11.

115. James Anderson, *Education of Blacks in the South*, 146.

116. Orr, *History of Education in Georgia*, 305.

117. Orr, 306.

118. Bacote, *Story of Atlanta University*, 29.

119. Bacote, 34.

120. Bacote, 30.

121. Bacote, 143. In 1930, Atlanta University, under the presidency of John Hope, "in connection with the Department of Education, would operate a laboratory school with a kindergarten, eight elementary grades, and a four-year high school." Bacote, *Story of Atlanta University*, 293. The high school portion was closed by the 1942-43 school year. See Bacote, 335-57.

122. Bacote, *Story of Atlanta University*, 257.

123. Jewell, *Race, Social Reform, and the Making of a Middle Class*. See also James Anderson, *Education of Blacks in the South*, 238-78.

124. Higginbotham, *Righteous Discontent*, 45.

125. Walker, *Their Highest Potential*, 205. See also Walker, *Hello Professor*; Walker, *Lost Education of Horace Tate*.

Chapter Two

1. Pressly, *Formative Years*, 121.

2. Kruse, *White Flight*, 173.

3. "The Physical Development of the School," RG 5.01, box 1, folder: Administrative Records 1956-1961, Office of the President [Restricted], Pressly, Dr. William L., Beck Archives-Westminster.

4. McGrath, "From Tokenism to Community Control," 845.

5. Minutes, November 12, 1958, RG 4.03, box 1, folder: Minutes—September 1957-June 1959. Board of Trustees [Restricted], Minutes, Beck Archives-Westminster.

6. Clipping, ca. March 1958, Roland M. Frye Biographical Files, Rose Library.

7. Kruse, *White Flight*, 138-39; Lassiter, *Silent Majority*.

8. Minutes, December 10, 1958, RG 4.03, box 1, folder: Minutes—September 1957-June 1959. Board of Trustees [Restricted], Minutes, Beck Archives-Westminster.

9. Minutes, December 10, 1958.

10. Minutes, January 14, 1959, RG 4.03, box 1, folder: Minutes—September 1957-June 1959. Board of Trustees [Restricted], Minutes, Beck Archives-Westminster.

11. "Both Sides Given to School Crisis," *Atlanta Journal*, April 3, 1959, 28, Roland M. Frye Biographical Materials, Rose Library.

12. Minutes, January 14, 1959.

13. Gong, "Race, Class, and Atlanta Public School Integration, 54.

14. McGrath, "Great Expectations," 157.

15. NCIS, "Legislation—National Defense Education Act," *NCISR*, no. 3 (June 1959): 6.

16. NCIS, "New Schools in the South," *NCISR*, no. 52 (March 1959): 2.

17. NCIS, 2-3.

18. NCIS, "Help for New Schools: A Manual," *NCISR*, no. 53 (June 1959): 3.

19. NCIS, "The Growth of Private Schools," *NCISR*, no. 86 (March 1960): 8.

20. See Liva Baker, *Second Battle of New Orleans*; Pratt, *Color of Their Skin*.

21. Roche, *Restructured Resistance*, xi. As indicated by Roche, Sibley had served as general counsel for Coca-Cola and president of the Atlanta-based Trust Company Bank and was a partner in one of the South's premier law firms, King and Spalding.

22. Roche, *Restructured Resistance*, 164, 166; O'Brien, "Georgia's Response to *Brown v. Board of Education*," 253.

23. O'Brien, "Georgia's Response to *Brown v. Board of Education*," 275.

24. Roche, *Restructured Resistance*, 183.

25. Kean, *Desegregating Private Higher Education in the South*, 182.

26. Kean, 182.

27. Kean, 184.

28. Minutes, GACHR Executive Committee, January 5, 1961, Eliza K. Paschall Papers, Rose Library.

29. Minutes, April 12, 1961, 8, RG 4.03, box 1, folder: Minutes—September 1959-June 1961, Board of Trustees [Restricted], Minutes, Beck Archives-Westminster.

30. NCIS, "National Defense Education Act Amendments," *NCISR*, no. 57 (March 1960): 6.

31. NCIS, "Legislation and Taxation—National Defense Education Act," *NCISR*, no. 60 (December 1960): 4.

32. NCIS, "Legislation and Taxation—Federal Legislation," *NCISR*, no. 62 (April 1961): 1.

33. "School Supports Child's Home," *Mark Sheet*, December 2, 1958, 2, RG 21.05, Beck Archives-Westminster.

34. "Dwike Mitchell and Willie Ruff Perform at Dual Assembly; Students Cheer Disc Stars," *Mark Sheet*, October 24, 1958, 1, RG 21.05, Beck Archives-Westminster.

35. "Midnighters Entertain at Two Dances and Jam Session during Big Jazz Weekend," *Mark Sheet*, February 13, 1959, 1, RG 21.05, Beck Archives-Westminster.

36. *Mark Sheet*, April 22, 1960, 3, RG 21.05, Beck Archives-Westminster.

37. "Noted R&B Expert Comments on Bo Diddley," *Mark Sheet*, February 17, 1961, 1, RG 21.05, Beck Archives-Westminster.

38. "Any Disturbance Affects Students throughout US," *Westminster Chimes*, October 1958, 2, RG 21.04, Beck Archives-Westminster.

39. "Informed Students to Decide between Nixon and Kennedy," *Westminster Chimes*, October 1960, 1, RG 21.04, Beck Archives-Westminster; "Editor's Desk: Students Must Think on National Scenes," *Westminster Chimes*, October 1960, 2, RG

21.04, Beck Archives-Westminster; Eudora Simmons, "Letter to the Editor: Awareness of Events Advocated by Students," *Westminster Chimes*, February 1961, 2, RG 21.04, Beck Archives-Westminster.

40. "Keep Public Schools Open," *Mark Sheet*, December 19, 1958, 2, RG 21.05, Beck Archives-Westminster.

41. "The Problem of Tolerance," *Mark Sheet*, December 17, 1959, 2, RG 21.05, Beck Archives-Westminster.

42. Nan Pendergrast, interview by author, July 29, 2009, Atlanta, Ga.

43. John Pendergrast, "Separate but Equal?," *Mark Sheet*, February 12, 1960, 2, RG 21.05, Beck Archives-Westminster.

44. Pendergrast, 2.

45. McGrath, "Great Expectations," 165.

46. McGrath, 166-67.

47. Liva Baker, *Second Battle of New Orleans*, 371; Pratt, *Color of Their Skin*, 36-37; Hoppe and Speck, *Maxine Smith's Unwilling Pupils*, 33.

48. McGrath, "Great Expectations," 168.

49. McGrath, 185.

50. Hornsby, "Black Public Education in Atlanta, Georgia," 28.

51. McGrath, "Great Expectations," 172.

52. McGrath, 177.

53. Minutes, GACHR Executive Committee, January 5, 1961, Eliza K. Paschall Papers, Rose Library.

54. Though ten were granted transfers in the spring of 1961, only nine actually transferred.

55. Kruse, *White Flight*, 151.

56. Kruse, 156-57.

57. Kruse, 159-60.

58. Minutes, September 13, 1961, RG 4.03, box 1, folder: Minutes—August 1961-July 1964. Board of Trustees [Restricted], Minutes, Beck Archives-Westminster.

59. Minutes, GACHR Board of Directors, September 12, 1961, Eliza K. Paschall Papers, Rose Library.

60. NCIS, "Legislation—Survey of School Opinion," *NCISR*, no. 64 (September 1961): 1.

61. Minutes, October 11, 1961, RG 4.03, box 1, folder: Minutes—August 1961-July 1964. Board of Trustees [Restricted], Minutes, Beck Archives-Westminster.

62. NCIS, "Legislation—Federal Legislation," *NCISR*, no. 62 (April 1961): 2-3.

63. The slave auction was mentioned again in the article, "Boys' School Prepares for Child's Home Drive," *Mark Sheet*, November 18, 1960, 1, RG 21.05, Beck Archives-Westminster.

64. Richard Weiss, *Mark Sheet*, October 13, 1961, 1, RG 21.05, Beck Archive-Westminster.

65. Parents' Council Meeting Minutes, November 7, 1961, RG 5.01, box 3a, folder: Parents Council Meetings 1961-1970, Office of the President [Restricted], Pressly, Dr. William L., Beck Archives-Westminster.

66. Daniel, *Lost Revolutions*, 148.

67. Ralph McGill Jr., "Prejudice?," *Mark Sheet*, October 13, 1961, 2, RG 21.05, Beck Archives-Westminster.

68. McGill Jr., 2.

69. Brooks Griffin, "Discrimination," *Mark Sheet*, November 22, 1961, 2, RG 21.05, Beck Archives-Westminster.

70. Mal Dunlevie, "Criticism," *Mark Sheet*, November 22, 1961, 2, RG 21.05, Beck Archives-Westminster.

71. Robert Dornbush, "Freshman Charges Student Council with Partiality," *Mark Sheet*, December 19, 1961, 2, RG 21.05, Beck Archives-Westminster.

72. GACHR Newsletter, *School News*, March 1962, Eliza K. Paschall Papers, Rose Library.

73. Eliza Paschall to William Pressly, May 30, 1962, Eliza K. Paschall Papers, Rose Library.

74. Parents' Council Meeting Minutes, April 22, 1962, RG 5.01, box 3a, folder: Parents Council Meetings, 1961-1970, Office of the President [Restricted], Pressly, Dr. William L., Beck Archives-Westminster.

75. President's Report to the Board, November 1962, RG 5.01, box 12, folder: 1962, Dr. William L. Pressly Papers, Office of the President [Restricted], Pressly, Dr. William L., Beck Archives-Westminster.

76. Nan Pendergrast, interview by author, July 29, 2009, Atlanta, Ga.

77. Jordan-Taylor, "Graduate Study and Jim Crow."

78. NCIS, "Introduction: NCIS-ISEB," *NCISR*, no. 67 (April 1962): 1.

79. Hornsby, "Black Public Education in Atlanta, Georgia," 30.

80. Hornsby, 30.

81. Kean, *Desegregating Private Higher Education in the South*, 185-86.

82. Kruse, *White Flight*, 209.

83. Kruse, 210.

84. "Prospectus in Human Relations in Greater Atlanta," 1963, Eliza K. Paschall Papers, Rose Library.

85. Gannon, "From White Flight to Open Admissions," 73.

86. Gannon, 80. Also because of age, Martin Luther King III was not tested for admission to Trinity; children had to be six years old to enroll at Trinity. See Gannon, "From White Flight to Open Admissions," 78.

87. Quoted in Kruse, *White Flight*, 175.

88. *Atlanta Journal*, March 16, 1963, 3, quoted in Gannon, "From White Flight to Open Admissions," 95. For more on Lovett, see Wade, "Forcing Progress."

89. Eliza Paschall to Kay Hocking, Nancy Perkins, and Anne Nelson, February 20, 1963, Eliza K. Paschall Papers, Rose Library.

90. Gannon, "From White Flight to Open Admissions," 108.

91. Two Year Report on Independent Schools Talent Search Program, box 13, Anne C. Stouffer Foundation Records, SHCUNC.

92. NAIS, "Broadening Educational Opportunities-Independent Schools Talent Search Program," *Report*, May 1964, 7-8.

93. NAIS, 7-8; Two Year Report on Independent Schools Talent Search Program.

94. NAIS, "Civil Rights," *NAISR*, no. 6 (October 1963): 7-8.

95. Kruse, *White Flight*, 205.

Chapter Three

1. Minutes, October 9, 1964, RG 4.03, box 1, folder: Minutes—August 1961-July 1964. Board of Trustees [Restricted], Minutes, Beck Archives-Westminster.

2. In the fall of 1963, the *Westminster Chimes* and the *Mark Sheet* merged to become the *Westminster Bi-Line*.

3. "Christian Attitude Is Strongly Urged," *Westminster Bi-Line*, November 1963, 4, RG 21.06, Beck Archives-Westminster.

4. Evans, "The Drag Line," *Westminster Bi-Line*, December 20, 1963, 2, RG 21.06, Beck Archives-Westminster.

5. Mallery, *Negro Students in Independent Schools*, 5.

6. Advice came from heads of schools such as the Wooster School in Danbury, Connecticut, Emma Willard School in Troy, New York, Commonwealth School in Boston, Massachusetts, the Friends School in Haverford, Pennsylvania, Shady Hill in Cambridge, Massachusetts, Francis Parker in Chicago, Illinois, and Phillips Exeter in New Hampshire.

7. Mallery, *Negro Students in Independent Schools*, 20.

8. Gannon, "From White Flight to Open Admissions," 109.

9. Gannon, 81-82.

10. Kruse, *White Flight*, 214.

11. Eliza Paschall to William Pressly, December 9, 1963, Eliza K. Paschall Papers, Rose Library.

12. Brown-Nagin, *Courage to Dissent*, 221-23.

13. Kruse, *White Flight*, 216.

14. Kruse, 219.

15. "Council on Human Relations of Greater Atlanta, Newsletter, January 1964," Eliza K. Paschall Papers, Rose Library.

16. Eliza Paschall to Max Taylor, March 26, 1964, Eliza K. Paschall Papers, Rose Library.

17. Eliza Paschall to members of the GACHR Board, confidential memorandum, n.d., Eliza K. Paschall Papers, Rose Library.

18. Kruse, *White Flight*, 137.

19. Rabbi Jacob M. Rothschild to William Pressly, April 20, 1964, RG 5.01, box 8, folder: Correspondence 1961-1966, Office of the President [Restricted], Pressly, Dr. William L., Beck Archives-Westminster.

20. Liva Baker, *Second Battle of New Orleans*, 472.

21. Baker, 472.

22. NAIS, "Broadening Educational Opportunities, Independent Schools Talent Search Program, Dartmouth ABC Program," *NAISR*, no. 9 (May 1964): 8.

23. "Two Year Report on Independent Schools Talent Search Program," box 13, Anne C. Stouffer Foundation Records, SHCUNC.

24. Pressly, *Formative Years*, 148.

25. Gannon, "From White Flight to Open Admissions," 110.

26. Memorandum to the Faculty, January 5, 1965, RG 5.01, box 1, folder: Administrative Records 1963-1965, Office of the President [Restricted], Pressly, Dr. William L., Beck Archives-Westminster.

27. NAIS, "Legislation," *NAISR*, no. 3 (December 1962): 6; NAIS, "Legislation," *NAISR*, no. 4 (April 1963): 6-7; NAIS, "Legislation," *NAISR*, no. 5 (June 1963): 4-5; NAIS, "Legislation," *NAISR*, no. 6 (October 1963): 5-6; NAIS, "Legislation," *NAISR*, no. 9 (May 1964): 8-9; NAIS, "Legislation," *NAISR*, no. 10 (September 1964): 5. See also Frank B. Keith, "Federal Aid and Non-Public Schools," *ISB* Series '61-'62, no. 2 (January 1962): 69-70.

28. The loan-forgiveness portion of the act had been extended to private school teachers; independent school teachers became eligible for stipends while they attended NDEA institutes for advanced study; and the institutes (originally only for foreign languages and counseling) were broadened to include "history, geography, modern foreign languages, reading, and English, as well as for teachers of disadvantaged youth, librarians, and educational media specialists." See NAIS, "Legislation—National Defense Education Act," *NAISR*, no. 12 (February 1965): 6-7.

29. NAIS, "Legislation—Federal Aid," *NAISR*, no. 13 (May 1965): 5.

30. NAIS, "Legislation—Federal Aid," 5-6; NAIS, "Legislation—Elementary and Secondary Education Act of 1965," *NAISR*, no. 14 (September 1965): 6.

31. NAIS, "The White House Conference—Three Observations," *NAISR*, no. 14 (September 1965): 2.

32. NAIS, "The White House Conference," 2.

33. NAIS, "Broadening Educational Opportunities—Independent Schools Talent Search Program, *NAISR*, no. 12 (February 1965): 8.

34. See James Anderson, *Education of Blacks in the South*; Watkins, *White Architects of Black Education*.

35. NAIS, "Broadening Educational Opportunities," 8.

36. Speede-Franklin, "Ethnic Diversity," 23.

37. "Education Conference," *ISB* 24, no. 3 (April, 1965): 57.

38. Moynihan, "Negro Family," 23.

39. Moynihan, 33.

40. Hornsby, "Black Public Education in Atlanta, Georgia," 32.

41. Gannon, "From White Flight to Open Admissions," 109.

42. Bob Bradbury, "Letter to the Editor," *Westminster Bi-Line*, October 11, 1965, 2, RG 21.06, Beck Archives-Westminster.

43. "Civil Rights: Segregation: Federal Income Tax: Exemptions and Deductions," 1412.

44. "Civil Rights: Segregation," 1432.

45. Minutes, October 14, 1965, RG 4.03, box 1, folder: September 1964-June 1967. Board of Trustees [Restricted], Minutes, Beck Archives-Westminster.

46. Pressly, *Formative Years*, 149.

47. Pressly, 150.

48. Minutes, November 11, 1965, RG 4.03, box 1, folder: September 1964-June 1967. Board of Trustees [Restricted], Minutes, Beck Archives-Westminster.

49. "Westminster Sets Desegregation," *Westminster Bi-Line*, December 16, 1965, 1, RG 21.06, Beck Archives-Westminster; Wayne Kelley, "Westminster Board Sets Desegregation," *Atlanta Constitution*, November 14, 1965, 55, Beck Archives-Westminster.

50. Pressly, *Formative Years*, 149.

51. Pressly, 150.

52. Pressly, 150.

53. Kelley reported that "private Catholic schools were desegregated here and throughout North Georgia in 1962," in "Westminster Board Sets Desegregation," 55.

54. Pressly, *Formative Years*, 149.

55. Minutes, December 8, 1965, RG 4.03, box 1, folder: September 1964-June 1967. Board of Trustees [Restricted], Minutes, Beck Archives-Westminster.

56. Minutes, December 8, 1965.

57. William Pressly to Robert Woodruff, November 12, 1965, Robert Winship Woodruff Papers, Rose Library.

58. "Westminster Sets Desegregation," *Westminster Bi-Line*, 1.

59. "Letter from the Editors," *Westminster Bi-Line*, December 16, 1965, 2, RG 21.06, Beck Archives-Westminster.

60. J. Cohen and Pendergrast, "Senior Students Examine Birch, Bigotry, and Tolerance," *Westminster Bi-Line*, November 8, 1965, 2, RG 21.06, Beck Archives-Westminster.

61. D. Field, "Minority Scapegoat Idea Needs to Be Cast Aside," *Westminster Bi-Line*, December 16, 1965, 2, RG 21.06, Beck Archives-Westminster.

62. Thomas M. Mikula, "Education of the Disadvantaged," *ISB* 25, no. 2 (December 1965): 17.

63. Mikula, 18.

64. Edward Blair, "Community Service," *ISB* 25, no. 2 (December 1965): 21.

65. Blair, 22.

66. NAIS, "Summary Report on Enrollment of Negro Students," March 1967, RG 26.01, box 21, folder: 1: Educational Testing Service Nominating Committee (ETS), Special Collections, Pressly, Dr. William L., Beck Archives-Westminster.

67. Nevin and Bills, *The Schools That Fear Built*, 8.

68. Minutes, April 12, 1967, RG 4.03, box 1, folder: September 1964-June 1967. Board of Trustees [Restricted], Minutes, Beck Archives-Westminster.

69. Minutes, May 10, 1967, RG 4.03, box 1, folder: September 1964-June 1967. Board of Trustees [Restricted], Minutes, Beck Archives-Westminster.

70. Mallery, *Negro Students in Independent Schools*, 21-22.

71. Handwritten notes from Pressly for faculty meeting [ca 1966], RG 5.01, box 2a, folder: Faculty Meeting [1966] Integration, Office of the President [Restricted], Pressly, Dr. William L., Beck Archives-Westminster.

72. Pressly, *Formative Years*, 152-53.

73. Pressly, 153.

74. Hill Martin, email message to author, March 28, 2010.

75. "Student Council Conducts Fund Raising Day for AFS," *Westminster Bi-Line*, December 16, 1966, 1, RG 21.06, Beck Archives-Westminster; "Juniors Plan Dance with

Malibus, Rebs," *Westminster Bi-Line*, April 25, 1966, 1, RG 21.06, Beck Archives-Westminster.

76. Bill Rothschild, "Julian Bond Issue: Beyond the Joke," *Westminster Bi-Line*, February 4, 1966, 2, RG 21.06, Beck Archives-Westminster.

77. "Unless Conditions Are Improved Violence in Ghettos Will Continue," *Westminster Bi-Line*, October 5, 1966, 2, RG 21.06, Beck Archives-Westminster.

78. "Unless Conditions Are Improved," 2.

79. Sarah Craig, "Project Head Start Gives Challenge to Students," *Westminster Bi-Line*, March 9, 1966, 4, RG 21.06, Beck Archives-Westminster.

80. "Three Senior Girls Tell of Head Start Summer," *Westminster Bi-Line*, October 5, 1966, 3, RG 21.06, Beck Archives-Westminster.

81. "All Precincts Reported That Bo Leads the Pack," *Westminster Bi-Line*, November 7, 1966, 5, RG 21.06, Beck Archives-Westminster.

82. "Callaway Speaks for Assembly," *Westminster Bi-Line*, November 7, 1966, 8, RG 21.06, Beck Archives-Westminster; "Callaway Talks of Cities, Education in Interview," *Westminster Bi-Line*, November 7, 1966, 4, RG 21.06, Beck Archives-Westminster.

83. Grady-Willis, *Challenging U.S. Apartheid*, 85.

84. Grady-Willis, 133.

85. "Valedictory," Headmasters' Meeting, February 1967, RG 26.01, box 22, folder: 10: "Valedictory" Headmaster's Meeting, 2-67, Special Collections, Pressly, Dr. William L., Beck Archives-Westminster.

86. Pressly, "Meanwhile, Georgia Schools Are Getting Better," 26.

87. Pressly, 26.

88. Harold Howe, "The Need for Entangling Alliances," *ISB* 26, no. 4 (May 1967): 16.

89. Minutes, March 6, 1967, RG 4.03, box 1, folder: September 1964-June 1967. Board of Trustees [Restricted], Minutes, Beck Archives-Westminster.

90. Pressly, *Formative Years*, 164.

91. Mira B. Wilson, "Colored Students Are an Asset," *ISB* Series '48-'49, no. 3 (February 1949): 12.

92. "What the Schools Are Doing," *ISB* Series '55-'56, no. 4 (May 1956): 25.

93. Mallery, *Negro Students*, 17

94. Mallery, 15.

95. Quoted in Mallery, 69: John D. Verdery, "We Wanted Negro Students." Reprinted from the *College Board Review* (Spring 1962).

96. Arthur Powell, *Lessons from Privilege*, 98.

97. Powell, 97.

98. Snyder and Snyder, "Dreams and Dilemmas."

99. "Southerner Aids 140 Black Students," *Ebony Magazine*, December 1975, 136, box 7, folder 6, Anne C. Stouffer Foundation Records, SHCUNC.

100. "Southerner Aids 140 Black Students," 142.

101. John Ehle to William Pressly, December 5, 1966, Jannard Wade, Stouffer Foundation Student File, Anne C. Stouffer Foundation Records, SHCUNC. Please note that Wade granted the author permission to access this restricted file.

102. Dr. Shirley McBay also worked at the National Science Foundation and became the first black female dean of students at the Massachusetts Institute of Tech-

nology. She is founder and past president of Quality Education for Minorities, a nonprofit organization based in Washington, D.C.

103. Michael McBay, email message to author, September 4, 2010.

104. McBay, email message.

105. McBay, email message.

106. Quoted in Mallery, *Negro Students*, 7.

107. John Ehle and A. Hollis Edens to Mr. Jannard Frederick Douglas Wade, January 31, 1967, Jannard Wade, Stouffer Foundation Student File, Anne C. Stouffer Foundation Records, SHCUNC. Isaac Clark was also chosen as a scholarship recipient and would attend Westminster in the fall of 1967.

108. Information Form for Referral to Preparatory School, Jannard Wade, Stouffer Foundation Student File, Anne C. Stouffer Foundation Records, SHCUNC.

109. Information Form for Referral to Preparatory School.

110. Jannard Wade, interview with author, June 30, 2009, Atlanta, Ga.

111. Wade, interview. According to the Collier Heights website, "Collier Heights has the distinction of being one of the few communities in the nation built exclusively by African American planners for the upcoming Atlanta African American middle class at a time when most housing for African Americans was 'transitioned' away from whites." See Collier Heights, "About Collier Heights," accessed April 2, 2011 (website). For additional historical accounting of the neighborhood as it transitioned from white to black, see Bayor, *Race and the Shaping of Twentieth-Century Atlanta*, 64-69; Kruse, *White Flight*, 97-104.

112. The school was named for Alonzo F. Herndon, a black Atlanta businessman and leader. In 1905, he established the Atlanta Mutual Insurance Association. According to historian Ron Bayor, "The Atlanta Life Insurance Company, as it came to be called, grew into one of the leading black-owned companies in the country and made Herndon a millionaire." See Bayor, *Race and the Shaping of Twentieth-Century Atlanta*, 94.

113. John Ehle to William Pressly, December 5, 1966, Jannard Wade, Stouffer Foundation Student File, Anne C. Stouffer Foundation Records, SHCUNC.

114. Jannard Wade, interview with author, June 30, 2009, Atlanta, Ga.

115. Dawn Clark, phone interview with author, March 26, 2010.

116. Elaine Jackson, interview with author, June 19, 2009, Lanham, Md.

117. Wanda Ward, interview with author, December 10, 2008, Arlington, Va.

118. D. P. Burch to Elaine Ward, March 14, 1966; Personal Collection of Dr. Wanda Ward.

119. Ward, interview, December 10, 2008.

120. Ward, interview.

121. Zweigenhaft and Domhoff, *Blacks in the White Elite*.

Chapter Four

1. John Ehle to William Pressly, December 5, 1966, Jannard Wade, Stouffer Foundation Student File, Stouffer Foundation Records, SHCUNC.

2. Michael McBay, email message to author, September 4, 2010.

3. Ron McBay, email message to author, May 24, 2009.

4. "Growth of Student Body," President's Report to the Board, November 1972, RG 5.01, box 13, folder: Report to the Board—November 1972—"The Development of the Westminster Schools," Office of the President [Restricted]. Pressly, Dr. William L., Beck Archives-Westminster.

5. U.S. Department of Commerce, Bureau of the Census, "Median Income in 1967 of Male Year-Round Full-Time Workers 25 years Old and Over" (figure), *Current Population Survey*, series P-60, no. 60, June 30, 1969; "Letter to Faculty and Staff," March 1967, RG 5.01, box 7a, folder: Correspondence Outgoing, Office of the President [Restricted], Pressly, Dr. William L., Beck Archives-Westminster.

6. Between 1955 and 1971, the ten colleges and universities most attended by Westminster alumni included the University of Georgia, Vanderbilt University, the University of North Carolina-Chapel Hill, Emory University, Duke University, Hollins, Georgia Tech, Washington and Lee, Sweet Briar, and the University of Virginia. Yale University and Princeton University were numbers eleven and fifteen, respectively. See "List of Colleges Attended by Westminster Graduates Since 1955," RG 5.01, box 2, folder: College Admissions Report, 1972, Office of the President [Restricted], Pressly, Dr. William L., Beck Archives-Westminster.

7. "The Westminster Schools," RG 5.01, box 1, folder: Administrative Records, 1963-1965, Office of the President [Restricted], Pressly, Dr. William L., Beck Archives-Westminster.

8. Orfield and Eaton, *Dismantling Desegregation*, xxi-xxii. See also *Green v. County School Board of New Kent County*, 391 U.S. 430 (1968); *Alexander v. Holmes County [Mississippi] Board of Education*, 396 U.S. 19 (1969).

9. Hedges et al., "The Question of School Resources and Student Achievement," 152.

10. San Miguel and Valencia, "From the Treaty of Guadalupe Hidalgo to *Hopwood*," 368.

11. Dawn Clark, phone interview with author, March 26, 2010.

12. Clark, phone interview.

13. Clark, phone interview.

14. Clark, phone interview.

15. Clark, phone interview.

16. "Annual Christmas Fund Drive Is Huge Success," *Westminster Bi-Line*, February 9, 1968, 3, RG 21.06, Beck Archives-Westminster; *Lynx* (Yearbook), 1965, 25; 1967, 8; 1968, 11, RG 21.02, Beck Archives-Westminster.

17. *Lynx*, 1968, 166; "A Thank You to a Great Inspiration," *Westminster Bi-Line*, December 8, 1967, 5, RG 21.06, Beck Archives-Westminster.

18. Joseph, *Waiting 'Til the Midnight Hour*, 127.

19. Rogers, *Black Campus Movement*, 95.

20. Grady-Willis, *Challenging U.S. Apartheid*, 143-48 (quote on 147).

21. Jannard Wade, interview with author, June 30, 2009, Atlanta, Ga.

22. Wade, interview.

23. Wanda Ward, interview with author, December 10, 2008, Arlington, Va.

24. *Lynx*, 1968, 44, 152, 172, 180.

25. Ron McBay, email message to author, May 24, 2009.

26. McBay, email message.

27. McBay, email message.

28. McBay, email message.

29. Ron McBay, email message to author, May 27, 2009.

30. Ron McBay, email message to author, June 8, 2009.

31. Ron McBay, email message, May 27, 2009.

32. Ron McBay, email message, June 8, 2009.

33. Ron McBay, email message, May 27, 2009.

34. Norfolk State College is now Norfolk State University. Originally named the Norfolk Unit of Virginia Union University, the institution began in 1935. In 1942, the school became Norfolk Polytechnic College, and in 1944, it came under the control of Virginia State College. By 1956, Norfolk State offered its first bachelor's degree. By 1969, Norfolk State College was a separate entity, and in 1979, the school was granted university status. Norfolk State University, "About" (website).

35. Malcolm Ryder, phone interview with author, May 18, 2009.

36. Ryder, phone interview.

37. Ryder, phone interview.

38. Interview report from Douglas R. Lewis, December 12, 1967, Malcolm Ryder, Stouffer Foundation Student File, Stouffer Foundation Records, SHCUNC. Please note that Ryder granted the author permission to access this restricted file.

39. Malcolm Ryder, email message to author, May 18, 2009.

40. Kenneth M. Smathers, "ABC Report, Duke University, 1968," box 13, Stouffer Foundation Records, SHCUNC.

41. Smathers, "ABC Report."

42. Rita Kiger to Whom It May Concern, November 1970, box 8, folder: Quail Roost Conference, Stouffer Foundation Records, SHCUNC.

43. Ryder, phone interview, May 18, 2009.

44. William L. Pressly to Parents of Boarding Students, May 17, 1968, RG 5.01, box 7a, folder: Correspondence Outgoing August 1967-June 1968, Office of the President [Restricted], Pressly, Dr. William L., Beck Archives-Westminster.

45. William L. Pressly to Parents of Boarding Students, May 17, 1968.

46. *Lynx* (Yearbook), 1969, 10, RG 21.02, Beck Archives–Westminster.

47. *Lynx*, 1969, 150, 152, 171.

48. Jannard Wade, interview with author, Atlanta, Ga., June 30, 2009.

49. *Lynx*, 1969, 132-33.

50. Wade, interview with author, June 30, 2009.

51. Wade, interview.

52. *Lynx*, 1969, 163.

53. Public Relations Committee Meeting, September 18, 1968, RG 5.01, box 2a, folder: Faculty Committee 1968-1970, Office of the President [Restricted], Pressly, Dr. William L., Beck Archives-Westminster.

54. Betsy Barge, "Dr. William Borders Speaks to Students," *Westminster Bi-Line*, October 30, 1968, 1, RG 21.06, Beck Archives-Westminster; *Lynx*, 1969, 8.

55. *Lynx*, 1969, 116, 190, 199.

56. Wanda Ward, interview with author, December 10, 2008, Arlington, Va.

57. "Vine City Workers Bridge Race Chasm," *Westminster Bi-Line*, September 27, 1968, 1, RG 21.06, Beck Archives-Westminster.

58. "Vine City Workers Bridge Race Chasm," 1.

59. Jill Heazelwood, "Ghetto Children Given Great Holiday Party," *Westminster Bi-Line*, January 28, 1969, 4, RG 21.06, Beck Archives-Westminster; Letter to Editor, *Westminster Bi-Line*, January 28, 1969, 2, RG 21.06, Beck Archives-Westminster.

60. "Girls National Honor Society Begins Tutoring Program for Underprivileged," *Westminster Bi-Line*, December 9, 1968, 6, RG 21.06, Beck Archives-Westminster.

61. Report to the Board, November 13, 1968, RG 5.01, box 13, folder: Report to the Board—1968 Nov 13, Office of the President [Restricted], Pressly, Dr. William L., Beck Archives-Westminster.

62. 10th Anniversary Convocation Speech at the Arlington School, February 4, 1969, RG 26.01, box 24, folder: Arlington School, 2-4-69; 10th Anniversary Convocation Speech, Special Collections, Pressly, Dr. William L. Beck Archives-Westminster.

63. Mary Perl Azrael, "Amy, Francisco, and Reggie: Their Homes *Versus* the School," *ISB* 27, no. 1 (October 1967): 16-18; Edith Nash, "The Story of an Integrated School," *ISB* 27, no. 2 (December 1967): 18-23; Michael L. Lasser, "The Independent Schools and the Multiracial World: An Interview with Elliott Shapiro," *ISB* 27, no. 3 (February 1968): 10-13.

64. NAIS, "Open Enrollment: A Statement of the Board of Directors," *NAISR*, no. 26 (October 1968): 1-2.

65. NAIS, 1-2.

66. Joia Johnson, phone interview with author, March 30, 2010.

67. Aaron Johnson is now a retired management consultant and health care administrator; his last position was vice president of Georgia Baptist Health as well as independent consultant. Dr. Joyce Johnson is a retired professor of music at Spelman College; she had also been department chair. Dr. Johnson continues to serve as the college organist.

68. Aaron Johnson, phone interview with author, May 13, 2010.

69. Joia Johnson, phone interview with author, March 30, 2010.

70. Johnson, phone interview.

71. Johnson, phone interview.

72. Dawn Clark, phone interview with author, March 26, 2010.

73. Ron McBay, email message to author, May 29, 2009.

74. *Lynx* (Yearbook), 1970, 26-27, RG 21.02, Beck Archives-Westminster.

75. Malcolm Ryder, phone interview with author, May 25, 2009.

76. Ryder, phone interview.

77. Ryder, phone interview.

78. Ryder, phone interview.

79. Irvine, *Educating Teachers for Diversity*, 10.

80. Jannard Wade, phone interview with author, June 30, 2009.

81. Wanda Ward, interview with author, December 10, 2008, Arlington, Va.

82. Ward, interview.

83. Ryder, phone interview with author, May 25, 2009.

84. *Lynx*, 1970, 120, 133, 145.

85. *Lynx*, 1970, 130, 188.

86. Ward, interview with author, December 10, 2008.

87. John Howard Griffin, *Black Like Me*; Paton, *Cry, the Beloved Country*.

88. "Interesting Courses Provide Opportunities," *Westminster Bi-Line*, November 1969, 6, RG 21.06, Beck Archives-Westminster.

89. "Vine City Group Sets Up Store; Projects Help Area Residents," *Westminster Bi-Line*, February 1970, 3, RG 21.06, Beck Archives-Westminster.

90. "Harper Students Make Return Visit," *Westminster Bi-Line*, December 1969, 6, RG 21.06, Beck Archives-Westminster.

91. "Letter to the Editor," *Westminster Bi-Line*, January 28, 1969, 2, RG 21.06, Beck Archives-Westminster.

92. "Mardi Gras Expresses Simplicity," *Westminster Bi-Line*, March 1970, 6, RG 21.06, Beck Archives-Westminster.

93. Patti Paschall, "Mr. Vernon Jordan Speaks to Students," *Westminster Bi-Line*, February 1970, 6, RG 21.06, Beck Archives-Westminster.

94. Linda McLean, "The Black Student in the White Independent School," *ISB* (February 1969): 68.

95. McLean, 69.

96. McLean, 70.

97. McLean, 72.

98. William Dandridge, interview with author, December 11, 2008, Boston, Mass.

99. Dandridge, interview.

100. William Dandridge, interview with author, October 22, 2009, Philadelphia, Pa.

101. Dandridge, interview with author, December 11, 2008.

Chapter Five

1. NAIS, "NAIS and Governmental Relations—The Establishment of a Special Committee," *NAISR*, no. 28 (February 1969): 2.

2. Nevin and Bills, *Schools That Fear Built*, 9.

3. Nevin and Bills, 12-13.

4. "Civil Rights: Segregation: Federal Income Tax: Exemptions and Deductions," 1411; *Green v. Kennedy* 309 F. Supp. 1127, 1970 U.S. District Court.

5. *Green v. Kennedy* 309 F. Supp. 1127, 1970 U.S. District Court. Interestingly, a similar case was also filed in 1969 in the U.S. District Court in Philadelphia. The plaintiffs, which included the NAACP, sought "a permanent injunction against the use of state

funds for support of sectarian schools and other private schools whose policies, 'by purpose or effect,' discriminate against persons by reason of race or religions, and goes on to assert that the defendant schools and nonpublic schools generally are *de facto* segregated and that aid to them will perpetuate such segregation." In NAIS, "Schools Politics, and the Law," *NAISR*, no. 30 (October 1969): 2.

6. *Green v. Kennedy*.

7. Dick Ritter, "Tax Exempt Status Seen Doubtful," *Federal Times*, July 15, 1970, 27, RG 26.01, box 12a, folder: 3a: Historical Society Clipping and Integration Clipping, Special Collections, Pressly, Dr. William L., Beck Archives-Westminster.

8. Testimony Prepared for Select Senate Committee on Equal Educational Opportunity, RG 26.01, box 24, folder: Testimony for Senate Committee on Equal Education Opportunity, June 1970, Special Collections, Pressly, Dr. William L., Beck Archives-Westminster.

9. "The Judicial Role in Attacking Racial Discrimination in Tax-Exempt Private Schools," 380.

10. NAIS, "Minority Affairs," *NAISR*, no. 41 (May 1972): 5.

11. Corliss Blount Denman, phone interview with author, July 20, 2009.

12. From Anne R. Forsyth and John Ehle to Corliss Blount, January 31, 1970, Corliss Blount, Stouffer Foundation Student File, Stouffer Foundation Records, SHCUNC (please note that Blount Denman granted the author permission to access this restricted file); John Ehle, interview with author, June 26, 2009, Winston-Salem, N.C.

13. From John Ehle to Dr. Donald Westmoreland, January 31, 1970, Corliss Blount, Stouffer Foundation Student file, Stouffer Foundation Records, SHCUNC.

14. Corliss Blount Denman, phone interview with author.

15. Denman, phone interview.

16. Denman, phone interview.

17. Denman, phone interview.

18. *Lynx* (Yearbook), 1971, 32-33, 110, 120, 122, 133, 148, 149, 151, 176, 179, 181, 183, 188, 196, 198, RG 21.02, Beck Archives-Westminster.

19. Jean Martin, "Ward, Timberlake Selected 1971 AFS Students," *Westminster Bi-Line*, June 5, 1971, 3, RG 21.06, Beck Archives-Westminster.

20. Joan Towles, "Fifth District Race Proves to Be Close," *Westminster Bi-Line*, November 3, 1970, 2, RG 21.06, Beck Archives-Westminster; "Paper Endorses Candidates," *Westminster Bi-Line*, November 3, 1970, 4, RG 21.06, Beck Archives-Westminster; Moria Egan, "Vinings Group Begins Tutoring," *Westminster Bi-Line*, December 18, 1970, 2, RG 21.06, Beck Archives-Westminster.

21. Graham, *Young Activists*, 34.

22. Graham, 63.

23. Malcolm Ryder, phone interview with author, May 18, 2009.

24. See Danns, "Chicago High School Students"; Danns, *Something Better for Our Children*; Franklin, "Black High School Student Activism"; Graham, *Young Activists*; Wright, "Black Pride Day, 1968."

25. For McBay's cartoons, see *Westminster Bi-Line*, October 14, 1970, 4; November 3, 1970, 4; November 30, 1970, 4; November 30, 1970, 5; October 1, 1971, 4; November 1971, 4, RG 21.06, Beck Archives-Westminster.

26. Michael McBay, "McBay Voices Black Frustrations," *Westminster Bi-Line*, June 5, 1971, RG 21.06, Beck Archives-Westminster.

27. William Dandridge, interview with author, February 20, 2010, Atlanta, Ga.

28. William Dandridge, interview with author, December 11, 2008, Boston, Mass.

29. William Dandridge, interview with author, October 22, 2009, Philadelphia, Pa.

30. Dandridge, interview with author, October 22, 2009.

31. Dandridge, interview.

32. Dandridge, interview.

33. Dandridge, interview.

34. Dandridge, interview, December 11, 2008.

35. David G. Erdmann, "Breaking the Myth Barrier," *ISB* (October 1970): 57.

36. William L. Dandridge, "The Real Question of Balance," *ISB* (October 1970): 59-60.

37. William L. Dandridge, "Black Reflections on the Independent School: 1. An Overview," *ISB* (December 1970): 9.

38. Dandridge, 9.

39. David Mallery, "Black Reflections on the Independent School: 2. Four Black Students Talk about School," *ISB* (December 1970): 13.

40. E. L. Belton, "Black Reflections on the Independent School: 3. The Black Teacher," *ISB* (December 1970): 15-17.

41. The Reverend Canon John T. Walker, "Black Reflections on the Independent School: 4. The Role of the Black Trustee," *ISB* (December 1970): 19-20.

42. Isaac Clark graduated a year early, in 1971, enrolling at Morehouse College and then Georgia Institute of Technology (Georgia Tech).

43. NAIS, "Minority Affairs," *NAISR*, no. 41 (May 1972): 5.

44. NAIS, 6.

45. NAIS, "Minority Affairs," *NAISR*, no. 40 (February 1972): 10.

46. Cora Pressly, "The Plunge into the White World," *ISB* (October 1971): 46.

47. Bill Prince, "Busing Is Imperative despite Cost, Impracticality, Objections," *Westminster Bi-Line*, October 1, 1971, 4, RG 21.06, Beck Archives-Westminster.

48. Michael McBay, "Sly's There's a Riot Goin' On," *Westminster Bi-Line*, February 1972, 4, RG 21.06, Beck Archives-Westminster; Michael McBay, "Angela Davis' Politics Render Justice Unlikely," *Westminster Bi-Line*, April 1972, 5-6, RG 21.06, Beck Archives-Westminster.

49. Tom Lumsden, "Noblesse Oblige Guides Student Response to Bond," *Westminster Bi-Line*, February 1972, 3, RG 21.06, Beck Archives-Westminster.

50. *Lynx* (Yearbook), 1972, 32, 50-55, 121, 183, RG 21.02, Beck Archives-Westminster.

51. "The Frances Isabelle Outler Award," Personal Collection of Dr. Wanda Ward.

52. Wanda Ward, interview with author, December 10, 2008, Arlington, Va.

53. Malcolm Ryder, "First Black Grads," *Westminster Bi-Line*, June 1972, 3, RG 21.06, Beck Archives-Westminster.

54. Jannard Wade, interview with author, June 30, 2009, Atlanta, Ga.

55. Wade, interview.

56. Wanda Ward, interview with author, December 10, 2008, Arlington, Va.

57. Elaine Jackson, interview with author, June 19, 2009, Lanham, Md.

58. Jane Haverty, interview with author, September 16, 2009, Atlanta, Ga.

59. Hill Martin, email message to author, March 28, 2010.

60. Malcolm Ryder, phone interview with author, May 25, 2009.

61. Donata Russell Ross, phone interview with author, May 12, 2010.

62. Ross, phone interview.

63. Corliss Blount Denman, phone interview with author, July 20, 2009.

64. Denman, phone interview.

65. William Dandridge, interview with author, December 11, 2008, Boston, Mass.

66. Dandridge, interview.

67. William Dandridge, interview with author, October 22, 2009, Philadelphia, Pa.

68. Dandridge, interview, December 11, 2008.

69. Dandridge, interview, October 22, 2009.

70. Dandridge, interview.

71. William Dandridge, interview with author, February 20, 2010, Atlanta, Ga.

72. Dandridge, interview, December 11, 2008.

73. Dandridge, interview. Please note that committee names may have changed over time.

74. Dandridge, interview.

75. Dandridge, interview, October 22, 2009.

76. Hornsby, "Black Public Education in Atlanta, Georgia," 37.

77. Gong, "Race, Class, and Atlanta Public School Integration," 157.

78. Gong, 157.

79. Hornsby, 40; Jackson, "Desegregation: Atlanta Style," 48–49; Plank and Turner, "Changing Patterns in Black School Politics," 600. Also, for a history of Atlanta since the 1970s, see Hobson, *Legend of the Black Mecca*.

80. Dawn Clark, phone interview with author, March 31, 2010.

81. Ron McBay, e-mail message to author, May 27, 2009.

Epilogue

1. See Appendix: "The Fearless Firsts since Graduating from Westminster" and Secret, "The Way to Survive."

2. "Transcript: Read Michelle Obama's Full Speech from the 2016 DNC."

3. Bell, *Silent Covenants*, 69.

4. Carter, "Educational Equality Is a Multifaceted Issue," 145.

5. Patel, "Youth Held at the Border," 4.

6. Khan, *Privilege*, 101.

7. For a recent examination of the relationship between racist ideas and racist policies in the United States, see Kendi, *Stamped from the Beginning*.

8. Accounts that provide a wider sociocultural perspective on school choice include Rofes and Stulberg, *Emancipatory Promise of Charter Schools*; and Stulberg, *Race, Schools, and Hope*. Also see Hannah-Jones, "Choosing a School."

9. Wells et al., *Both Sides Now*, 270.

10. Examples include Andrews, "Black Achievers' Experiences with Racial Spotlighting and Ignoring," and DeCuir and Dixson, "'So When It Comes Out, They Aren't That Surprised That It Is There.'"

11. Ladson-Billings, "From the Achievement Gap to the Educational Debt."

12. Paris, "Culturally Sustaining Pedagogy," 95.

13. Beadie, "Federal Role in Education and the Rise of Social Science Research," 33.

Bibliography

Manuscript and Archival Collections

Atlanta, Georgia
- Lewis H. Beck Archives, The Westminster Schools
  - Board of Trustee Records [Restricted], Record Group 4
    - Minutes, Record Group 4.03
    - President's Report to the Board of Trustees, Record Group 4.04
    - Correspondence, Record Group 4.05
  - Office of the President [Restricted], Record Group 5
    - Pressly, Dr. William L., Record Group 5.01
  - Office of Institutional Advancement, Record Group 13
    - Campaigns and Promotional Materials, Record Group 13.07
  - Student Publications, Record Group 21
    - *Lynx* (Yearbook), Record Group 21.02
    - *Westminster Tattler*, Record Group 21.03
    - *Westminster Chimes*, Record Group 21.04
    - *Mark Sheet*, Record Group 21.05
    - *Westminster Bi-Line*, Record Group 21.06
  - Special Collections, Record Group 26
    - William L. Pressly Papers, Record Group 26.01
- Stuart A. Rose Manuscript, Archives, and Rare Book Library, Emory University
  - Emory University Biographical Files, Circa 1880-1990
    - Roland M. Frye
  - Eliza K. Paschall Papers, 1860-1990
  - Robert Winship Woodruff Papers, 1819-1996 (Bulk 1924-1986)

Chapel Hill, North Carolina
- Southern Historical Collection, Louis Round Wilson Special Collections Library, University of North Carolina at Chapel Hill
  - Anne C. Stouffer Foundation Records #04556

National Independent School Materials

Independent School Bulletin (ISB)
National Association of Independent Schools Report
National Council of Independent Schools Report
Reports of the Annual Meeting of the National Association of Independent Schools

Interviews by Author

Clark, Dawn. Telephone interviews, March 26, 2010; March 31, 2010.

Clark, Johnnie. Telephone interview, May 11, 2010.

Dandridge, William. Interview, Boston, Mass., December 11, 2008; Interview, Philadelphia, Pa., October 22, 2009; Interview, Atlanta, Ga., February 20, 2010.

Denman, Corliss Blount. Telephone interview, July 20, 2009.

Ehle, John. Interview, Winston-Salem, N.C., June 26, 2009.

Haverty, Jane. Interview, Atlanta, Ga., September 16, 2009.

Jackson, Elaine. Interview, Lanham, Md., June 19, 2009.

Johnson, Aaron. Telephone interview, May 13, 2010.

Johnson, Joia. Telephone interview, March 30, 2010.

Kahn, Bobette Reed. Telephone interview, February 23, 2010.

Martin, Hill. Email interview, March 28, 2010; Telephone interview, March 28, 2010.

McBay, Michael. Email interviews, May 28, 2009; September 4, 2010.

McBay, Ron. Email interviews, May 24, 2009; May 27, 2009; May 29, 2009; May 31, 2009; June 8, 2009; June 13, 2009; June 16, 2009; April 26, 2010.

Pendergrast, Nan. Interview, Atlanta, Ga., July 29, 2009.

Ross, Donata Russell. Telephone interview, May 12, 2010.

Ryder, Malcolm. Email interview, May 18, 2009; Telephone interviews, May 18, 2009; May 25, 2009.

Wade, Jannard. Interview, Atlanta, Ga., June 30, 2009.

Walters, Bill. Interview, Durham, N.C., February 27, 2010.

Ward, Wanda. Interview, Arlington, Va., December 10, 2008; Telephone interview, July 23, 2009.

Wells, Jere. Interview, Atlanta, Ga., June 15, 2009.

Unpublished Work

Brown, Robbie. "'Opening the Gates': The Integration of the Westminster Schools, 1951-1972." Unpublished paper, Emory University, Atlanta, Ga., n.d.

Government Document

Jones, Thomas Jesse. *Negro Education: A Study of the Private and Higher Schools for Colored People in the United States.* 2 vols. U.S. Department of the Interior, Bureau of Education, Bulletins 38 and 39. Washington, D.C.: U.S. Government Printing Office, 1917.

Websites

Center for Education Reform. "K-12 Facts." Accessed October 5, 2015. https://www.edreform.com/2012/04/k-12-facts.

Collier Heights. Accessed April 2, 2011. http://collierheights.org/about/.

National Association of Independent Schools. "NAIS Independent School Facts at a Glance." Accessed October 5, 2015. http://www.nais.org/Statistics/Pages/NAIS -Independent-School-Facts-at-a-Glance.aspx.

———. "What Is the Difference between Independent Schools and Other Private Schools?" Accessed December 8, 2005. http://www.nais.org/resources/faq.cfm ?ItemNumber=144101&sn.ItemNumber=14616.

National Center for Education Statistics. "Digest of Education Statistics." Accessed October 5, 2015. http://nces.ed.gov/programs/digest/d13/tables/dt13_205.10.asp ?current=yes.

———. "SAT Scores." April 21, 2017. https://nces.ed.gov/fastfacts/display.asp?id=171.

Norfolk State University. Accessed April 2, 2011. http://www.nsu.edu/about/history .html.

Pilgrim, David. "The Pickaninny Caricature." Accessed November 16, 2008. http:// www.ferris.edu/news/jimcrow/picaninny/.

United States Census. "Number of Inhabitants, United States Summary." In *Census of Population*, vol. 1. 1950 Census. Accessed March 18, 2017. http://www2.census .gov/prod2/decennial/documents/23761117v1ch03.pdf.

———. "Statistics of Population." In *Twelfth Census of the United States—1900*. Census Reports Vol. 1. Population, Part 1. Accessed March 18, 2017. http://www2 .census.gov/prod2/decennial/documents/33405927v1ch01.pdf.

The Westminster Schools. "About Us: History." Accessed January 14, 2016. http:// classic.westminster.net/about_us_history/index.aspx.

———. "Tuition and Financial Aid." Accessed April 4, 2017. https://www .westminster.net/tuition_financial_aid.

Secondary Sources

Adair, Alvis V. *Desegregation: The Illusion of Black Progress*. Lanham, Md.: University Press of America, 1984.

Adams, David. *Education for Extinction: American Indians and the Boarding School Experience, 1875-1928*. Lawrence: University Press of Kansas, 1995.

Adamson, June N. "Few Black Voices Heard: The Black Community and the 1956 Desegregation Crisis in Clinton." In *Trial and Triumph: Essays in Tennessee's African American History*, edited by Carroll Van West, 334-49. Knoxville: University of Tennessee Press, 2002.

Alexander v. Holmes County [Mississippi] Board of Education, 396 U.S. 19 (1969).

Alridge, Derrick. *The Educational Thought of W. E. B. Du Bois: An Intellectual History*. New York: Teachers College Press, 2008.

Anderson, Eric, and Alfred A. Moss. *Dangerous Donations: Northern Philanthropy and Southern Black Education, 1902-1930*. Columbia: University of Missouri Press, 1999.

Anderson, James. *The Education of Blacks in the South, 1860-1935*. Chapel Hill: University of North Carolina Press, 1988.

Andrews, Dorinda J. Carter. "Black Achievers' Experiences with Racial Spotlighting and Ignoring in a Predominantly White High School." *Teachers College Record* 114, no. 10 (2012): 1–46.

Baird, Leonard L. *The Elite Schools: A Profile of Prestigious Independent Schools*. Lexington, Mass.: Lexington Books, 1977.

Baker, Liva. *The Second Battle of New Orleans: The Hundred-Year Struggle to Integrate the Schools*. New York: HarperCollins, 1996.

Baker, R. Scott. *Paradoxes of Desegregation: African American Struggles for Educational Equity in Charleston, South Carolina, 1926-1972*. Columbia: University of South Carolina Press, 2006.

Bates, Daisy. "The Long Shadow of Little Rock." In *The Eyes on the Prize Civil Rights Reader: Documents, Speeches, and Firsthand Accounts from the Black Freedom Struggle, 1954-1990*, edited by Clayborne Carson, David J. Garrow, Gerald Gill, Vincent Harding, and Darlene Clark Hine, 97-106. New York: Penguin Books, 1991.

Bayor, Ronald H. *Race and the Shaping of Twentieth-Century Atlanta*. Chapel Hill: University of North Carolina Press, 1996.

Beadie, Nancy. "The Federal Role in Education and the Rise of Social Science Research: Historical and Comparative Perspectives." *Review of Research in Education* 40 (March 2016): 1-37.

Bell, Derrick. *Silent Covenants: Brown v. Board of Education and the Unfilled Hopes for Racial Reform*. New York: Oxford University Press, 2004.

Biondi, Martha. *The Black Revolution on Campus*. Berkeley: University of California Press, 2012.

Bolton, Charles S. *The Hardest Deal of All: The Battle Over School Integration in Mississippi, 1870-1980*. Jackson: University Press of Mississippi, 2005.

Bond, Horace Mann. *The Education of the Negro in the American Social Order*. First published in 1934 by Prentice-Hall. New York: Octagon Books. 1966.

Borstelmann, Thomas. *The 1970s: A New Global History from Civil Rights to Economic Inequality*. Princeton, N.J.: Princeton University Press, 2012.

Bourdieu, Pierre. "The Forms of Capital." Translated by Richard Nice. In *Handbook of Theory and Research for Sociology of Education*, edited by John G. Richardson, 241-58. New York: Greenwood, 1985.

Brown v. Board of Education of Topeka I, 347 U.S. 483 (1954).

Brown v. Board of Education of Topeka II, 349 U.S. 294 (1955).

Brown-Nagin, Tomiko. *Courage to Dissent: Atlanta and the Long History of the Civil Rights Movement*. Oxford: Oxford University Press, 2011.

Bullock, Henry Allen. *A History of Negro Education in the South: From 1619 to the Present*. New York: Praeger Publishers, 1967.

Carter, Prudence L. "Educational Equality Is a Multifaceted Issue: Why We Must Understand the School's Sociocultural Context for Student Achievement." *RSF: The Russell Sage Foundation Journal of Social Sciences* 2, no. 5 (2016): 142-63.

Cary, Lorene. *Black Ice*. New York: Vintage Books, 1991.

Cecelski, David S. *Along Freedom Road: Hyde County, North Carolina, and the Fate of Black Schools in the South*. Chapel Hill: University of North Carolina Press, 1994.

Chamberlain, Ernest Barrett. *Our Independent Schools: The Private School in American Education*. New York: American Book, 1944.

Champagne, Anthony M. "The Segregation Academy and the Law." *Journal of Negro Education* 42, no. 1 (1973): 58-66.

Chubb, John E., and Terry M. Moe. *Politics, Markets, and America's Schools.* Washington, D.C.: The Brookings Institution, 1990.

"Civil Rights: Segregation: Federal Income Tax: Exemptions and Deductions: The Validity of Tax Benefits to Private Segregated Schools." *Michigan Law Review* 68, no. 7 (1970): 1410-38.

Cookson, Peter W., Jr., and Caroline Hodges Persell. *Preparing for Power: America's Elite Boarding Schools.* New York: Basic Books, 1985.

Cooper, Arnold. *Between Struggle and Hope: Four Black Educators in the South, 1894-1915.* Ames: Iowa State University Press, 1989.

Cornelius, Janet Duitsman. *"When I Can Read My Title Clear": Literacy, Slavery, and Religion in the Antebellum South.* Columbia: University of South Carolina Press, 1991.

Daniel, Pete. *Lost Revolutions: The South in the 1950s.* Chapel Hill: University of North Carolina Press, 2000.

Danns, Dionne. "Chicago High School Students' Movement for Quality Public Education, 1966-1971." *Journal of African American History* 88 (Spring 2003): 138-50.

———. *Desegregating Chicago's Public Schools: Policy Implementation, Politics, and Protest, 1965-1985.* New York: Palgrave Macmillan, 2014.

———. *Something Better for Our Children: Black Organizing in Chicago Public Schools, 1963-1971.* New York: Routledge, 2003.

Danns, Dionne, Michelle A. Purdy, and Christopher M. Span, eds. *Using Past as Prologue: Contemporary Perspectives on African American Educational History.* Charlotte, N.C.: Information Age, 2015.

DeCuir, Jessica T., and Adrienne D. Dixson. "'So When It Comes Out, They Aren't That Surprised That It Is There': Using Critical Race Theory as a Tool of Analysis of Race and Racism in Education." *Educational Researcher* 33, no. 5 (2004): 26-31.

Delmont, Matthew. *Why Busing Failed: Race, Media, and the National Resistance to School Desegregation.* Oakland: University of California Press, 2016.

De Schweinitz, Rebecca. *If We Could Change the World: Young People and America's Long Struggle for Racial Equality.* Chapel Hill: University of North Carolina Press, 2009.

Dilonardo, Mary Jo. "One Size Doesn't Fit All." *Atlanta* 45, no. 9 (January 2006): 78-84.

Dougherty, Jack. "From Anecdote to Analysis: Oral Interviews and New Scholarship in Educational History." *Journal of American History* 86, no. 2 (1999): 712-23.

———. *More Than One Struggle: The Evolution of Black School Reform in Milwaukee.* Chapel Hill: University of North Carolina Press, 2004.

Douglass, Davison M. *Reading, Writing, and Race: The Desegregation of Charlotte Schools.* Chapel Hill: University of North Carolina Press, 1991.

Du Bois, W. E. B. "Of Booker T. Washington and Others." In *The Souls of Black Folk,* 36-50.

————. *The Souls of Black Folk*. First published in 1903. New York: Penguin Books, 1989.

Erickson, Ansley. *Making the Unequal Metropolis: School Desegregation and Its Limits*. Chicago: The University of Chicago Press, 2016.

Fabrikant, Geraldine. "At Elite Prep Schools, College-Size Endowments." *New York Times*, January 26, 2008. http://www.nytimes.com/2008/01/26/business/26prep.html?ref=business.

Fairclough, Adam. "The Costs of *Brown*: Black Teachers and School Integration." *Journal of American History* 91, no. 1 (June 2004): 43-55.

Franklin, V. P. "Black High School Student Activism: An Urban Phenomenon?" *Journal of Research in Education* 10 (Fall 2000): 3-8.

————. "Introduction: *Brown v. Board of Education* — Fifty Years of Educational Change in the United States." *Journal of African American History* 90, no. 1/2 (Winter 2005): 1-8.

Franklin, V. P., and Edward P. McDonald. "Blacks in Urban Catholic Schools in the United States: A Historical Perspective." In *Visible Now: Blacks in Private Schools*, edited by Diana T. Slaughter and Deborah J. Johnson, 93-108. New York: Greenwood, 1988.

Franklin, V. P., and Carter Julian Savage, eds. *Cultural Capital and Black Education: African American Communities and the Funding of Black Schooling, 1865 to the Present*. Charlotte, N.C.: Information Age, 2004.

Fraser, James W., ed. *The School in the United States: A Documentary History*. New York: Routledge, 2014.

Freund, David M. P. "Marketing the Free Market: State Intervention and the Politics of Prosperity in Metropolitan America." In *The New Suburban History*, edited by Kevin M. Kruse and Thomas J. Sugrue, 11-32. Chicago: University of Chicago Press, 2006.

Friedman, Milton. "The Role of Government in Education." In *Capitalism and Freedom*, edited by Milton Friedman, 85-107. Chicago: University of Chicago Press, 1962.

Fultz, Michael. "African American Teachers in the South, 1890-1940: Powerlessness and the Ironies of Expectations and Protest." *History of Education Quarterly* 35, no. 4 (Winter 1995): 401-22.

————. "The Displacement of Black Educators Post-*Brown*: An Overview and Analysis." *History of Education Quarterly* 44, no. 1 (2004): 11-45.

Gadsden, Brett. *Between North and South: Delaware, Desegregation, and the Myth of American Exceptionalism*. Philadelphia: University of Pennsylvania Press, 2012.

Gannon, Michael. "From White Flight to Open Admissions: The Founding and Integration of Private Schools in the City of Atlanta, 1951-1967." Master's thesis, Georgia State University, 2004.

Gaztambide-Fernandez, Ruben. "What Is an Elite Boarding School?" *Review of Educational Research* 79 (September 2009): 1090-128.

Gong, Wei-ling. "Race, Class, and Atlanta Public School Integration, 1954-1991." PhD diss., Emory University, 1991.

Grady-Willis, Winston A. *Challenging U.S. Apartheid: Atlanta and Black Struggles for Human Rights, 1960-1977*. Durham, N.C.: Duke University Press, 2006.

Graham, Gael. *Young Activists: American High School Students in the Age of Protest.* DeKalb: Northern Illinois University Press, 2006.

Grant, Donald L., and Jonathan Grant. *The Way It Was in the South: The Black Experience in Georgia.* Athens: University of Georgia Press, 1993.

Green v. County School Board of New Kent County, 391 U.S. 430 (1968).

Green v. Kennedy, 309 F. Supp. 1127, 1970 U.S. District Court.

Griffin, John Howard. *Black Like Me.* New York: Penguin Putnam, 1960.

Griffin, Judith Berry. "Human Diversity and Academic Excellence: Learning from Experience." *Journal of Negro Education* 68, no. 1 (Winter 1999), 72-79.

Hager, Christopher. *Word by Word: Emancipation and the Art of Writing.* Cambridge, Mass.: Harvard University Press, 2013.

Hale, Grace Elizabeth. *Making Whiteness: The Culture of Segregation in the South, 1890-1940.* New York: Vintage Books, 1998.

Hale, Jon. *The Freedom Schools: Student Activists in the Mississippi Civil Rights Movement.* New York: Columbia University Press, 2016.

Hall, Diane M., and Howard C. Stevenson. "Double Jeopardy: Being African American and 'Doing Diversity' in Independent Schools." *Teachers College Record* 109 (2007): 1-23.

Hampton, Henry, and Steve Fayer, eds. *Voices of Freedom: An Oral History of the Civil Rights Movement from the 1980s through 1990s.* New York: Bantam Books, 1990.

Hannah-Jones, Nikole. "Choosing a School for My Daughter in a Segregated City." *New York Times,* June 9, 2016. https://www.nytimes.com/2016/06/12/magazine/choosing-a-school-for-my-daughter-in-a-segregated-city.html.

Hardiman, Rita, Bailey W. Jackson, and Pat Griffin. "Conceptual Foundations." In *Readings for Diversity and Social Justice,* edited by Maurianne Adams, Warren J. Blumenfeld, Carmelita (Rosie) Castaneda, Heather W. Hackman, Madeline L. Peters, and Ximena Zuniga, 26-35. New York: Routledge, 2013.

Hayes, Worth Kamili. "The Rise and Fall of a Black Private School: Holy Name of Mary and the Golden Age of Black Private Education in Chicago, 1940-1990." In *Using Past as Prologue: Contemporary Perspectives on African American Educational History,* edited by Dionne Danns, Michelle A. Purdy, and Christopher M. Span, 201-20. Charlotte, N.C.: Information Age, 2015.

Hedges, Larry, Terri D. Pigott, Joshua R. Polanin, Ann Marie Ryan, Charles Tocci, and Ryan T. Williams. "The Question of School Resources and Student Achievement: A History and Reconsideration." *Review of Research in Education* 44 (March 2016): 143-68.

Hein, Virginia. "The Image of 'A City Too Busy to Hate': Atlanta in the 1960s." *Phylon* 33 (1972): 205-21.

Higginbotham, Evelyn Brooks. *Righteous Discontent: The Women's Movement in the Black Baptist Church, 1880-1920.* Cambridge, Mass.: Harvard University Press, 1993.

Hobson, Maurice. *The Legend of the Black Mecca: Politics and Class in the Making of Modern Atlanta.* Chapel Hill: University of North Carolina Press, 2017.

Hoppe, Sherry L., and Bruce W. Speck. *Maxine Smith's Unwilling Pupils: Lessons Learned in Memphis's Civil Rights Classroom.* Knoxville: University of Tennessee Press, 2007.

Hornsby, Alton, Jr. "Black Public Education in Atlanta, Georgia, 1954-1973: From Segregation to Segregation." *Journal of Negro History* 76, no. 1 (1991): 21-47.

Irvine, Jacqueline Jordan. *Educating Teachers for Diversity: Seeing with a Cultural Eye*. New York: Teachers College Press, 2003.

Irvine, Jacqueline Jordan, and Michele Foster, eds. *Growing Up African American in Catholic Schools*. New York: Teachers College Press, 1996.

Jackson, Barbara L. "Desegregation: Atlanta Style." *Theory into Practice* 17, no. 1 (1978), 43-53.

Jewell, Joseph. *Race, Social Reform, and the Making of a Middle Class: The American Missionary Association and Black Atlanta, 1870-1900*. Lanham, Md.: Rowman & Littlefield, 2007.

Jones, Faustine Childress. *A Traditional Model of Educational Excellence: Dunbar High School of Little Rock, Arkansas*. Washington, D.C.: Howard University Press, 1981.

Jones, Jacqueline. *Soldiers of Light and Love: Northern Teachers and Georgia Blacks, 1865-1873*. Chapel Hill: University of North Carolina Press, 1980.

Jordan-Taylor, Donna. "Graduate Study and Jim Crow: The Circular Migration of Southern Black Educators, 1945-1970." In *Using Past as Prologue: Contemporary Perspectives on African American Educational History*, edited by Dionne Danns, Michelle A. Purdy, and Christopher M. Span, 117-40. Charlotte, N.C.: Information Age, 2015.

Joseph, Penial E. *Waiting 'Til the Midnight Hour: A Narrative History of Black Power in America*. New York: Holt Paperbacks, 2006.

"The Judicial Role in Attacking Racial Discrimination in Tax-Exempt Private Schools." *Harvard Law Review* 93, no. 2 (1979): 378-407.

Kaestle, Carl. *Pillars of the Republic: Common Schools and American Society, 1790-1860*. New York: Hill and Wang, 1983.

Kean, Melissa. *Desegregating Private Higher Education in the South: Duke, Emory, Rice, Tulane, and Vanderbilt*. Baton Rouge: Louisiana State University Press, 2008.

Kendi, Ibram X. *Stamped from the Beginning: The Definitive History of Racist Ideas in America*. New York: Nation Books, 2016.

Khan, Shamus Rahman. *Privilege: The Making of an Adolescent Elite at St. Paul's School*. Princeton, N.J.: Princeton University Press, 2011.

Klarman, Michael. "How *Brown* Changed Race Relations: The Backlash Thesis." *Journal of American History* 81, no. 1 (June 1994): 81-118.

Kluger, Richard. *Simple Justice: The History of Brown v. Board of Education and Black America's Struggle for Equality*. First published in 1975. New York: Vintage Books, 2004.

K'Meyer, Tracy E. *From Brown to Meredith: The Long Struggle for School Desegregation in Louisville, Kentucky, 1954-2007*. Chapel Hill: University of North Carolina Press, 2013.

Kraushaar, Otto F. *American Nonpublic Schools: Patterns of Diversity*. Baltimore, Md.: Johns Hopkins University Press, 1972.

Kruse, Kevin. "Beyond the Southern Cross: The National Origins of the Religious Right." In *The Myth of Southern Exceptionalism*, edited by Matthew D. Lassiter and Joseph Crespino, 286-307. Oxford: Oxford University Press, 2009.

————. *White Flight: Atlanta and the Making of Modern Conservatism*. Princeton, N.J.: Princeton University Press, 2005.

Ladson-Billings, Gloria. "From the Achievement Gap to the Educational Debt: Understanding Achievement in U.S. Schools." *Educational Researcher* 35, no. 7 (October 2006): 3-12.

————. "Landing on the Wrong Note: The Price We Paid for *Brown*." *Educational Researcher* 33, no. 7 (October 2004): 3-13.

Lassiter, Matthew D. *The Silent Majority: Suburban Politics in the Sunbelt South*. Princeton, N.J.: Princeton University Press, 2006.

Lassiter, Matthew D., and Joseph Crespino, eds. *The Myth of Southern Exceptionalism*. New York: Oxford University Press, 2010.

Lepore, Jill. "Historians Who Love Too Much: Reflections on Microhistory and Biography." *Journal of American History* 88, no. 1 (June 2001): 129-44.

Litwack, Leon. *Trouble in Mind: Black Southerners in the Age of Jim Crow*. New York: Vintage Books, 1998.

Mallery, David. *Negro Students in Independent Schools*. Boston: National Association of Independent Schools, 1963.

Martin, Harold H. *William Berry Hartsfield: Mayor of Atlanta*. Athens: University of Georgia Press, 1978.

Martin, Waldo E., Jr. Brown v. Board of Education: *A Brief History with Documents*. Boston: Bedford/St. Martin's, 1998.

McGrath, Susan M. "From Tokenism to Community Control: Political Symbolism in the Desegregation of Atlanta's Public Schools, 1961-1973." *Georgia Historical Quarterly* 79 (1995): 842-72.

McGrath, Susan Margaret. "Great Expectations: The History of School Desegregation in Atlanta and Boston, 1954-1990." PhD diss., Emory University, 1992.

McNeil, Genna Rae. *Groundwork: Charles Hamilton Houston and the Struggle for Civil Rights*. Philadelphia: University of Pennsylvania Press, 1983.

Merriam, Sharan B. *Qualitative Research and Case Study Applications in Education*. San Francisco: Jossey-Bass, 1998.

Miller, Arthur S. *Racial Discrimination and Private Education: A Legal Analysis*. Chapel Hill: University of North Carolina Press, 1957.

Mirel, Jeffrey E. *Patriotic Pluralism: Americanization Education and European Immigrants*. Cambridge, Mass.: Harvard University Press, 2010.

Morris, Wade H., Jr. "Forcing Progress: The Struggle to Integrate Southern Episcopal Schools." Master's thesis, Georgetown University, 2009.

Moss, Hilary J. *Schooling Citizens: The Struggle for African American Education in Antebellum America*. Chicago: University of Chicago Press, 2009.

Moynihan, Daniel Patrick. "The Negro Family: The Case for National Action." In *The Essential Neoconservative Reader*, edited by Mark Gerson, foreword by James O. Wilson, 23-28. Reading, Mass.: Addison-Wesley, 1996.

Nevin, David, and Robert Bills. *The Schools That Fear Built: Segregationist Academies in the South*. Washington, D.C.: Acropolis Books, 1976.

Noblit, George W., and Van O. Dempsey. *The Social Construction of Virtue: The Moral Life of Schools*. Albany: State University of New York Press, 1996.

O'Brien, Thomas V. *The Politics of Race and Schooling: Public Education in Georgia, 1900-1961*. Lanham, Md.: Lexington Books, 1999.

O'Brien, Thomas Victor. "Georgia's Response to *Brown v. Board of Education*: The Rise and Fall of Massive Resistance, 1949-1961." PhD diss., Emory University, 1992.

Orfield, Gary, and Susan Eaton, eds. *Dismantling Desegregation: The Quiet Reversal of Brown v. Board of Education*. New York: New Press, 1996.

Orfield, Gary, and Erica Frankenberg, with Jongyeon Ee and John Kuscera. Brown *at 60: Great Progress, a Long Retreat, and an Uncertain Future*. The Civil Rights Project. Accessed April 21, 2017. https://www.civilrightsproject.ucla.edu/research/k-12 -education/integration-and-diversity/brown-at-60-great-progress-a-long-retreat -and-an-uncertain-future/Brown-at-60-051814.pdf.

Orr, Dorothy. *A History of Education in Georgia*. Chapel Hill: University of North Carolina Press, 1950.

Orsini, Alfonso J. "A Context for Understanding Faculty Diversity." In *The Colors of Excellence: Hiring and Keeping Teachers of Color in Independent Schools*, edited by Pearl Rock Kane and Alfonso J. Orsini, 29-45. New York: Teachers College, 2003.

Parents Involved in Community Schools v. Seattle School District No. 1 (Nos. 05-908 and 05-915). 551 U.S. 701, 2007 U.S. Supreme Court.

Paris, Django. "Culturally Sustaining Pedagogy: A Needed Change in Stance, Terminology, and Practice." *Educational Researcher* 41, no. 3 (April 2012): 93-97.

Patel, Leigh. *Youth Held at the Border: Immigration, Education, and the Politics of Inclusion*. New York: Teachers College Press, 2012.

Patillo-Beals, Melba. *Warriors Don't Cry: A Searing Memoir of the Battle to Integrate Little Rock's Central High*. New York: Pocket Books, 1995.

Paton, Alan. *Cry, the Beloved Country*. New York: Charles Scribner's Sons, 1948.

Patterson, James T. Brown v. Board of Education: *A Civil Rights Milestone and Its Troubled Legacy*. Oxford: Oxford University Press, 2001.

Perkins, Linda M. "The First Black Talent Identification Program: The National Scholarship Service and Fund for Negro Students, 1947-1968." *Perspectives on the History of Higher Education* 29 (2012): 173-97.

Perrillo, Jonna. *Uncivil Rights: Teachers, Unions, and Race in the Battle for School Equity*. Chicago: University of Chicago Press, 2012.

Pierson, Sharon Gay. *Laboratory of Learning: HBCU Laboratory Schools and Alabama State College Lab High in the Era of Jim Crow*. New York: Peter Lang, 2014.

Plank, David N., and Marcia Turner. "Changing Patterns in Black School Politics: Atlanta, 1872-1973." *American Journal of Education* 95, no. 4 (1987): 584-608.

Podair, Jerald. *The Strike That Changed New York: Blacks, Whites, and the Ocean-Hill Brownsville Crisis*. New Haven, Conn.: Yale University Press, 2002.

Portelli, Alessandro. "Peculiarities of Oral History." *History Workshop Journal* 96 (Autumn 1981): 96–107.

Powell, Arthur G. *Lessons from Privilege: The American Prep School Tradition*. Cambridge, Mass.: Harvard University Press, 1996.

powell, john a., and Marguerite L. Spencer. "Response: *Brown* Is Not *Brown* and Educational Reform Is Not Reform If Integration Is Not a Goal." *New York University Review of Law and Change* 28 (2003): 343-51.

Pratt, Robert A. *The Color of Their Skin: Education and Race in Richmond, Virginia, 1954-1989*. Charlottesville: University Press of Virginia, 1992.

Pressly, William L. *The Formative Years at Atlanta's Westminster Schools*. Atlanta, Ga.: McGuire, 1991.

———. "Meanwhile, Georgia Schools Are Getting Better." *University: A Princeton Quarterly*, no. 32 (Spring 1967): 23-26.

Purdy, Michelle A. "Blurring Public and Private: The Pragmatic Desegregation Politics of an Elite Private School in Atlanta." *History of Education Quarterly* 56, no. 1 (February 2016): 61-89.

———. "Courageous Navigation: African American Students at an Elite Private School in the South, 1967-1972." In "Civil Rights, Black Power, and African American Education," special issue, *Journal of African American History* 100, no. 4 (Fall 2015): 610-35.

Reese, William J. "Changing Conceptions of 'Public' and 'Private' in American Educational History." In *History, Education, and the Schools*, edited by William J. Reese, 95-112. New York: Palgrave Macmillan, 2007.

Reynolds, Katherine C. "Charlotte Hawkins Brown and the Palmer Institute." In *Founding Mothers and Others: Women Educational Leaders during the Progressive Era*, edited by Alan R. Sadovnik and Susan F. Semel, 7-17. New York: Palgrave, 2002.

Rickford, Russell. *We Are an African People: Independent Education, Black Power, and the Radical Imagination*. Oxford: Oxford University Press, 2016.

Roche, Jeff. *Restructured Resistance: The Sibley Commission and the Politics of Desegregation in Georgia*. Athens: University of Georgia Press, 1998.

Rofes, Eric, and Lisa M. Stulberg, eds. *The Emancipatory Promise of Charter Schools: Toward a Progressive Politics of School Choice*. Albany: State University of New York Press, 2004.

Rogers, Ibram. *Black Campus Movement: Black Students and the Racial Reconstitution of Higher Education, 1965-1972*. New York: Palgrave Macmillan, 2012.

Sanchez, George. *Becoming Mexican American: Ethnicity, Culture, and Identity in Chicano Los Angeles, 1900-1945*. New York: Oxford University Press, 1993.

Sanders, Crystal. *A Chance for Change: Head Start and Mississippi's Black Freedom Struggle*. Chapel Hill: University of North Carolina Press, 2016.

Sanders, Katrina M. "Forgotten or Simply Ignored: A Historiography of African Americans and Catholic Education." In *Using Past as Prologue: Contemporary Perspectives on African American Educational History*, edited by Dionne Danns, Michelle A. Purdy, and Christopher M. Span, 57-85. Charlotte, N.C.: Information Age, 2015.

San Miguel, Guadalupe, Jr., and Richard R. Valencia. "From the Treaty of Guadalupe Hidalgo to *Hopwood*: The Educational Plight and Struggle of Mexican Americans in the Southwest." *Harvard Educational Review* 68, no. 3 (Fall 1998): 353-412.

Schulman, Bruce J. *From Cotton Belt to Sunbelt: Federal Policy, Economic Development, and the Transformation of the South, 1938-1980*. New York: Oxford University Press, 1991.

Schulman, Bruce J., and Julian E. Zelizer, eds. *Rightward Bound: Making America Conservative in the 1970s*. Cambridge, Mass.: Harvard University Press, 2008.

Secret, Mosi. "The Way to Survive It Was to Make A's." *New York Times*, September 7, 2017. https://www.nytimes.com/2017/09/07/magazine/the-way-to-survive-it-was-to-make-as.html.

Sizer, Theodore. "The Academies: An Interpretation." In *The Age of the Academies*, edited by Theodore Sizer, 1-49. New York: Bureau of Publications, Teachers College, Columbia University, 1964.

Slaughter, Diana T., and Deborah J. Johnson, eds. *Visible Now: Blacks in Private Schools*. New York: Greenwood, 1988.

Snyder, Ben, and Margot Snyder. "Dreams and Dilemmas." *Independent School* (Winter 1999): 66-72.

Sowell, Thomas. "Patterns of Black Excellence." *Public Interest* 43 (1976): 26-58.

Speede-Franklin, Wanda A. "Ethnic Diversity: Patterns and Implications of Minorities in Independent Schools." In *Visible Now: Blacks in Private Schools*, edited by Diana T. Slaughter and Deborah J. Johnson, 21-31. New York: Greenwood, 1988.

Steffes, Tracy L. *School, Society, and State: A New Education to Govern Modern America, 1890-1940*. Chicago: University of Chicago Press, 2012.

Stevens, Mitchell L. *Creating a Class: College Admissions and the Education of Elites*. Cambridge, Mass.: Harvard University Press, 2007.

Stewart, Allison. *First Class: The Legacy of Dunbar, America's First Black Public High School*. Chicago: Lawrence Hill Books, 2013.

Stulberg, Lisa M. *Race, Schools, and Hope: African Americans and School Choice after Brown*. New York: Teachers College Press, 2008.

Tamura, Eileen H. *Americanization, Acculturation, and Ethnic Identity: The Nisei Generation in Hawaii*. Champaign: University of Illinois Press, 1994.

Thuesen, Sarah Caroline. *Greater Than Equal: African American Struggles for Schools and Citizenship in North Carolina, 1919-1965*. Chapel Hill: University of North Carolina Press, 2013.

Todd-Breland, Elizabeth. "Control and Independence: Black Alternatives for Urban Education." In *Using Past as Prologue: Contemporary Perspectives on African American Educational History*, edited by Dionne Danns, Michelle A. Purdy, and Christopher M. Span, 253-74. Charlotte, N.C.: Information Age, 2015.

Tolley, Kim, and Nancy Beadie. "A School for Every Purpose: An Introduction to the History of Academies in the United States." In *Chartered Schools: Two Hundred Years of Independent Academies in the United States, 1727-1925*, edited by Nancy Beadie and Kim Tolley, 3-16. New York: RoutledgeFalmer, 2002.

Tushnet, Mark. *The NAACP's Legal Strategy against Segregated Education, 1925-1950*. Chapel Hill: University of North Carolina Press, 1987.

Wadelington, Charles Weldon, and Richard F. Knapp. *Charlotte Hawkins Brown & Palmer Memorial Institute: What One Young African American Woman Could Do*. Chapel Hill: University of North Carolina Press, 1999.

Walker, Vanessa Siddle. "Black Educators as Educational Advocates in the Decades before *Brown v. Board of Education.*" *Educational Researcher* 42, no. 2 (May 2013): 207-22.

———. *Hello Professor: A Black Principal and Professional Leadership in the Segregated South*. Chapel Hill: University of North Carolina Press, 2009.

———. *The Lost Education of Horace Tate: Uncovering the Hidden Heroes Who Fought for Justice in Schools*. New York: New Press, 2018.

———. *Their Highest Potential: An African American School Community in the Segregated South*. Chapel Hill: University of North Carolina Press, 1996.

Washington, Booker T. *Up from Slavery*. First published in 1901. New York: Dover, 1995.

Washington Post, July 26, 2016. "Transcript: Read Michelle Obama's Full Speech from the 2016 DNC." https://www.washingtonpost.com/news/post-politics/wp/2016 /07/26/transcript-read-michelle-obamas-full-speech-from-the-2016-dnc/?utm _term=.af878837500e.

Watkins, William H. *The White Architects of Black Education: Ideology and Power in America, 1865-1954*. New York: Teachers College Press, 2001.

Wells, Amy Stuart, Jennifer Jellison Holme, Anita Tijerina Revilla, and Awo Korantemaa Atanda. *Both Sides Now: The Story of School Desegregation's Graduates*. Berkeley: University of California Press, 2009.

Williams, Heather Andrea. *Self-Taught: African American Education in Slavery and Freedom*. Chapel Hill: University of North Carolina Press, 2005.

Williamson, Joy Ann. *Black Power on Campus: The University of Illinois, 1965-1975*. Urbana: University of Illinois Press, 2003.

Willis, Vincent. "'Let Me In, I Have the Right to Be Here': Black Youth Struggle for Equal Education and Full Citizenship after the *Brown* Decision, 1954–1969." *Citizenship Teaching & Learning* 9, no. 1 (December 2013): 53–70.

Wilson, Zebulon Vance, and J. Russell Frank. *They Took Their Stand: The Integration of Southern Private Schools*. Atlanta, Ga.: Mid-South Association of Independent Schools, 1983.

Woodson, Carter G. *The Education of the Negro Prior to 1861: A History of the Education of the Colored People of the United States from the Beginning of Slavery to the Civil War*. First published in 1915 by G. P. Putnam. Lexington: Traffic Output, 2015.

Wright, Dwayne C. "Black Pride Day, 1968: High School Student Activism in York Pennsylvania." *Journal of African American History* 88 (Spring 2003): 153-62.

Yow, Valerie Raleigh. *Recording Oral History: A Guide for the Humanities and Social Sciences*. New York: AltaMira, 2005.

Zweigenhaft, Richard L., and G. William Domhoff. *Blacks in the White Elite: Will the Progress Continue?* Lanham, Md.: Rowman & Littlefield, 2003.

Index

Page numbers in italics indicate illustrations.

within, 7, 19, 116, 143–44, 148, 161,
169; Dandridge network within,
169–73; federal legislation monitored
by, 87–88; formation of, 75;
leadership team of, 155; Minority
Affairs Committee established by,
116; open enrollment statement by,
132–34; Pressly as leader of, 6, 75,
97, 116; support of black students
by, 4, 88, 89, 117, 141–42, 156–57,
168–69
National Council for the Social Studies,
37
National Council of Independent
Schools (NCIS), 41–42, 60, 61;
expressed purposes of, 75; formation
of, 37, 38–39; monitoring of federal
government by, 59–60, 63–64; Pressly
as leader of, 23, 35–36
National Council of Teachers of
English, 37
National Council of Teachers of
Mathematics, 37
National Defense Education Act
(NDEA), 87; provisions of, 59–60, 63,
206n28
National Scholarship Service and Fund
for Negro Students (NSSFNS), 40, 79,
99, 106–7
Negro Students in Independent Schools
(Mallery), 83, 99–100, 106, 127, 165
Nevin, David, 97–98
New Orleans, La., 4, 61, 69, 86
New York, N.Y., 40; Independent
Schools Opportunity Project in, 161;
Prep for Prep project in, 107; Project
Broad Jump in, 107
noblesse oblige, 89, 131–32, 148
Norfolk State College (University), 45,
124, 211n34
Northern Congregational Church, 51
Northfield Academy, 106

Obama, Barack, 4, 5, 179
Obama, Malia and Sasha, 4, 179

Obama, Michelle, 4, 179
Ogden, Robert C., 49
Oglethorpe School, 53, 78, 108, 111,
122, 135
Organizations Assisting Schools in
September (OASIS), 70
Osgood, Esther E., 155

Paine College, 45
Palmer Institute, 51, 52
*Parents Involved in Community
Schools v. Seattle School District No. 1*,
9, 15
Parker, William, 91
Parkman, Francis, 39
Paris, Django, 182
Paschall, Eliza, 74, 77, 78–79, 83, 85
Patel, Leigh, 180
Peabody, George Foster, 49
Peabody Fund, 50
Pendergrast, John, 67, 68–69
Pendergrast, Nan, 67–68, 74
Pendergrast, Scott, 129
People's Association for Selective
Shopping, 83
Phelps-Stokes Fund, 50
Philadelphia, Penn.: Friends Council on
Education in, 161
Philanthropy, 49–50, 51, 200n102
Phillips, Renita Pace, 111
Phillips Academy, 4, 41
Pickaninny caricatures, 43–44
Pierce v. Society of Sisters, 37
Pilgrim, David, 43
Piney Woods School, 51
Plaut, Richard, 99–100
Plessy v. Ferguson, 27, 33, 47
political activism, 11, 14, 50, 151,
152–55. *See also* civil rights movement
Porter, James, 58
Porter, Janice, 106
Potter, Cary, 80, 88, 143–44, 155
Powell, Arthur, 37
Presbyterian Church North, 51
Pressly, Cora, 161–62

CPSIA information can be obtained
at www.ICGtesting.com
Printed in the USA
LVHW09*1201230918
590951LV00009BA/130/P